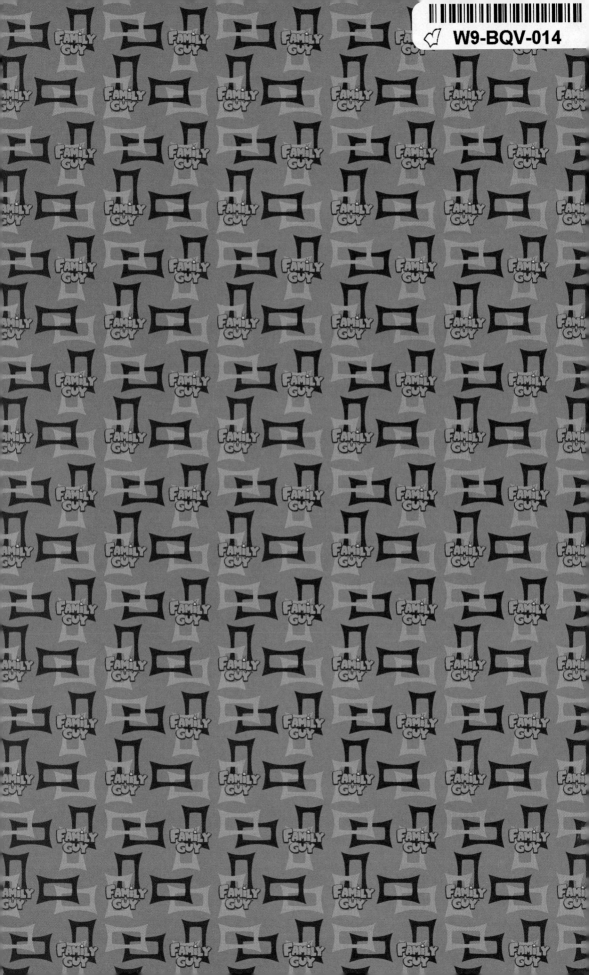

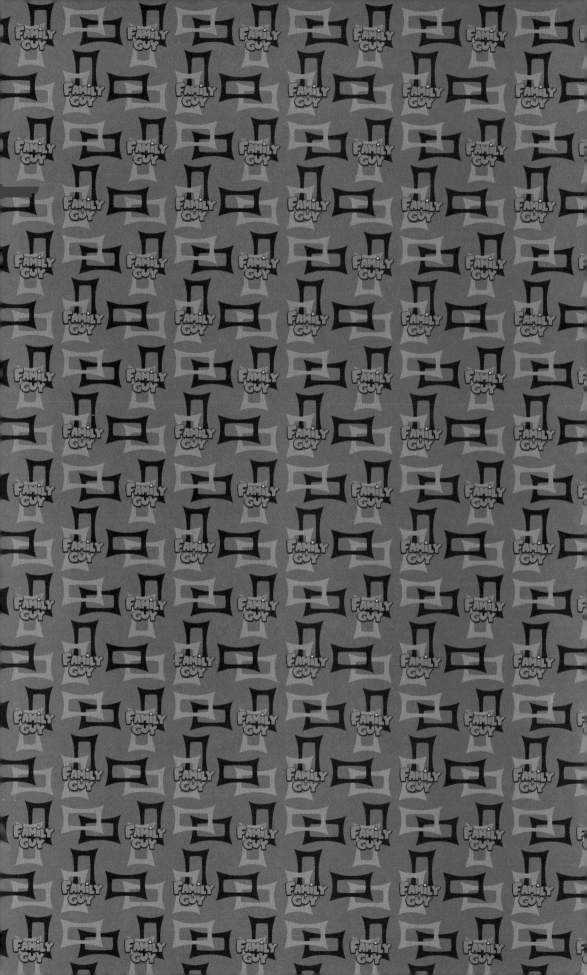

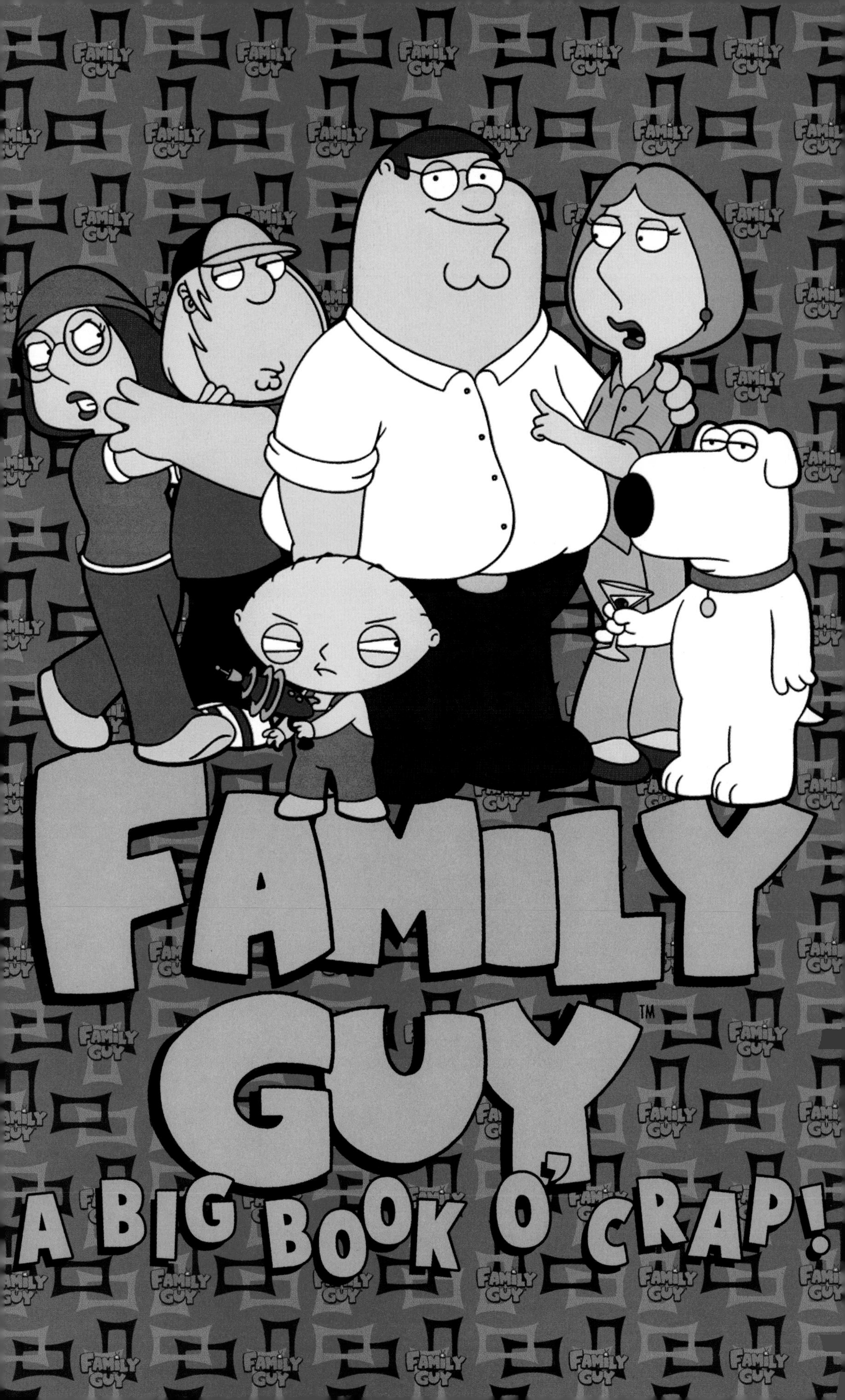
FAMILY GUY™
A BIG BOOK O' CRAP!

AS SEEN ON TV

FAMILY GUY™

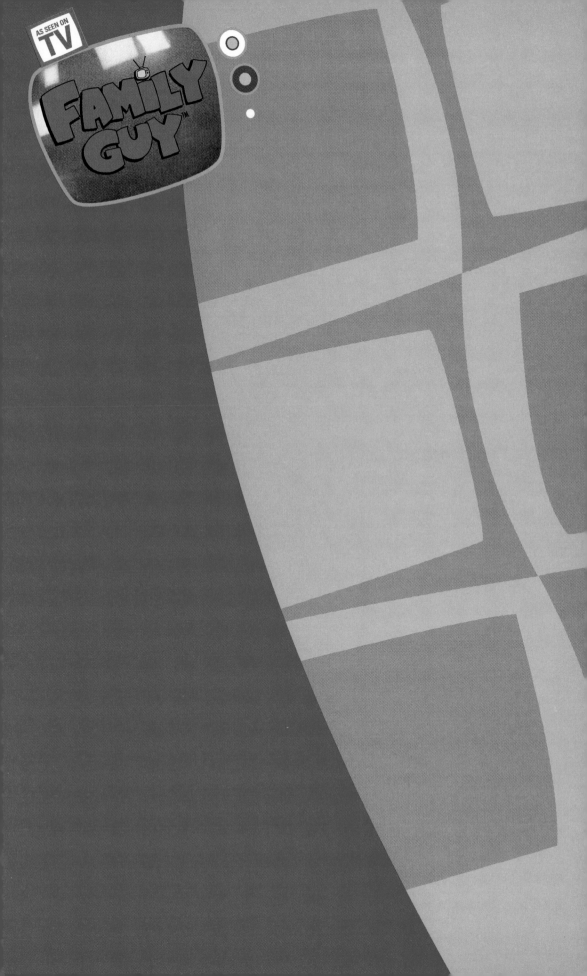

MATT FLECKENSTEIN
Writer

JASON AXTELL, YOUNG "MXMINE" BAEK, BAOWOW, ALDIN BAROZA, CLAYTON BROWN, MICK CASSIDY, CHAD E. COOPER, GARY L. GALLEGOS, LOUIS C. GALLEGOS, MARK GARCIA, ROBERT GRABE, KEN HAYASHI, JR., RICH KOSLOWSKI, DANTE LEANDADO, ANNIE MCMILLAN, ERIK MOXCEY, MIKE PHI, BEN PHILLIPS, DOMINIC POLCINO, MICHAELANGELO ROCCO, SHARON ROSS, RONALD SMITH, KEITH WONG
Linework

JOSH BLAYLOCK, KENDALL BRUNS, BRIAN J. CROWLEY, ERIC DOXTATOR, NICK GROBE, RUDY HALL, AARON HÜBRICH, MIKE O'SULLIVAN, KATIE SITAR, BRAD SOLTIS, DON STOUT, EVAN SULT, BRIAN TORNEY, YESFLAT
Colors

BRIAN J. CROWLEY
Letters

SEAN DOVE
Design

BRIAN TORNEY
Art & Editorial Assistance

MIKE O'SULLIVAN
Editor

RICH YOUNG
Licensing Manager

JOSH BLAYLOCK
Sick, Sick Little Moo Cow

Many thanks to DEBBIE OLSHAN at Fox & SHARON ROSS at Family Guy!

DEVIL'S DUE PUBLISHING

JOSH BLAYLOCK President

SAM WELLS Assistant Publisher   SUSAN BISHOP VP Marketing

MICHAEL O'SULLIVAN Senior Editor   CRANK! Computer Operations

TIM SEELEY Staff Artist   SEAN DOVE Art Director

BRIAN J. CROWLEY Staff Letterer   CAITLIN McKAY Webstore Manager

WWW.DEVILSDUE.NET

FAMILY GUY™ A BIG BOOK O' CRAP. OCTOBER, 2006. FIRST PRINTING. Published by Devil's Due Publishing, Inc. Office of publication 4619 N. Ravenswood Ave. #204, Chicago, IL 60640.

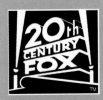

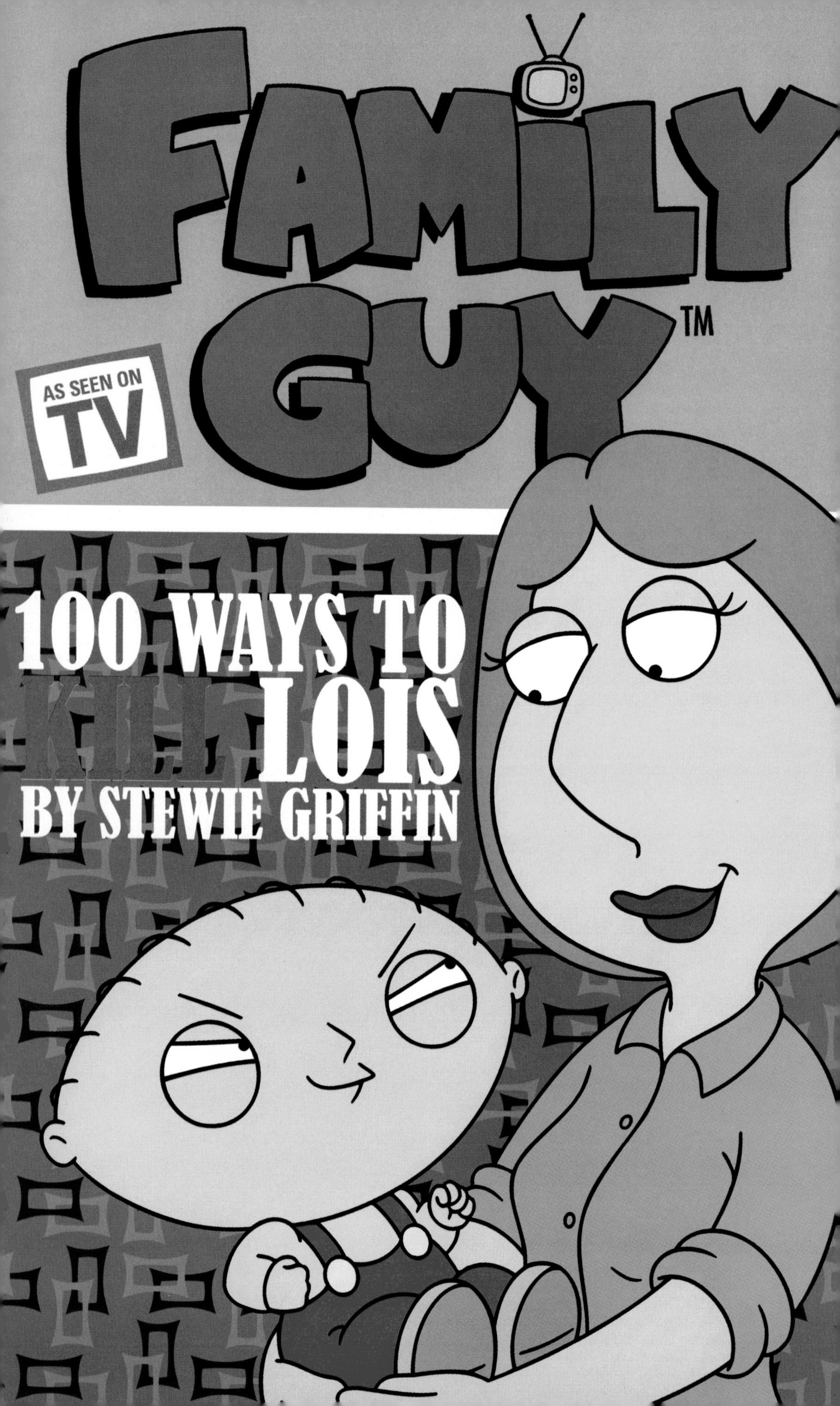
FAMILY GUY™
AS SEEN ON TV
100 WAYS TO KILL LOIS
BY STEWIE GRIFFIN

20TH CENTURY FOX & DEVIL'S DUE PUBLISHING PRESENT

100 WAYS TO KILL LOIS

HOSTED BY STEWIE GRIFFIN

HI, THERE. I'M *STEWIE GRIFFIN*.

100 WAYS TO KILL LOIS

HOSTED BY STEWIE GRIFFIN

AND WELCOME TO MY COUNTDOWN OF THE TOP 100 WAYS TO KILL LOIS.

OVER THE NEXT FEW PAGES, I'LL WALK YOU THROUGH THE INS AND OUTS OF HOW AND WHY I WANT TO KILL MY WRETCHED MOTHER, IN DELIGHTFUL, OVER-PRODUCED, CABLE SHOW-TYPE COUNTDOWN FORM.

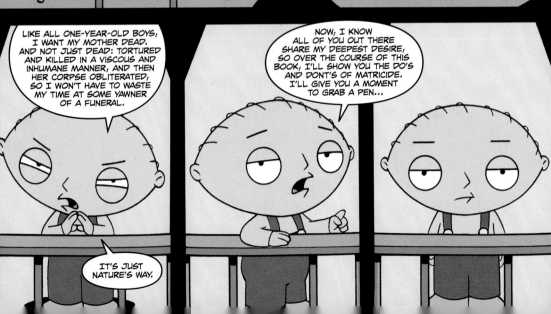

LIKE ALL ONE-YEAR-OLD BOYS, I WANT MY MOTHER DEAD. AND NOT JUST DEAD: TORTURED AND KILLED IN A VISCOUS AND INHUMANE MANNER, AND THEN HER CORPSE OBLITERATED, SO I WON'T HAVE TO WASTE MY TIME AT SOME YAWNER OF A FUNERAL.

IT'S JUST NATURE'S WAY.

NOW, I KNOW ALL OF YOU OUT THERE SHARE MY DEEPEST DESIRE, SO OVER THE COURSE OF THIS BOOK, I'LL SHOW YOU THE DO'S AND DONT'S OF MATRICIDE. I'LL GIVE YOU A MOMENT TO GRAB A PEN...

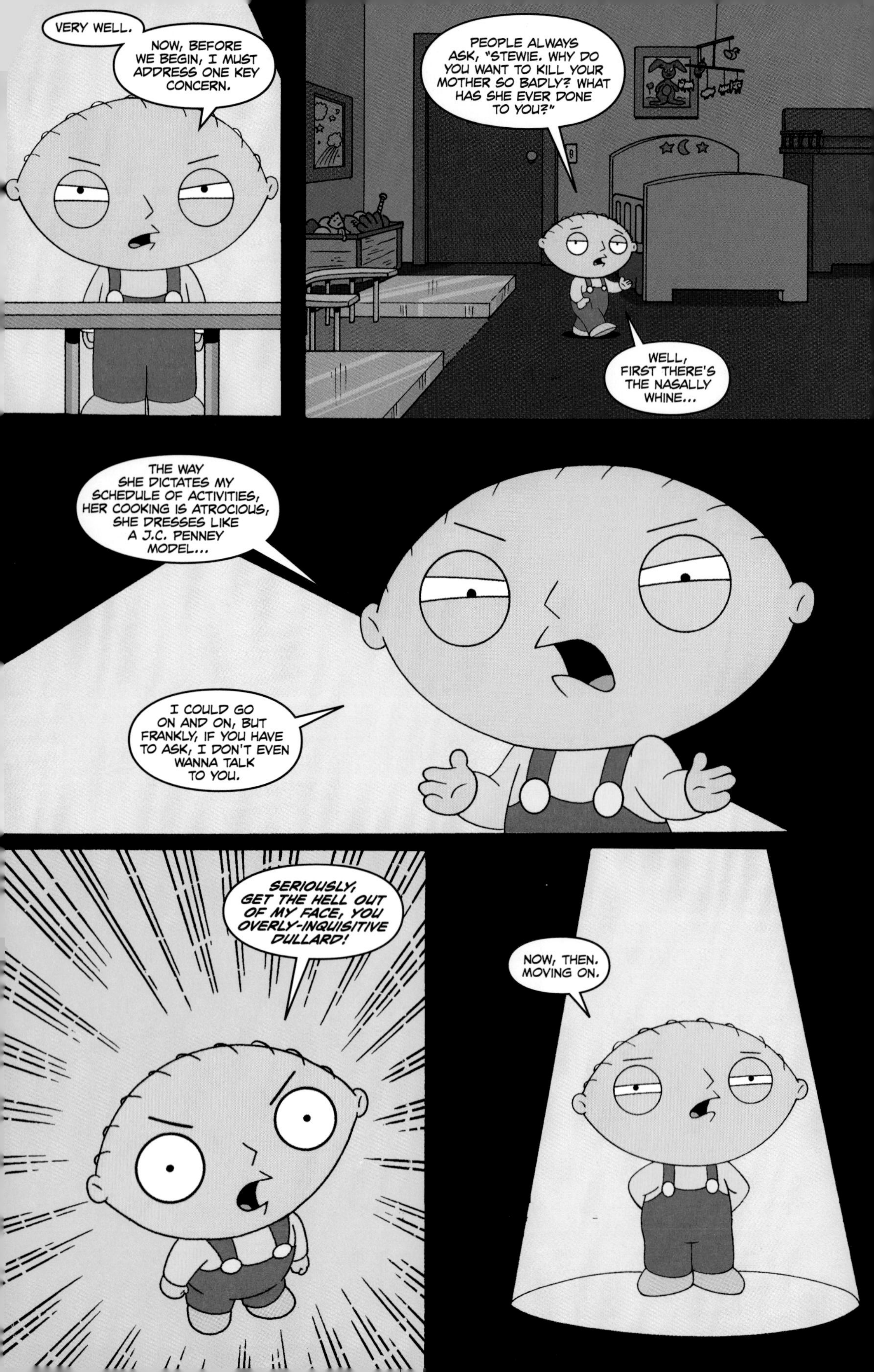
VERY WELL.
NOW, BEFORE WE BEGIN, I MUST ADDRESS ONE KEY CONCERN.
PEOPLE ALWAYS ASK, "STEWIE. WHY DO YOU WANT TO KILL YOUR MOTHER SO BADLY? WHAT HAS SHE EVER DONE TO YOU?"
WELL, FIRST THERE'S THE NASALLY WHINE...
THE WAY SHE DICTATES MY SCHEDULE OF ACTIVITIES, HER COOKING IS ATROCIOUS, SHE DRESSES LIKE A J.C. PENNEY MODEL...
I COULD GO ON AND ON, BUT FRANKLY, IF YOU HAVE TO ASK, I DON'T EVEN WANNA TALK TO YOU.
SERIOUSLY, GET THE HELL OUT OF MY FACE, YOU OVERLY-INQUISITIVE DULLARD!
NOW, THEN. MOVING ON.

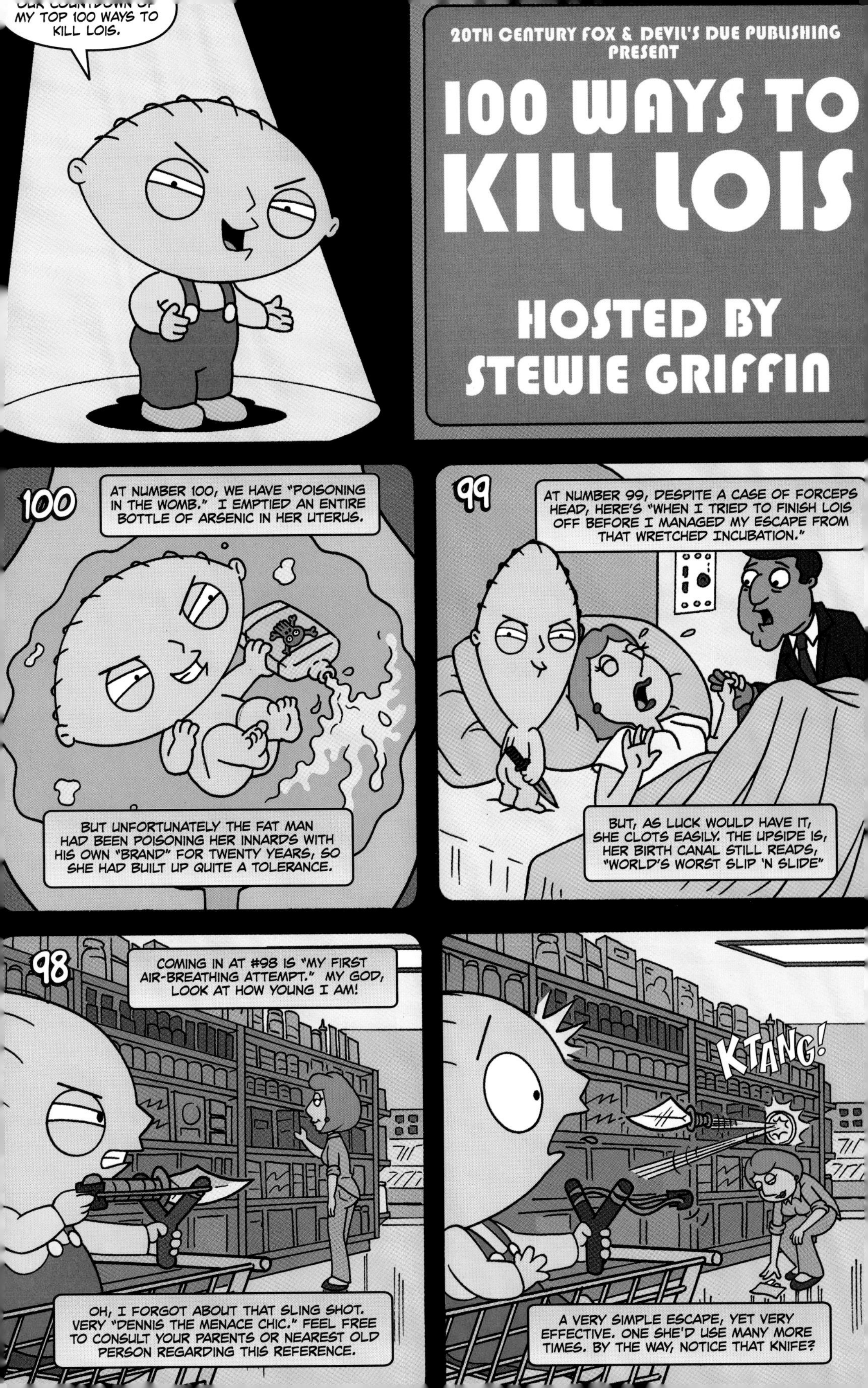

MY TOP 100 WAYS TO KILL LOIS.
20TH CENTURY FOX & DEVIL'S DUE PUBLISHING PRESENT
100 WAYS TO KILL LOIS
HOSTED BY STEWIE GRIFFIN
100
AT NUMBER 100, WE HAVE "POISONING IN THE WOMB." I EMPTIED AN ENTIRE BOTTLE OF ARSENIC IN HER UTERUS.
BUT UNFORTUNATELY THE FAT MAN HAD BEEN POISONING HER INNARDS WITH HIS OWN "BRAND" FOR TWENTY YEARS, SO SHE HAD BUILT UP QUITE A TOLERANCE.
99
AT NUMBER 99, DESPITE A CASE OF FORCEPS HEAD, HERE'S "WHEN I TRIED TO FINISH LOIS OFF BEFORE I MANAGED MY ESCAPE FROM THAT WRETCHED INCUBATION."
BUT, AS LUCK WOULD HAVE IT, SHE CLOTS EASILY. THE UPSIDE IS, HER BIRTH CANAL STILL READS, "WORLD'S WORST SLIP 'N SLIDE"
98
COMING IN AT #98 IS "MY FIRST AIR-BREATHING ATTEMPT." MY GOD, LOOK AT HOW YOUNG I AM!
OH, I FORGOT ABOUT THAT SLING SHOT. VERY "DENNIS THE MENACE CHIC." FEEL FREE TO CONSULT YOUR PARENTS OR NEAREST OLD PERSON REGARDING THIS REFERENCE.
KTANG!
A VERY SIMPLE ESCAPE, YET VERY EFFECTIVE. ONE SHE'D USE MANY MORE TIMES. BY THE WAY, NOTICE THAT KNIFE?

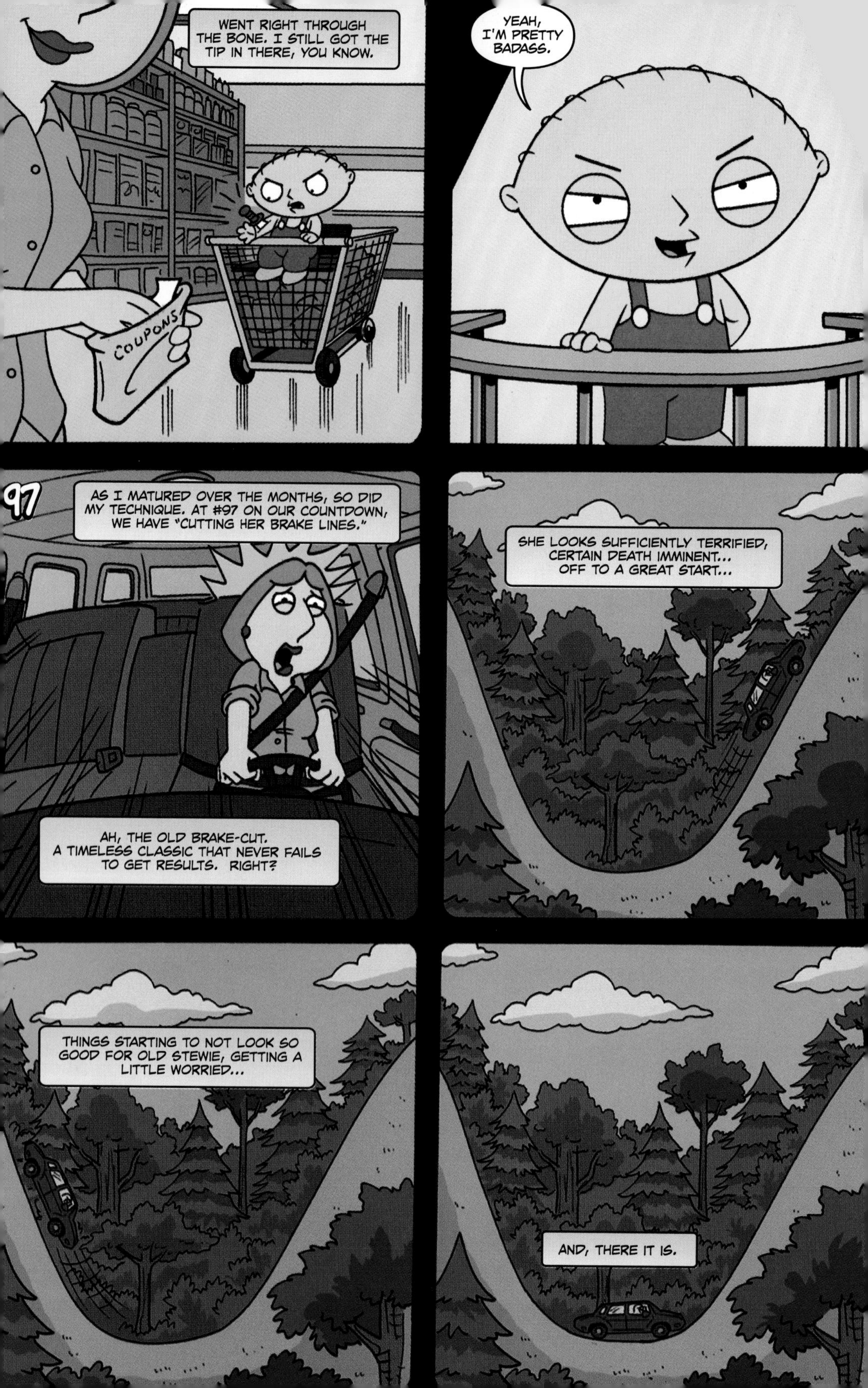
WENT RIGHT THROUGH THE BONE. I STILL GOT THE TIP IN THERE, YOU KNOW.
COUPONS
YEAH, I'M PRETTY BADASS.
97
AS I MATURED OVER THE MONTHS, SO DID MY TECHNIQUE. AT #97 ON OUR COUNTDOWN, WE HAVE "CUTTING HER BRAKE LINES."
AH, THE OLD BRAKE-CUT. A TIMELESS CLASSIC THAT NEVER FAILS TO GET RESULTS. RIGHT?
SHE LOOKS SUFFICIENTLY TERRIFIED, CERTAIN DEATH IMMINENT... OFF TO A GREAT START...
THINGS STARTING TO NOT LOOK SO GOOD FOR OLD STEWIE, GETTING A LITTLE WORRIED...
AND, THERE IT IS.

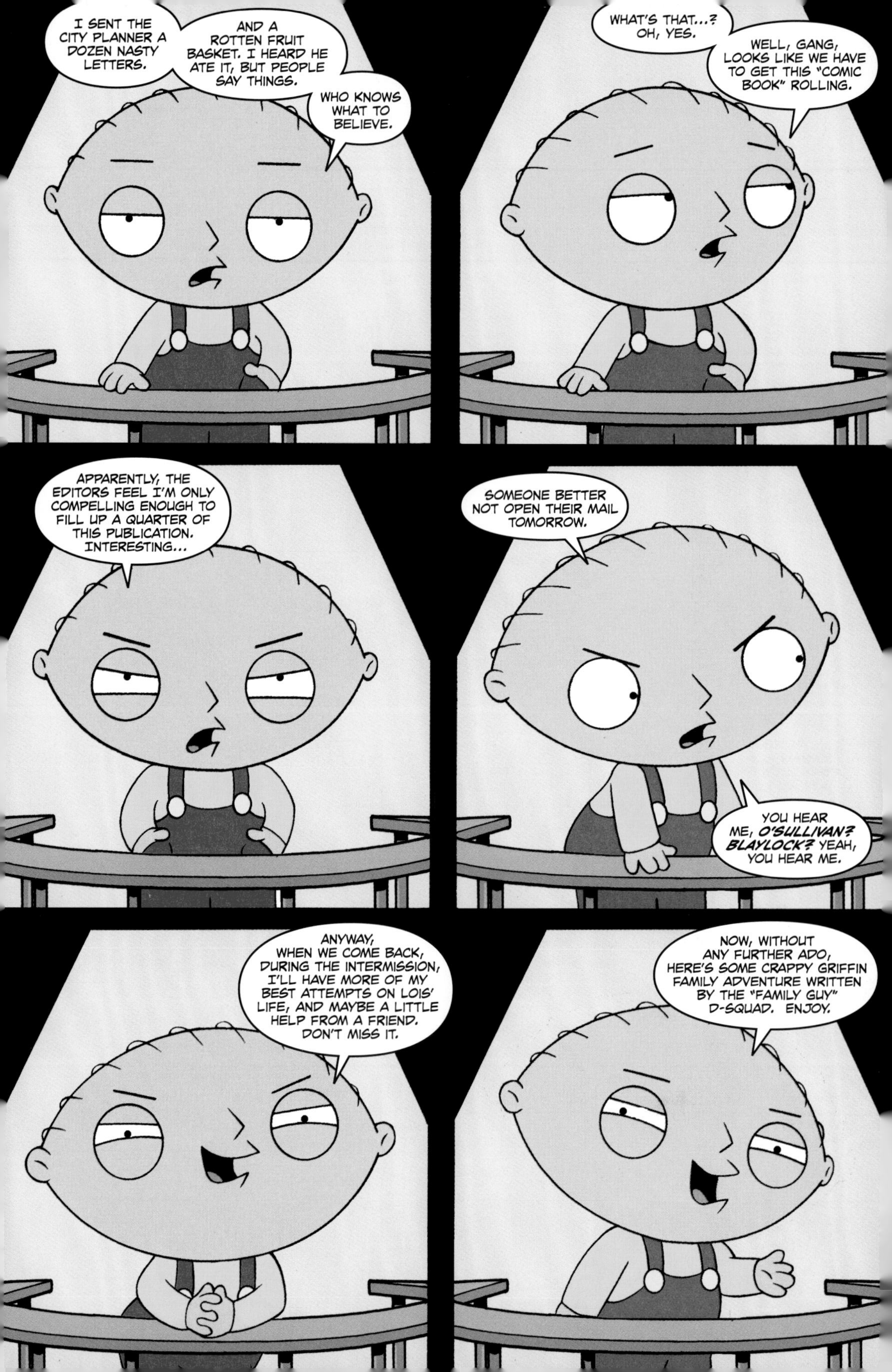
I SENT THE CITY PLANNER A DOZEN NASTY LETTERS.
AND A ROTTEN FRUIT BASKET. I HEARD HE ATE IT, BUT PEOPLE SAY THINGS.
WHO KNOWS WHAT TO BELIEVE.
WHAT'S THAT...? OH, YES.
WELL, GANG, LOOKS LIKE WE HAVE TO GET THIS "COMIC BOOK" ROLLING.
APPARENTLY, THE EDITORS FEEL I'M ONLY COMPELLING ENOUGH TO FILL UP A QUARTER OF THIS PUBLICATION. INTERESTING...
SOMEONE BETTER NOT OPEN THEIR MAIL TOMORROW.
YOU HEAR ME, O'SULLIVAN? BLAYLOCK? YEAH, YOU HEAR ME.
ANYWAY, WHEN WE COME BACK, DURING THE INTERMISSION, I'LL HAVE MORE OF MY BEST ATTEMPTS ON LOIS' LIFE, AND MAYBE A LITTLE HELP FROM A FRIEND. DON'T MISS IT.
NOW, WITHOUT ANY FURTHER ADO, HERE'S SOME CRAPPY GRIFFIN FAMILY ADVENTURE WRITTEN BY THE "FAMILY GUY" D-SQUAD. ENJOY.

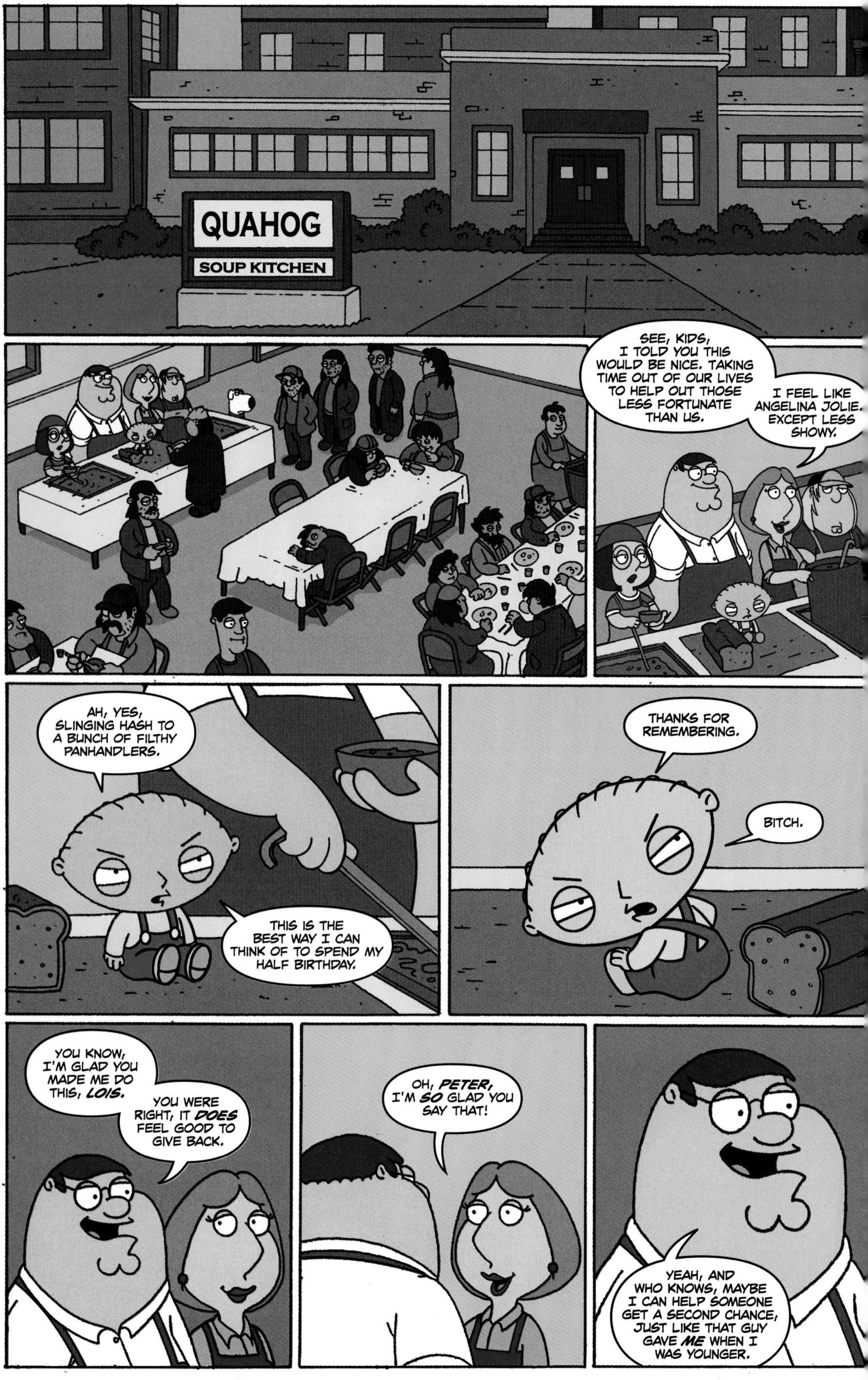

QUAHOG
SOUP KITCHEN
SEE, KIDS, I TOLD YOU THIS WOULD BE NICE. TAKING TIME OUT OF OUR LIVES TO HELP OUT THOSE LESS FORTUNATE THAN US.
I FEEL LIKE ANGELINA JOLIE. EXCEPT LESS SHOWY.
AH, YES, SLINGING HASH TO A BUNCH OF FILTHY PANHANDLERS.
THIS IS THE BEST WAY I CAN THINK OF TO SPEND MY HALF BIRTHDAY.
THANKS FOR REMEMBERING.
BITCH.
YOU KNOW, I'M GLAD YOU MADE ME DO THIS, *LOIS.*
YOU WERE RIGHT, IT *DOES* FEEL GOOD TO GIVE BACK.
OH, *PETER,* I'M *SO* GLAD YOU SAY THAT!
YEAH, AND WHO KNOWS, MAYBE I CAN HELP SOMEONE GET A SECOND CHANCE, JUST LIKE THAT GUY GAVE *ME* WHEN I WAS YOUNGER.

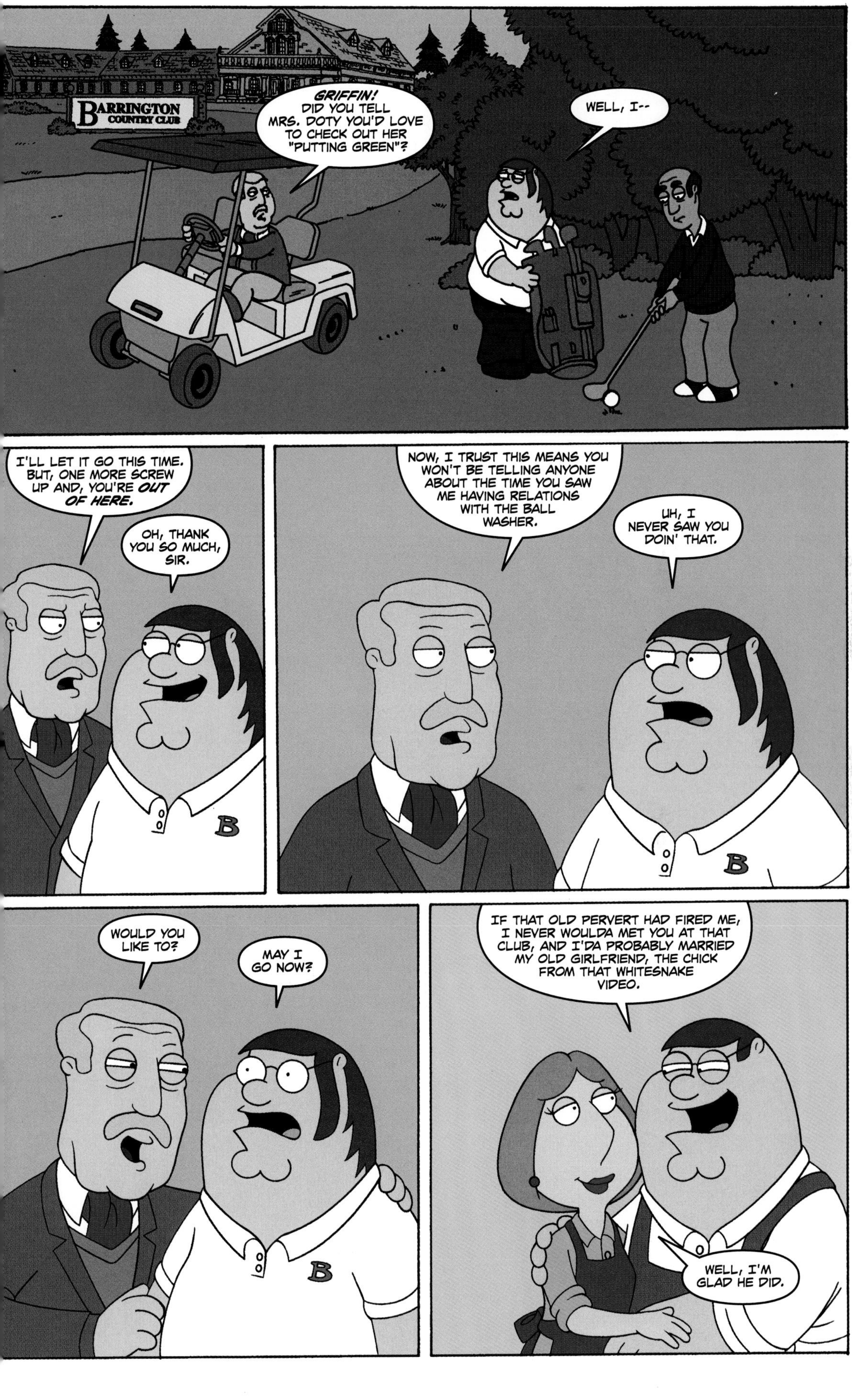

BARRINGTON COUNTRY CLUB
GRIFFIN! DID YOU TELL MRS. DOTY YOU'D LOVE TO CHECK OUT HER "PUTTING GREEN"?
WELL, I--
I'LL LET IT GO THIS TIME. BUT, ONE MORE SCREW UP AND, YOU'RE OUT OF HERE.
OH, THANK YOU SO MUCH, SIR.
NOW, I TRUST THIS MEANS YOU WON'T BE TELLING ANYONE ABOUT THE TIME YOU SAW ME HAVING RELATIONS WITH THE BALL WASHER.
UH, I NEVER SAW YOU DOIN' THAT.
WOULD YOU LIKE TO?
MAY I GO NOW?
IF THAT OLD PERVERT HAD FIRED ME, I NEVER WOULDA MET YOU AT THAT CLUB, AND I'DA PROBABLY MARRIED MY OLD GIRLFRIEND, THE CHICK FROM THAT WHITESNAKE VIDEO.
WELL, I'M GLAD HE DID.

QUAGMIRE?

WHAT THE HELL ARE YOU DOING?

OH, HEY, *BRIAN.* JUST SCAMMIN' ON SOME *VERY* EAGER TAIL.

YOU'RE HITTING ON HOMELESS WOMEN?

THAT'S SICK. SOME OF THESE PEOPLE HAVE MENTAL PROBLEMS.

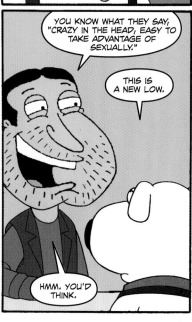

YOU KNOW WHAT THEY SAY, "CRAZY IN THE HEAD, EASY TO TAKE ADVANTAGE OF SEXUALLY."

THIS IS A NEW LOW.

HMM. YOU'D THINK.

BRETT BUTLER

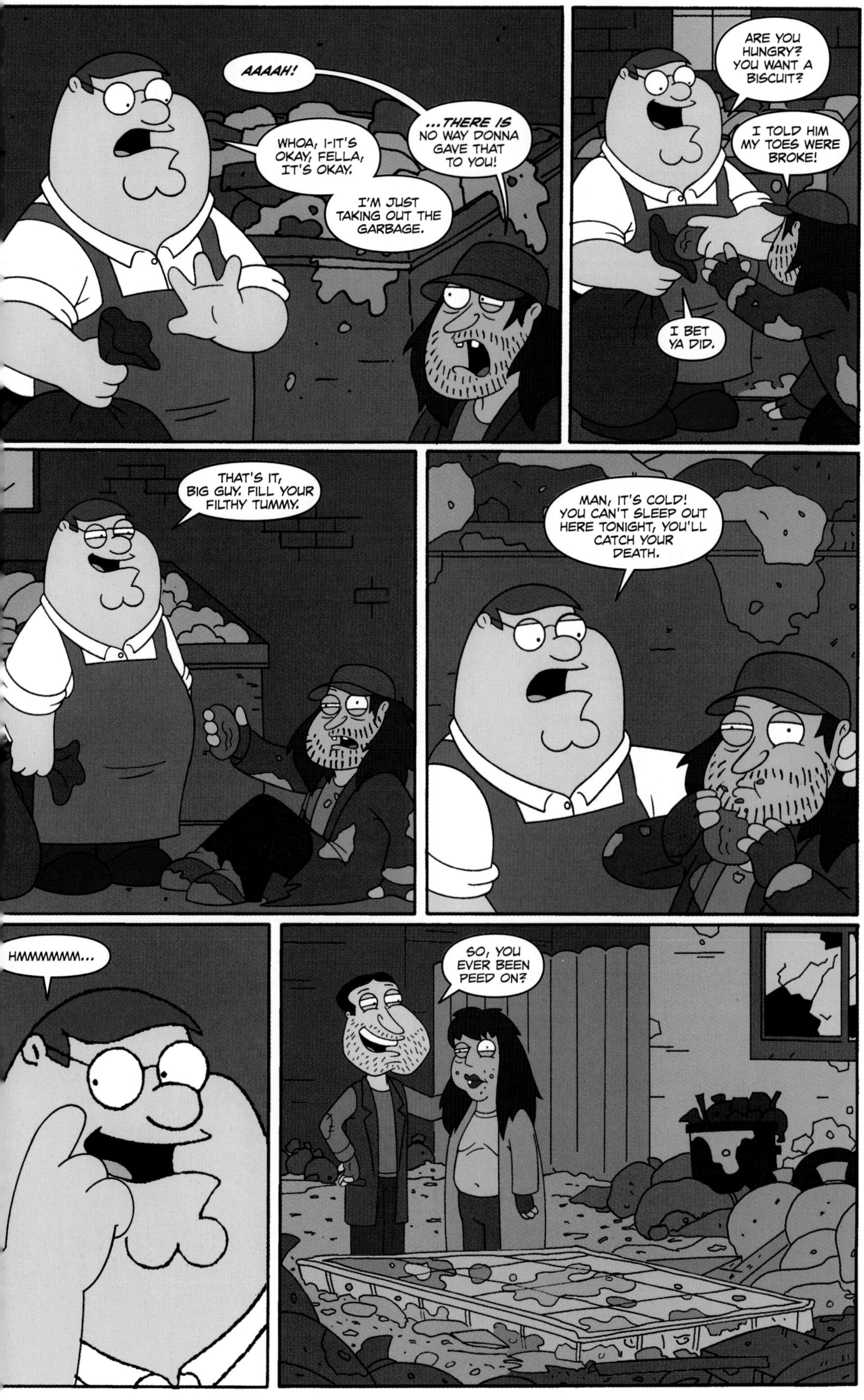
AAAAH!
...THERE IS NO WAY DONNA GAVE THAT TO YOU!
WHOA, I-IT'S OKAY, FELLA, IT'S OKAY.
I'M JUST TAKING OUT THE GARBAGE.
ARE YOU HUNGRY? YOU WANT A BISCUIT?
I TOLD HIM MY TOES WERE BROKE!
I BET YA DID.
THAT'S IT, BIG GUY. FILL YOUR FILTHY TUMMY.
MAN, IT'S COLD! YOU CAN'T SLEEP OUT HERE TONIGHT, YOU'LL CATCH YOUR DEATH.
HMMMMMMM...
SO, YOU EVER BEEN PEED ON?

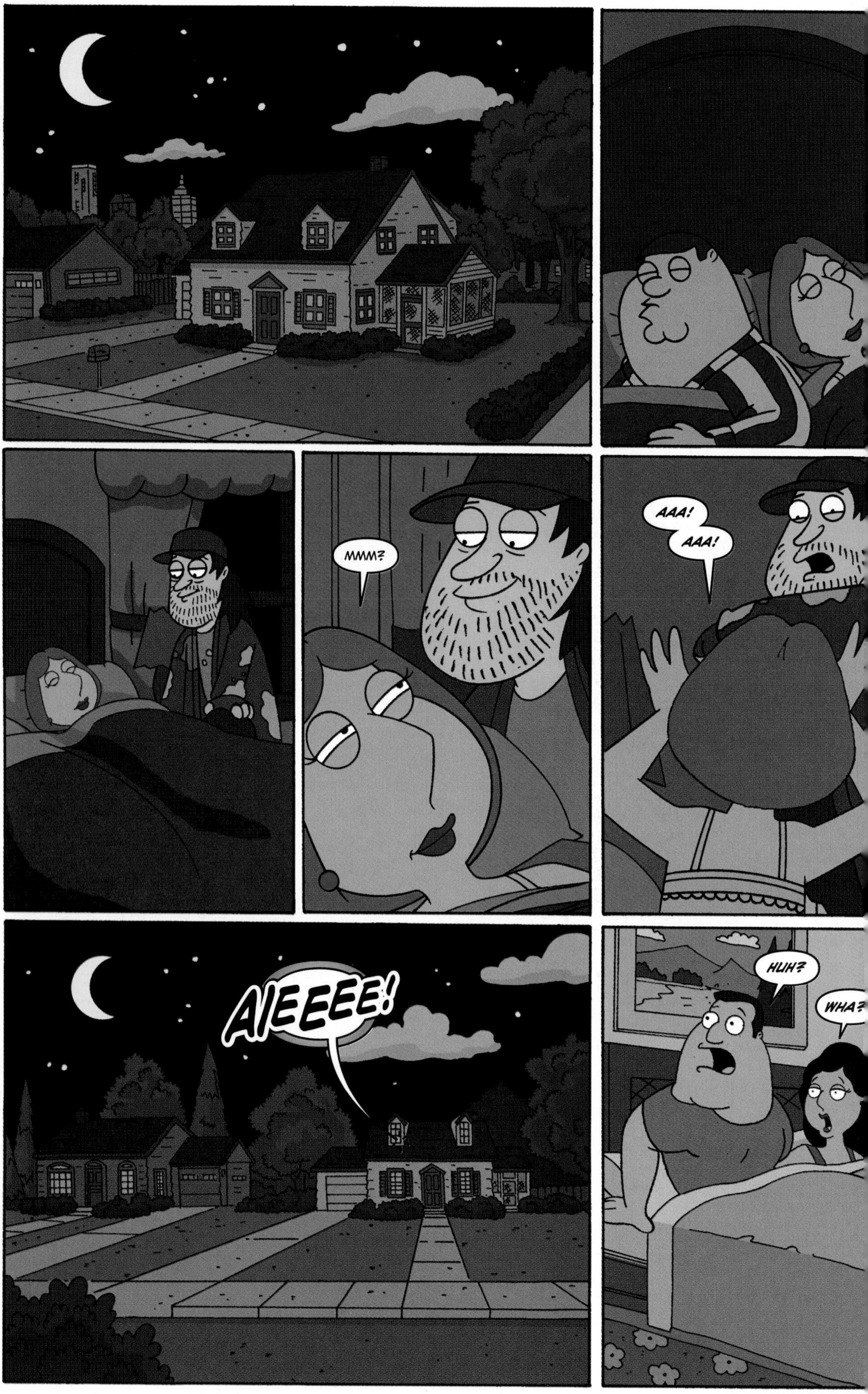
MMM?
AAA!
AAA!
AIEEEE!
HUH?
WHA?

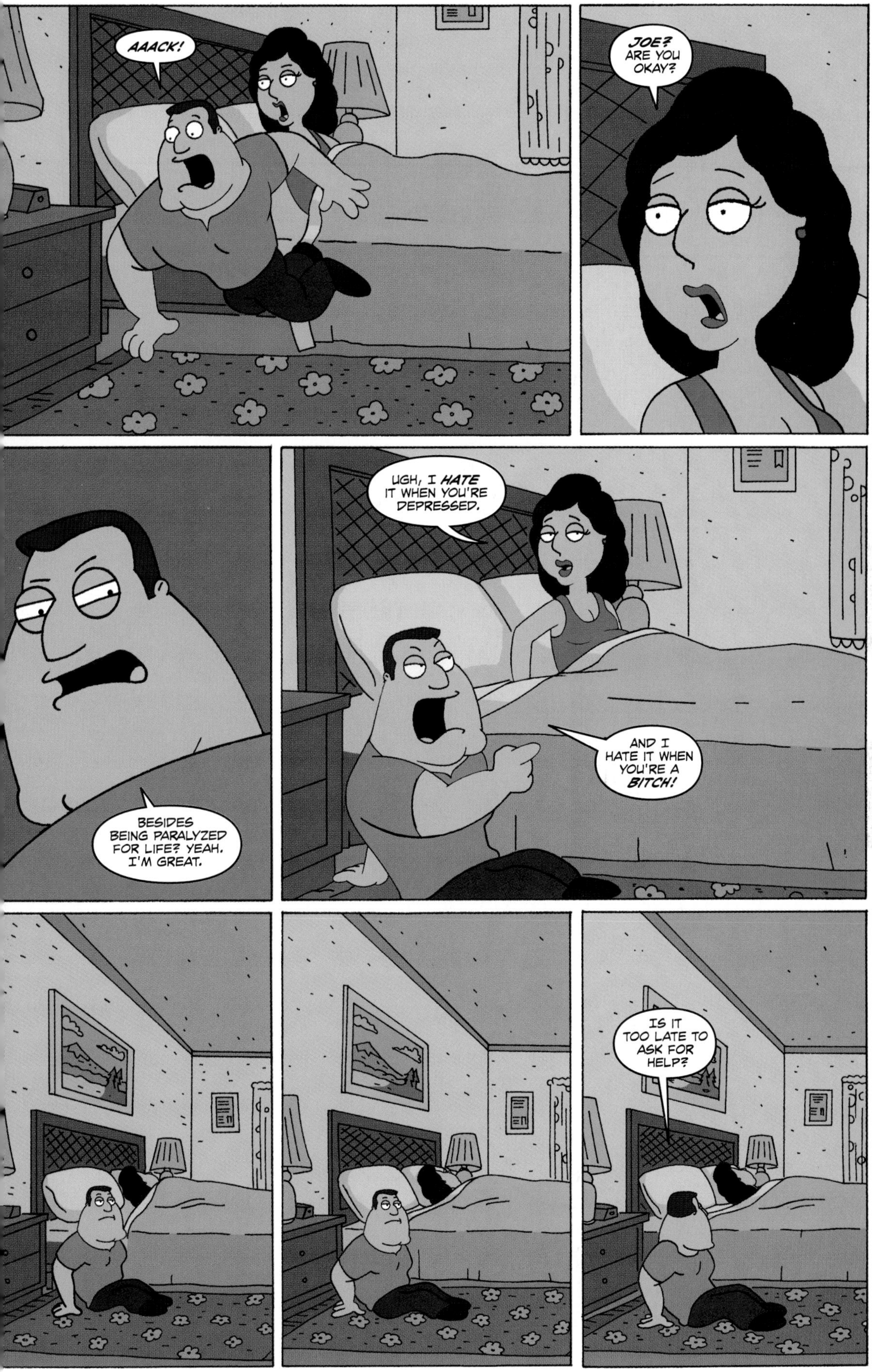
AAACK!
JOE? ARE YOU OKAY?
BESIDES BEING PARALYZED FOR LIFE? YEAH. I'M GREAT.
UGH, I HATE IT WHEN YOU'RE DEPRESSED.
AND I HATE IT WHEN YOU'RE A BITCH!
IS IT TOO LATE TO ASK FOR HELP?

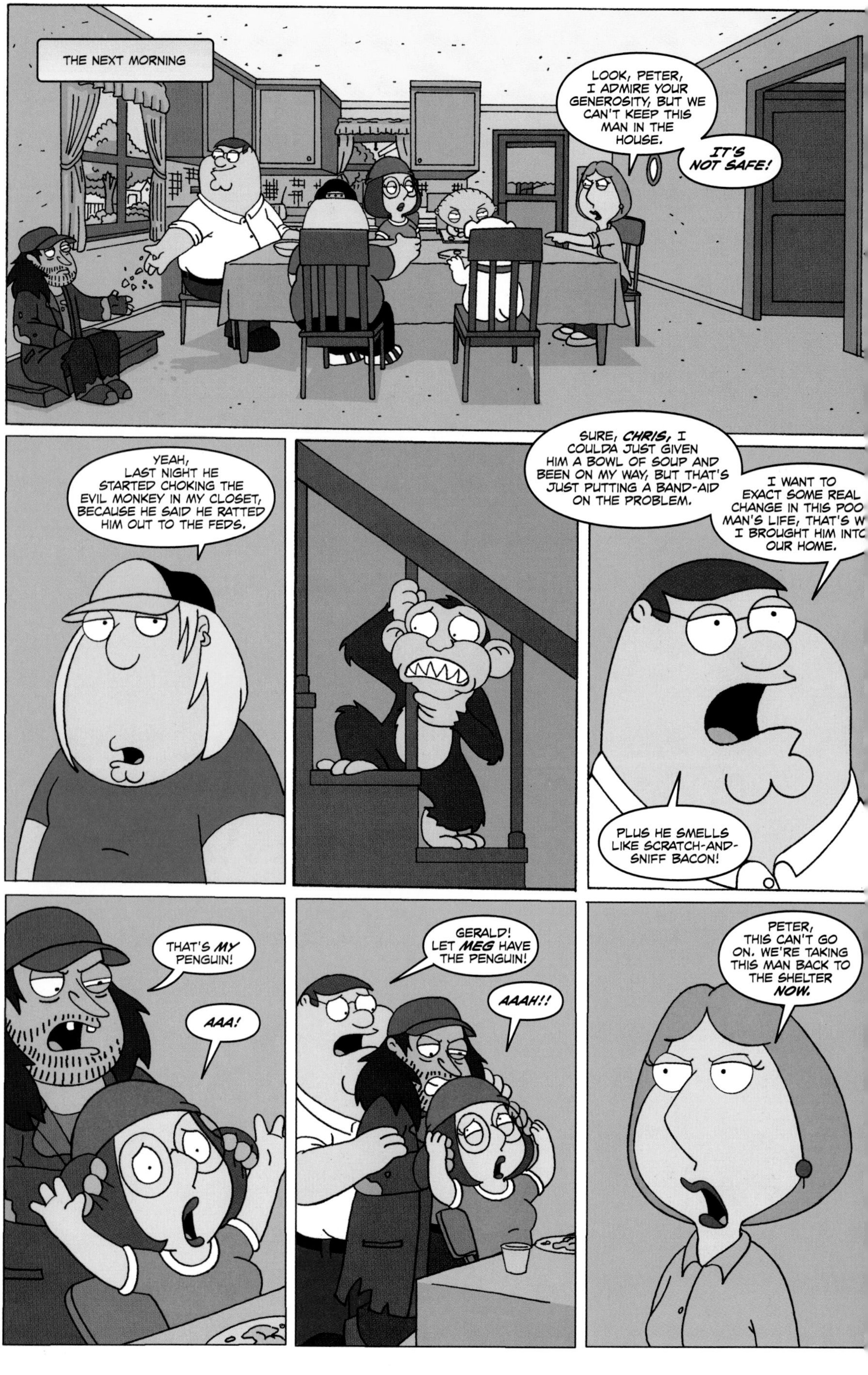
THE NEXT MORNING
LOOK, PETER, I ADMIRE YOUR GENEROSITY, BUT WE CAN'T KEEP THIS MAN IN THE HOUSE.
IT'S NOT SAFE!
YEAH, LAST NIGHT HE STARTED CHOKING THE EVIL MONKEY IN MY CLOSET, BECAUSE HE SAID HE RATTED HIM OUT TO THE FEDS.
SURE, CHRIS, I COULDA JUST GIVEN HIM A BOWL OF SOUP AND BEEN ON MY WAY, BUT THAT'S JUST PUTTING A BAND-AID ON THE PROBLEM.
I WANT TO EXACT SOME REAL CHANGE IN THIS POO MAN'S LIFE, THAT'S W I BROUGHT HIM INTO OUR HOME.
PLUS HE SMELLS LIKE SCRATCH-AND-SNIFF BACON!
THAT'S MY PENGUIN!
AAA!
GERALD! LET MEG HAVE THE PENGUIN!
AAAH!!
PETER, THIS CAN'T GO ON. WE'RE TAKING THIS MAN BACK TO THE SHELTER NOW.

"THIS MAN," LOIS? IF YOU WEREN'T SO BUSY BEING ANGRY, YOU'DA REALIZED I NAMED HIM *GERALD.*

PETER, YOU NAMED HIM?!

PETER, LOIS IS RIGHT. THIS MAN DOESN'T NEED A PLACE TO STAY, HE NEEDS INTENSE PSYCHOLOGICAL HELP.

NO, BRIAN, ALL HE NEEDS IS A LITTLE *PCP.*

DON'T YOU MEAN *TLC?*

WHY? WHAT'D I SAY?

PCP.

WHAT'S PCP?

IT'S A TYPE OF DRUG.

DRUGS, EH?

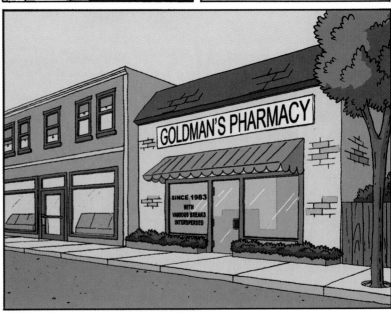

GOLDMAN'S PHARMACY

SINCE 1983 WITH VARIOUS BREAKS INTERSPERSED

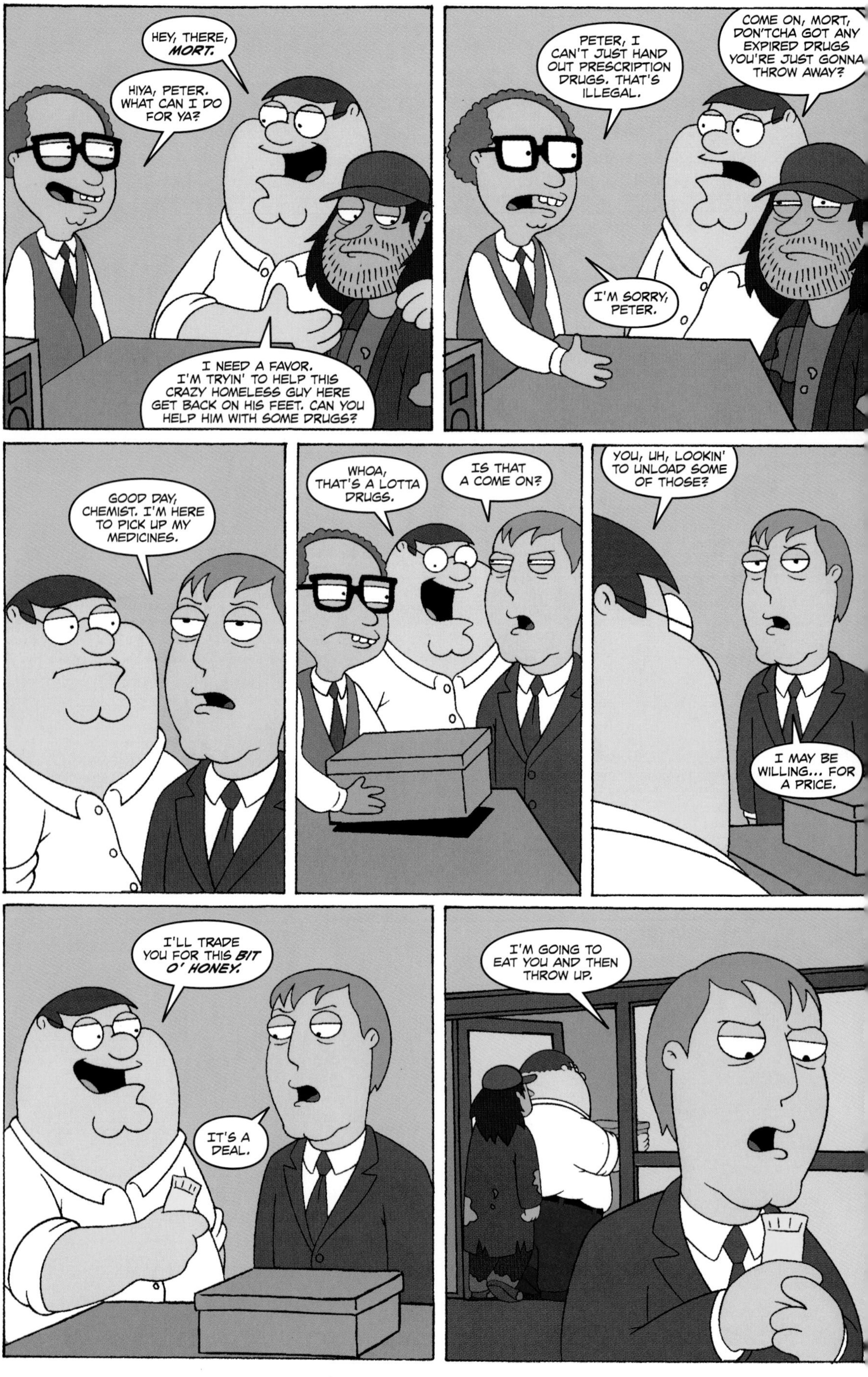
HEY, THERE, *MORT.*
HIYA, PETER. WHAT CAN I DO FOR YA?
I NEED A FAVOR. I'M TRYIN' TO HELP THIS CRAZY HOMELESS GUY HERE GET BACK ON HIS FEET. CAN YOU HELP HIM WITH SOME DRUGS?
PETER, I CAN'T JUST HAND OUT PRESCRIPTION DRUGS. THAT'S ILLEGAL.
COME ON, MORT, DON'TCHA GOT ANY EXPIRED DRUGS YOU'RE JUST GONNA THROW AWAY?
I'M SORRY, PETER.
GOOD DAY, CHEMIST. I'M HERE TO PICK UP MY MEDICINES.
WHOA, THAT'S A LOTTA DRUGS.
IS THAT A COME ON?
YOU, UH, LOOKIN' TO UNLOAD SOME OF THOSE?
I MAY BE WILLING... FOR A PRICE.
I'LL TRADE YOU FOR THIS *BIT O' HONEY.*
IT'S A DEAL.
I'M GOING TO EAT YOU AND THEN THROW UP.

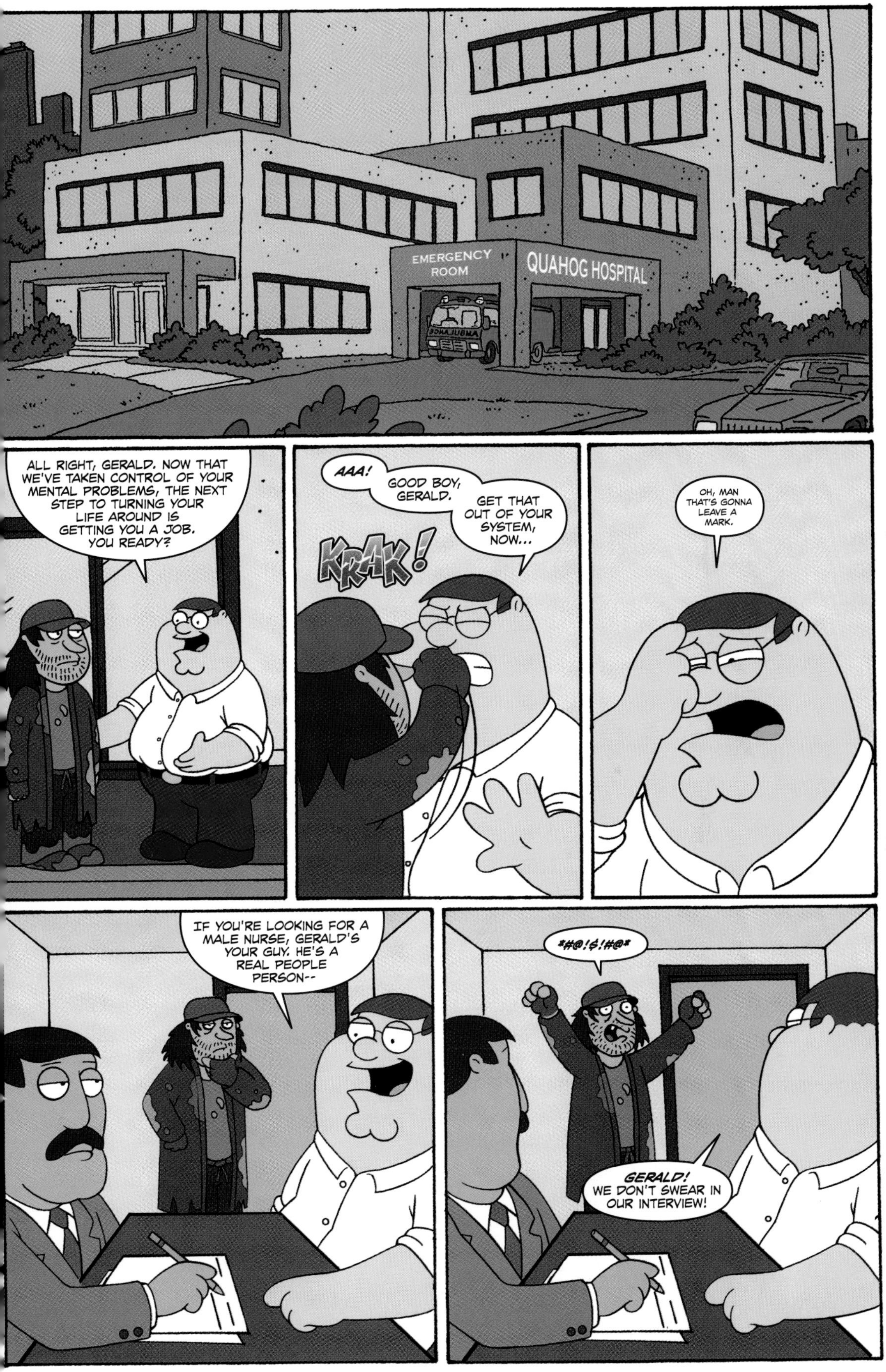
EMERGENCY ROOM
QUAHOG HOSPITAL
AMBULANCE
ALL RIGHT, GERALD. NOW THAT WE'VE TAKEN CONTROL OF YOUR MENTAL PROBLEMS, THE NEXT STEP TO TURNING YOUR LIFE AROUND IS GETTING YOU A JOB. YOU READY?
AAA!
GOOD BOY, GERALD.
GET THAT OUT OF YOUR SYSTEM, NOW...
KRAK!
OH, MAN THAT'S GONNA LEAVE A MARK.
IF YOU'RE LOOKING FOR A MALE NURSE, GERALD'S YOUR GUY. HE'S A REAL PEOPLE PERSON--
#@!$!#@
GERALD! WE DON'T SWEAR IN OUR INTERVIEW!

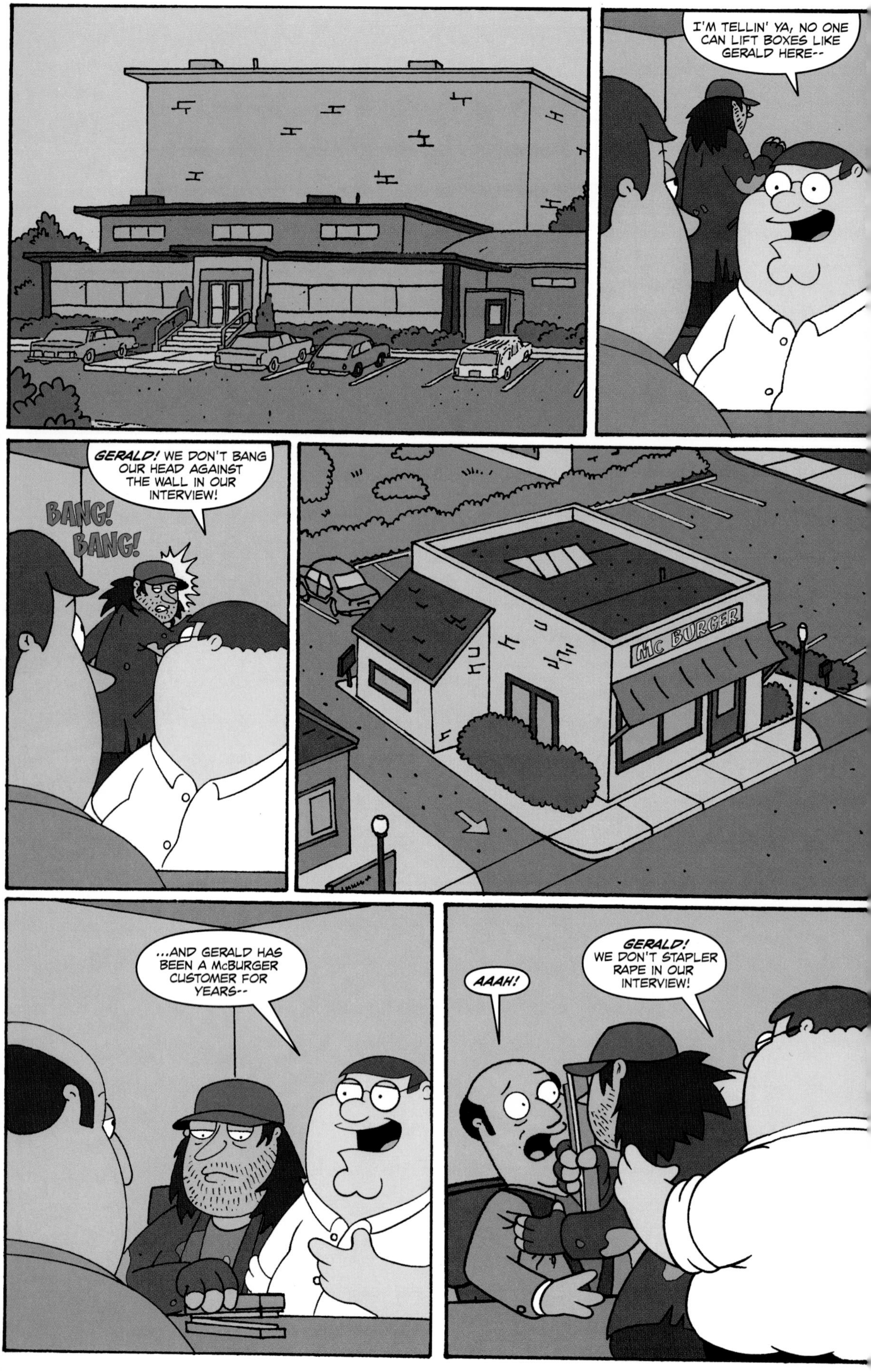
I'M TELLIN' YA, NO ONE CAN LIFT BOXES LIKE GERALD HERE--
BANG! BANG!
GERALD! WE DON'T BANG OUR HEAD AGAINST THE WALL IN OUR INTERVIEW!
MC BURGER
...AND GERALD HAS BEEN A McBURGER CUSTOMER FOR YEARS--
AAAH!
GERALD! WE DON'T STAPLER RAPE IN OUR INTERVIEW!

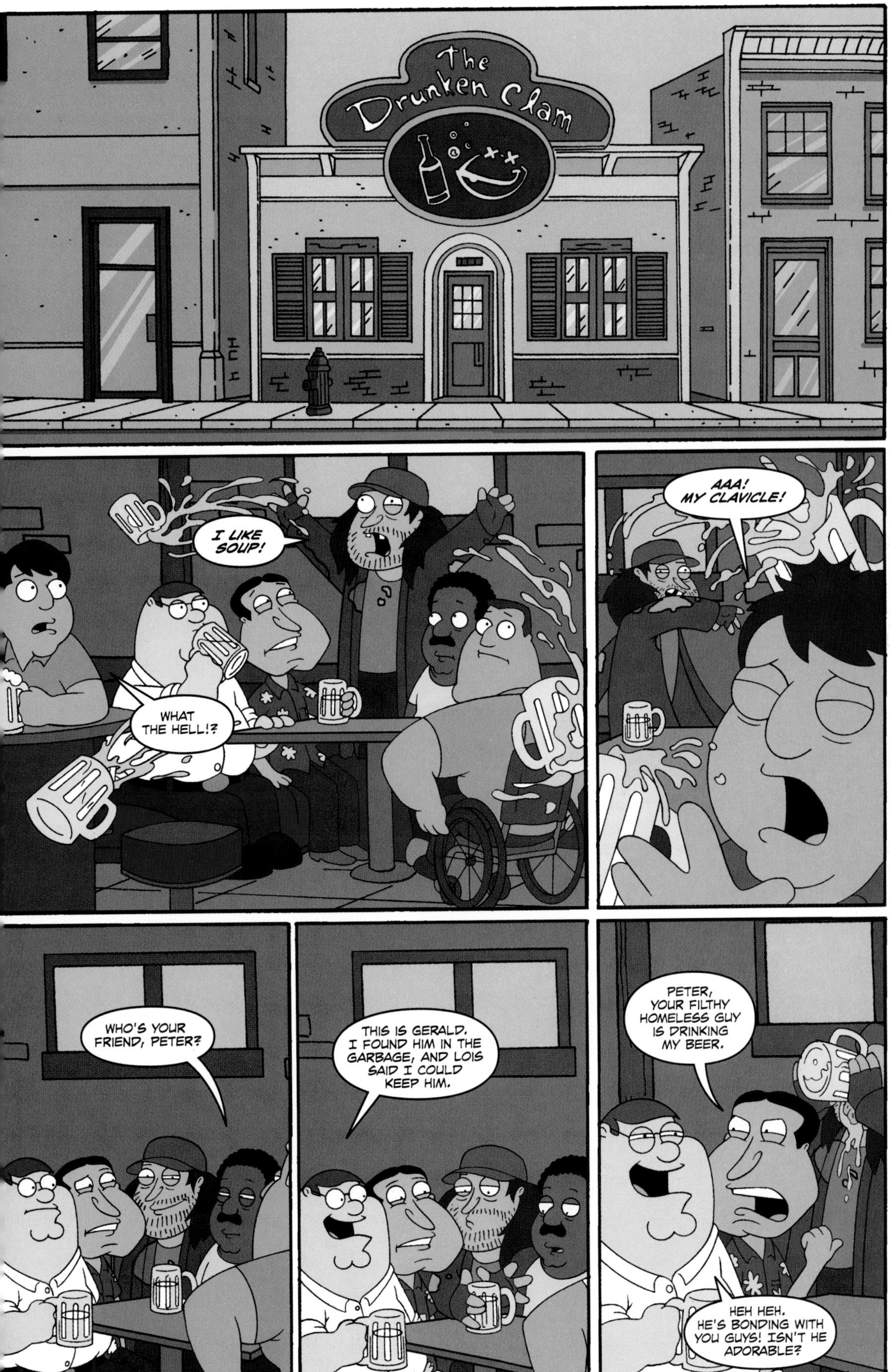
The Drunken Clam
I LIKE SOUP!
WHAT THE HELL!?
AAA! MY CLAVICLE!
WHO'S YOUR FRIEND, PETER?
THIS IS GERALD. I FOUND HIM IN THE GARBAGE, AND LOIS SAID I COULD KEEP HIM.
PETER, YOUR FILTHY HOMELESS GUY IS DRINKING MY BEER.
HEH HEH. HE'S BONDING WITH YOU GUYS! ISN'T HE ADORABLE?

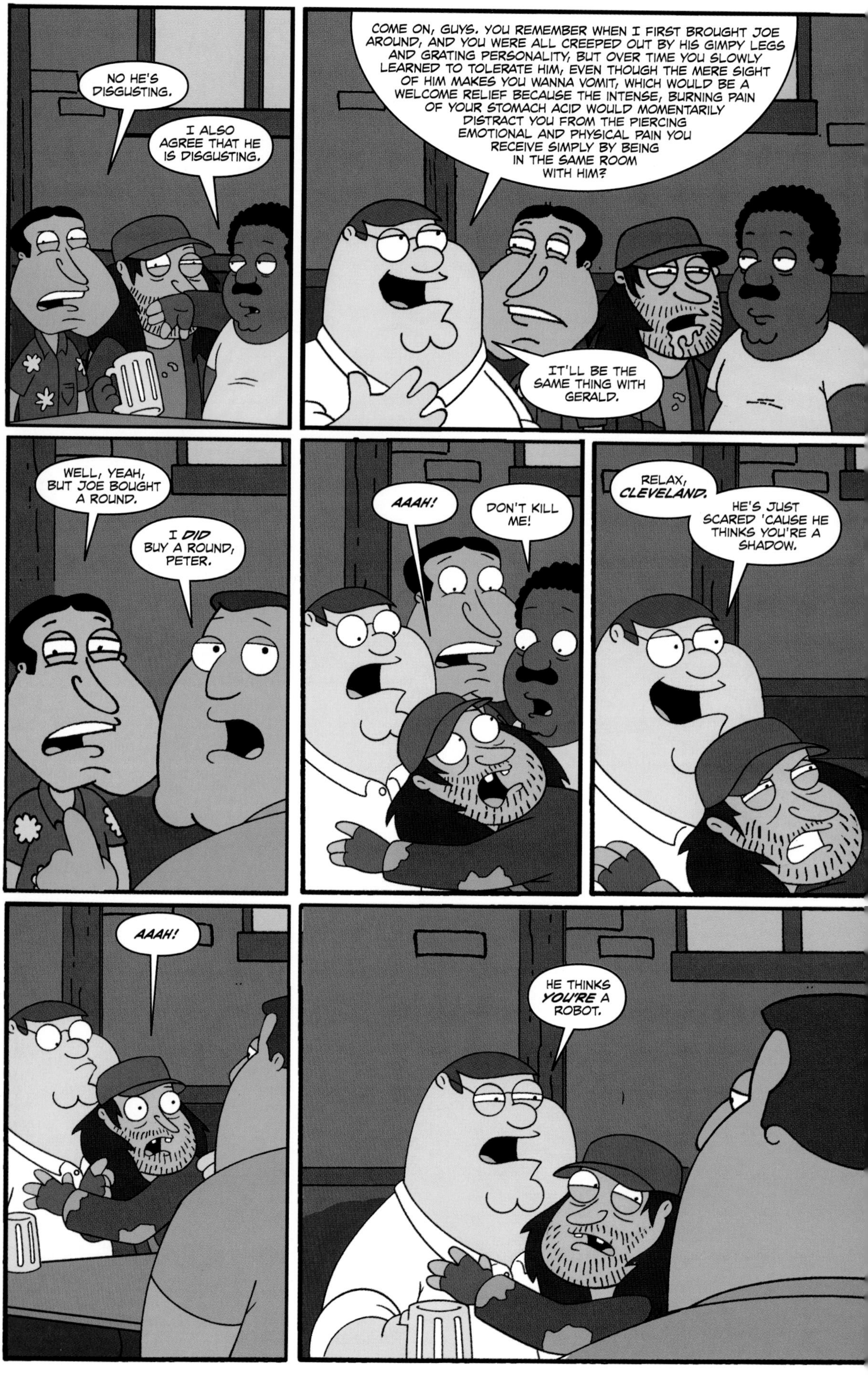
NO HE'S DISGUSTING.
I ALSO AGREE THAT HE IS DISGUSTING.
COME ON, GUYS. YOU REMEMBER WHEN I FIRST BROUGHT JOE AROUND, AND YOU WERE ALL CREEPED OUT BY HIS GIMPY LEGS AND GRATING PERSONALITY, BUT OVER TIME YOU SLOWLY LEARNED TO TOLERATE HIM, EVEN THOUGH THE MERE SIGHT OF HIM MAKES YOU WANNA VOMIT, WHICH WOULD BE A WELCOME RELIEF BECAUSE THE INTENSE, BURNING PAIN OF YOUR STOMACH ACID WOULD MOMENTARILY DISTRACT YOU FROM THE PIERCING EMOTIONAL AND PHYSICAL PAIN YOU RECEIVE SIMPLY BY BEING IN THE SAME ROOM WITH HIM?
IT'LL BE THE SAME THING WITH GERALD.
WELL, YEAH, BUT JOE BOUGHT A ROUND.
I *DID* BUY A ROUND, PETER.
AAAH!
DON'T KILL ME!
RELAX, ***CLEVELAND.***
HE'S JUST SCARED 'CAUSE HE THINKS YOU'RE A SHADOW.
AAAH!
HE THINKS ***YOU'RE*** A ROBOT.

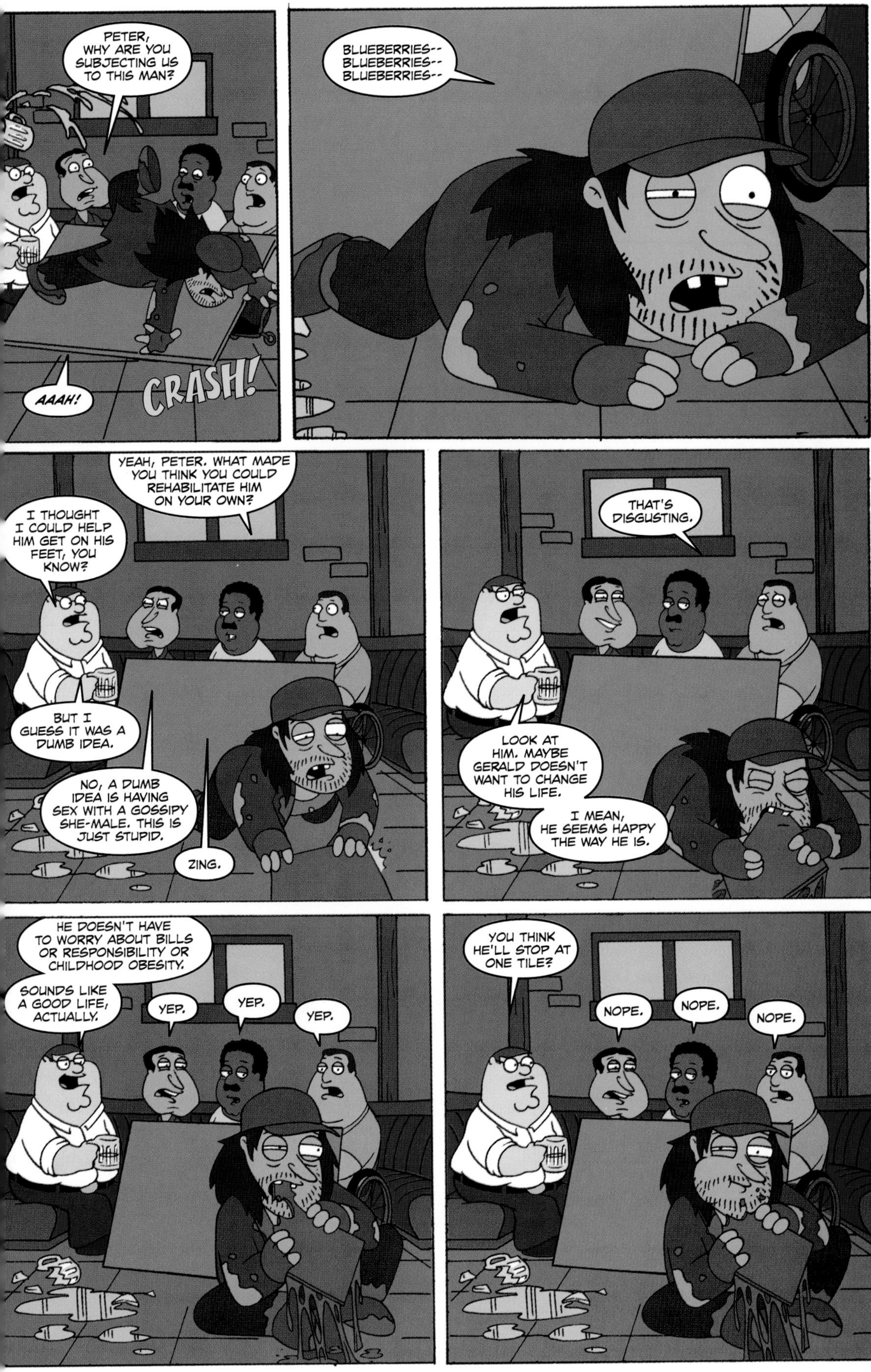
PETER, WHY ARE YOU SUBJECTING US TO THIS MAN?
AAAH!
CRASH!
BLUEBERRIES-- BLUEBERRIES-- BLUEBERRIES--
YEAH, PETER. WHAT MADE YOU THINK YOU COULD REHABILITATE HIM ON YOUR OWN?
I THOUGHT I COULD HELP HIM GET ON HIS FEET, YOU KNOW?
BUT I GUESS IT WAS A DUMB IDEA.
NO, A DUMB IDEA IS HAVING SEX WITH A GOSSIPY SHE-MALE. THIS IS JUST STUPID.
ZING.
THAT'S DISGUSTING.
LOOK AT HIM. MAYBE GERALD DOESN'T WANT TO CHANGE HIS LIFE.
I MEAN, HE SEEMS HAPPY THE WAY HE IS.
HE DOESN'T HAVE TO WORRY ABOUT BILLS OR RESPONSIBILITY OR CHILDHOOD OBESITY.
SOUNDS LIKE A GOOD LIFE, ACTUALLY.
YEP.
YEP.
YEP.
YOU THINK HE'LL STOP AT ONE TILE?
NOPE.
NOPE.
NOPE.

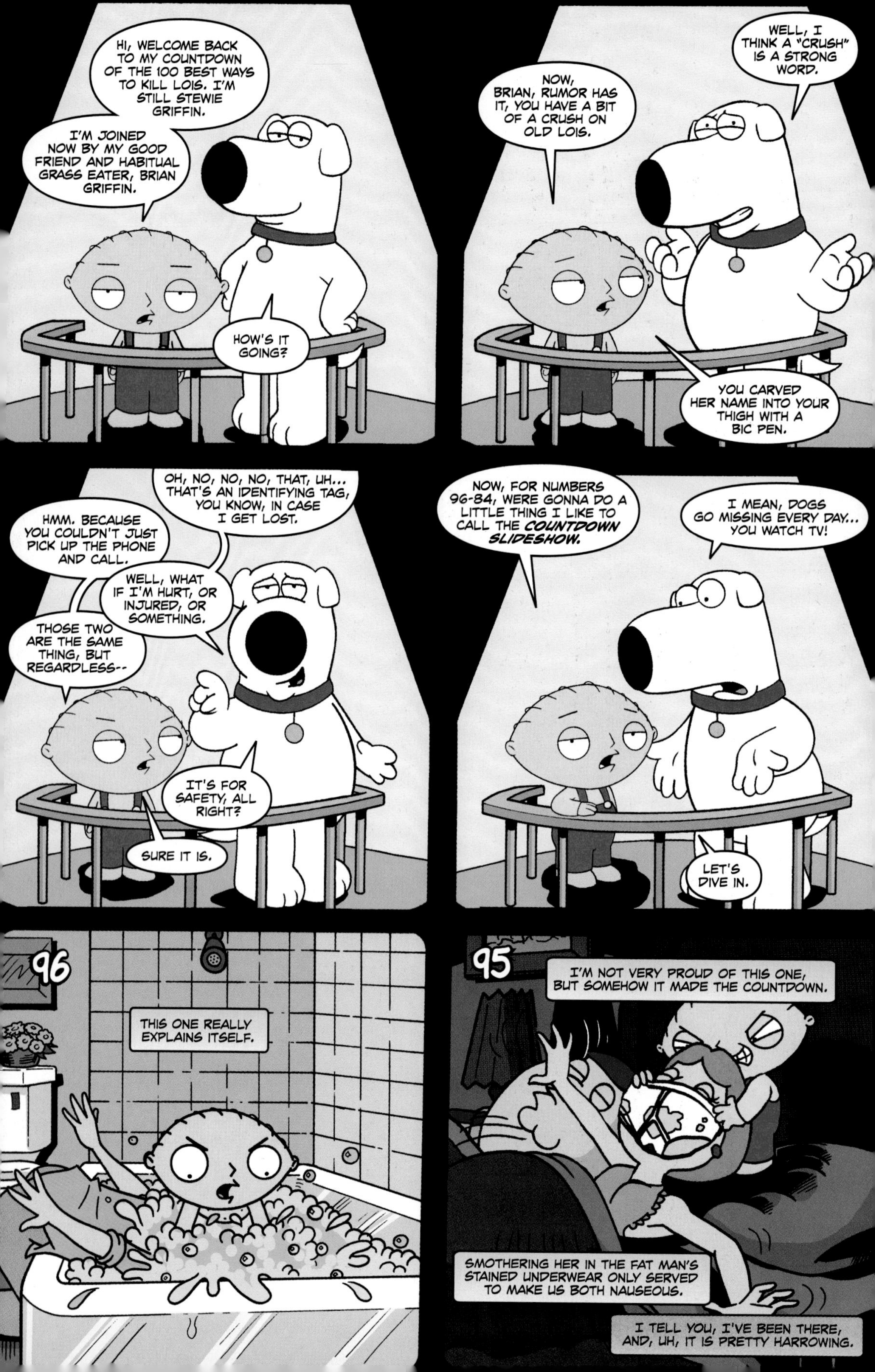
HI, WELCOME BACK TO MY COUNTDOWN OF THE 100 BEST WAYS TO KILL LOIS. I'M STILL STEWIE GRIFFIN.
I'M JOINED NOW BY MY GOOD FRIEND AND HABITUAL GRASS EATER, BRIAN GRIFFIN.
HOW'S IT GOING?
NOW, BRIAN, RUMOR HAS IT, YOU HAVE A BIT OF A CRUSH ON OLD LOIS.
WELL, I THINK A "CRUSH" IS A STRONG WORD.
YOU CARVED HER NAME INTO YOUR THIGH WITH A BIC PEN.
OH, NO, NO, NO, THAT, UH... THAT'S AN IDENTIFYING TAG, YOU KNOW, IN CASE I GET LOST.
HMM. BECAUSE YOU COULDN'T JUST PICK UP THE PHONE AND CALL.
WELL, WHAT IF I'M HURT, OR INJURED, OR SOMETHING.
THOSE TWO ARE THE SAME THING, BUT REGARDLESS--
IT'S FOR SAFETY, ALL RIGHT?
SURE IT IS.
I MEAN, DOGS GO MISSING EVERY DAY... YOU WATCH TV!
NOW, FOR NUMBERS 96-84, WERE GONNA DO A LITTLE THING I LIKE TO CALL THE COUNTDOWN SLIDESHOW.
LET'S DIVE IN.
96
THIS ONE REALLY EXPLAINS ITSELF.
95
I'M NOT VERY PROUD OF THIS ONE, BUT SOMEHOW IT MADE THE COUNTDOWN.
SMOTHERING HER IN THE FAT MAN'S STAINED UNDERWEAR ONLY SERVED TO MAKE US BOTH NAUSEOUS.
I TELL YOU, I'VE BEEN THERE, AND, UH, IT IS PRETTY HARROWING.

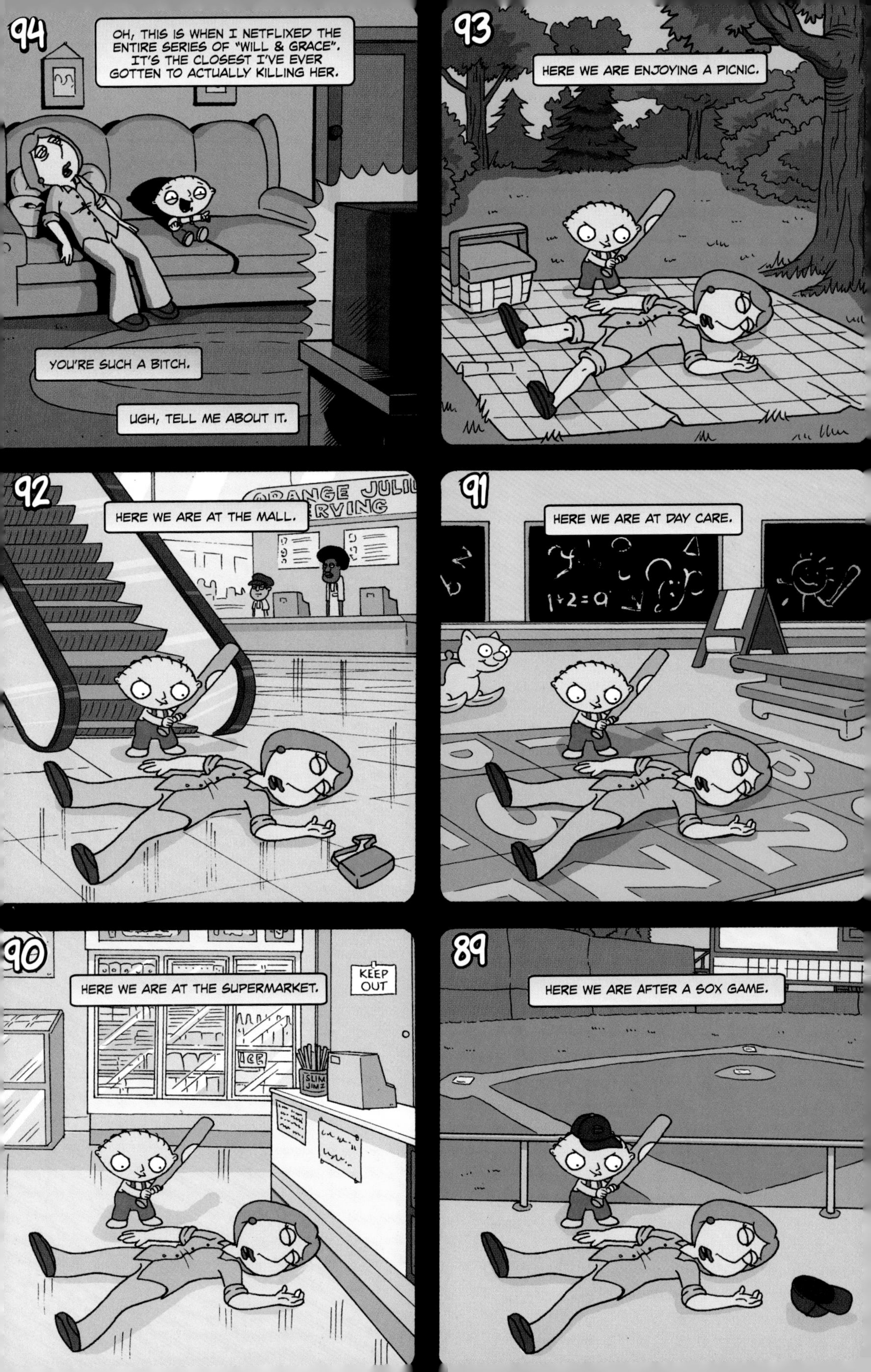
94
OH, THIS IS WHEN I NETFLIXED THE ENTIRE SERIES OF "WILL & GRACE". IT'S THE CLOSEST I'VE EVER GOTTEN TO ACTUALLY KILLING HER.
YOU'RE SUCH A BITCH.
UGH, TELL ME ABOUT IT.
93
HERE WE ARE ENJOYING A PICNIC.
92
HERE WE ARE AT THE MALL.
91
HERE WE ARE AT DAY CARE.
90
HERE WE ARE AT THE SUPERMARKET.
KEEP OUT
ICE
SLIM JIMZ
89
HERE WE ARE AFTER A SOX GAME.

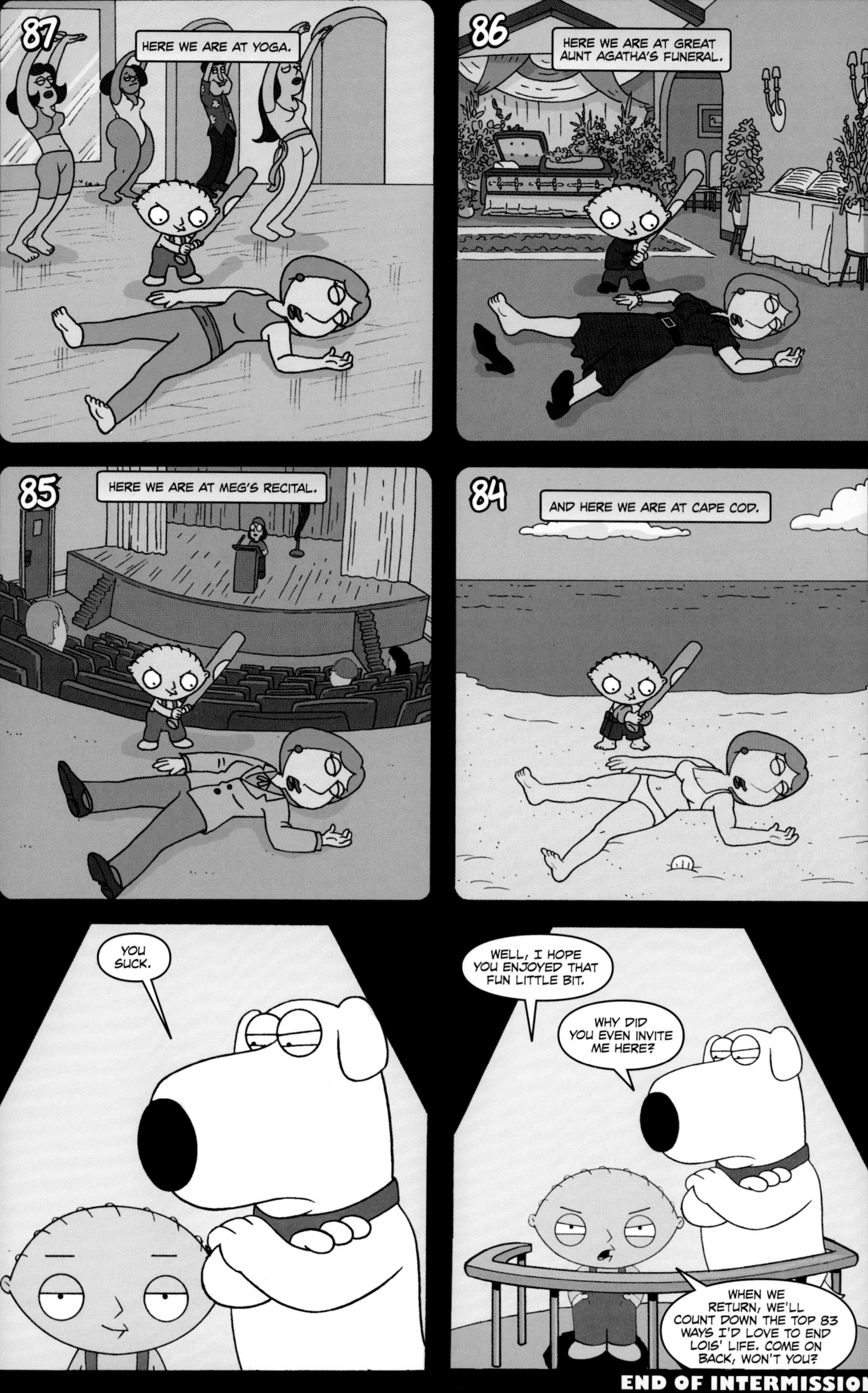
87
HERE WE ARE AT YOGA.
86
HERE WE ARE AT GREAT AUNT AGATHA'S FUNERAL.
85
HERE WE ARE AT MEG'S RECITAL.
84
AND HERE WE ARE AT CAPE COD.
YOU SUCK.
WELL, I HOPE YOU ENJOYED THAT FUN LITTLE BIT.
WHY DID YOU EVEN INVITE ME HERE?
WHEN WE RETURN, WE'LL COUNT DOWN THE TOP 83 WAYS I'D LOVE TO END LOIS' LIFE. COME ON BACK, WON'T YOU?
END OF INTERMISSIO

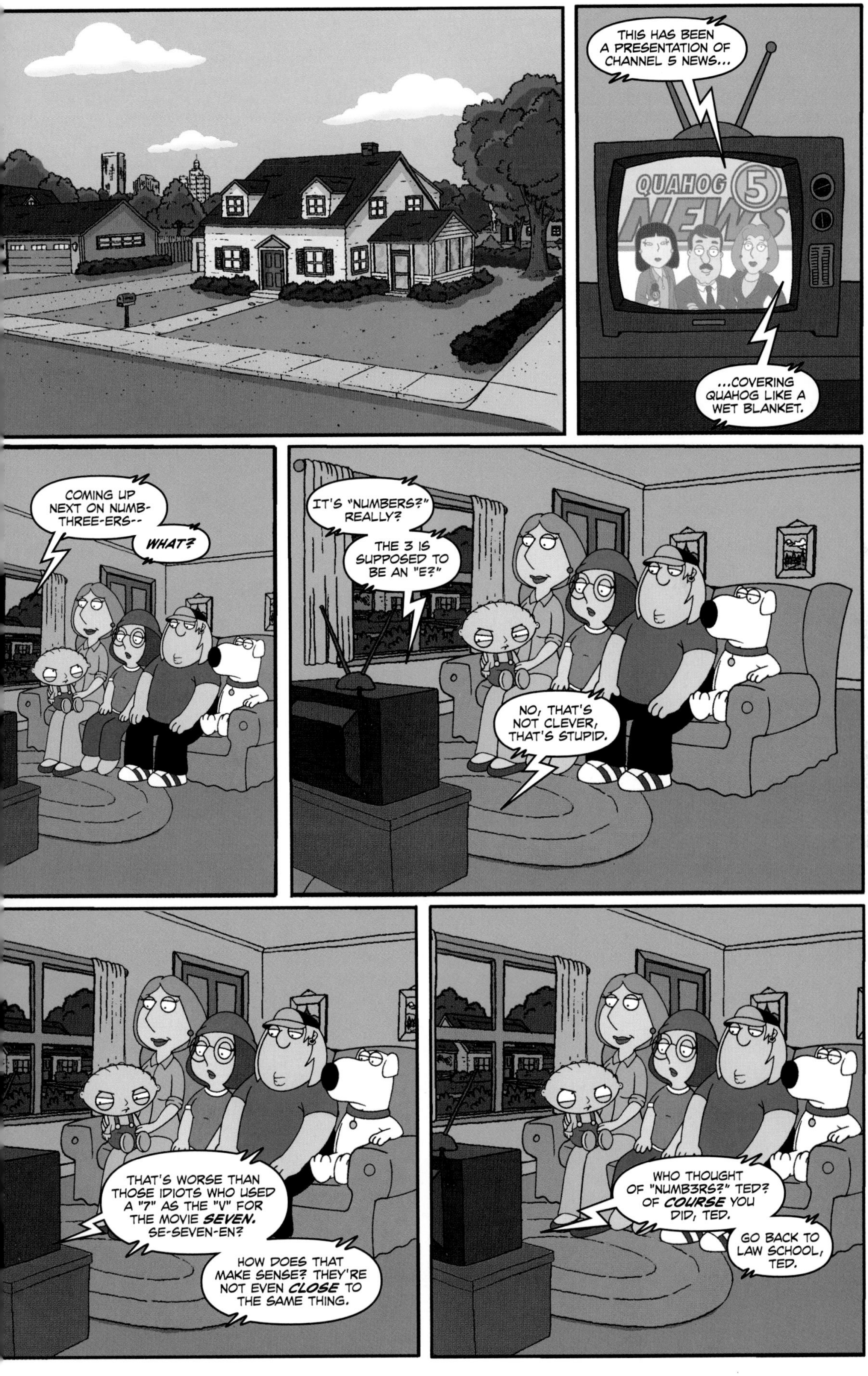
THIS HAS BEEN A PRESENTATION OF CHANNEL 5 NEWS...
QUAHOG 5 NEWS
...COVERING QUAHOG LIKE A WET BLANKET.
COMING UP NEXT ON NUMB-THREE-ERS--
WHAT?
IT'S "NUMBERS?" REALLY?
THE 3 IS SUPPOSED TO BE AN "E?"
NO, THAT'S NOT CLEVER, THAT'S STUPID.
THAT'S WORSE THAN THOSE IDIOTS WHO USED A "7" AS THE "V" FOR THE MOVIE SEVEN. SE-SEVEN-EN?
HOW DOES THAT MAKE SENSE? THEY'RE NOT EVEN CLOSE TO THE SAME THING.
WHO THOUGHT OF "NUMB3RS?" TED? OF COURSE YOU DID, TED.
GO BACK TO LAW SCHOOL, TED.

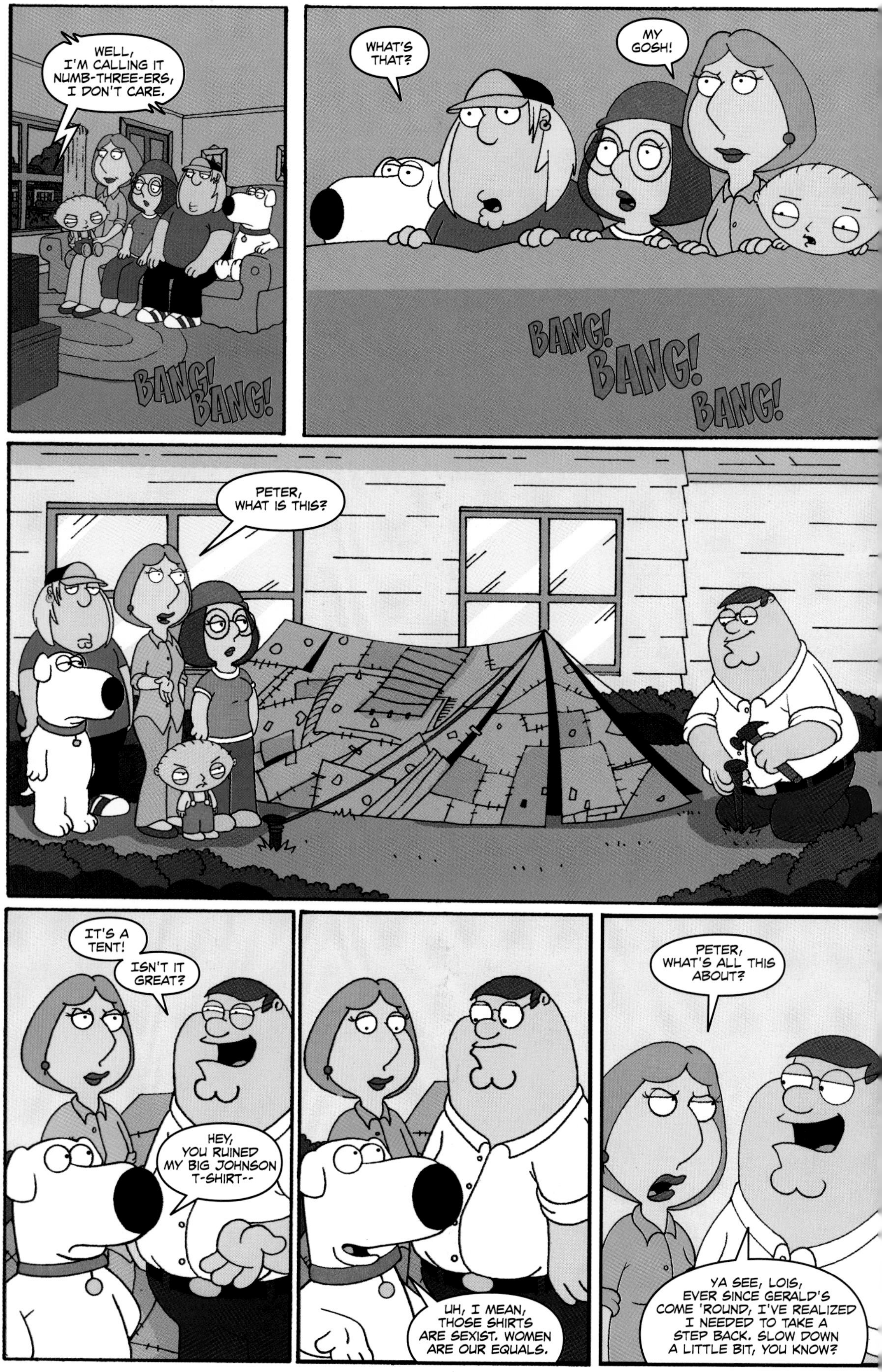
WELL, I'M CALLING IT NUMB-THREE-ERS, I DON'T CARE.
BANG! BANG!
WHAT'S THAT?
MY GOSH!
BANG! BANG! BANG!
PETER, WHAT IS THIS?
IT'S A TENT!
ISN'T IT GREAT?
HEY, YOU RUINED MY BIG JOHNSON T-SHIRT--
UH, I MEAN, THOSE SHIRTS ARE SEXIST. WOMEN ARE OUR EQUALS.
PETER, WHAT'S ALL THIS ABOUT?
YA SEE, LOIS, EVER SINCE GERALD'S COME 'ROUND, I'VE REALIZED I NEEDED TO TAKE A STEP BACK. SLOW DOWN A LITTLE BIT, YOU KNOW?

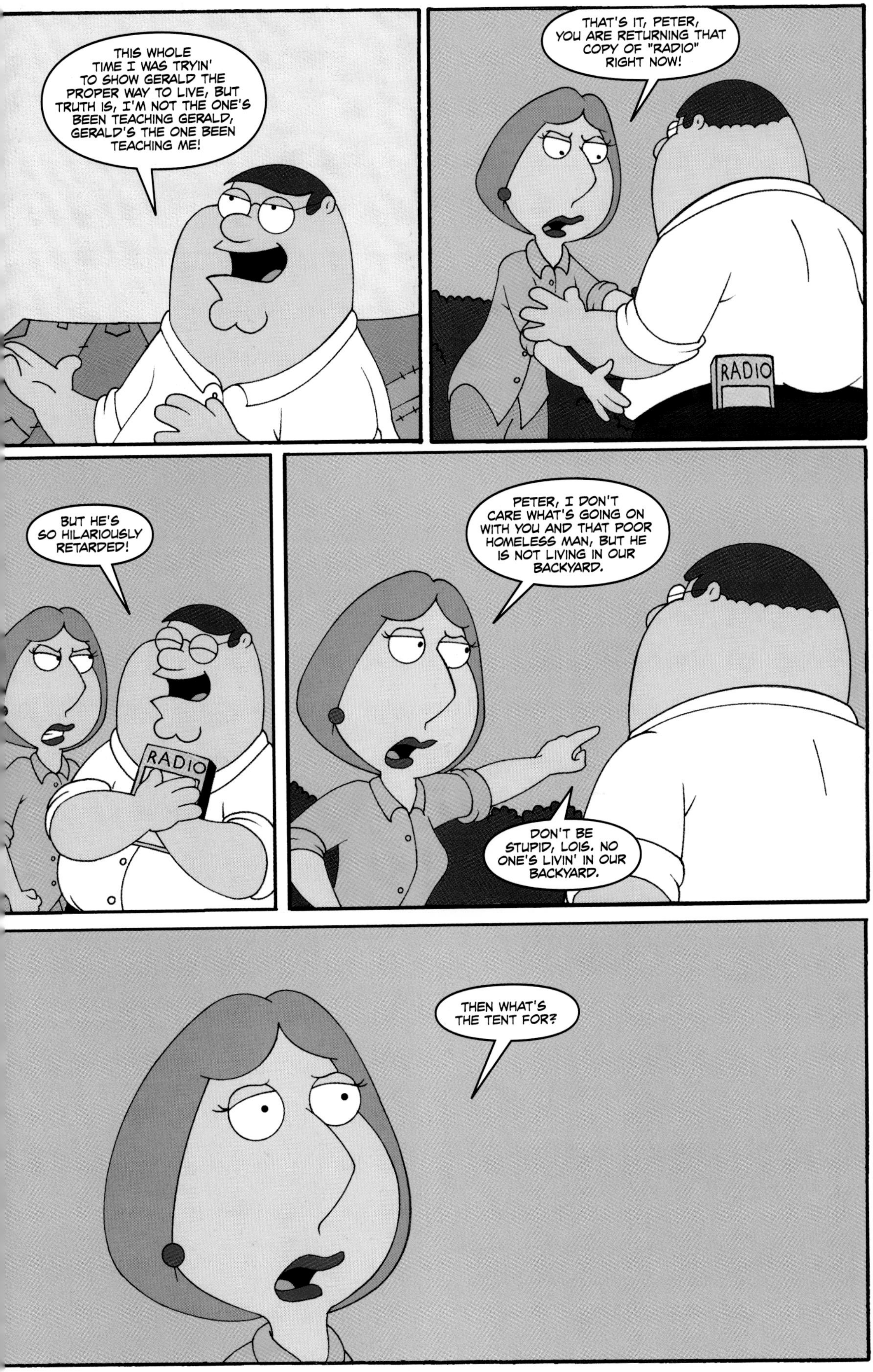
THIS WHOLE TIME I WAS TRYIN' TO SHOW GERALD THE PROPER WAY TO LIVE, BUT TRUTH IS, I'M NOT THE ONE'S BEEN TEACHING GERALD, GERALD'S THE ONE BEEN TEACHING ME!
THAT'S IT, PETER, YOU ARE RETURNING THAT COPY OF "RADIO" RIGHT NOW!
RADIO
BUT HE'S SO HILARIOUSLY RETARDED!
RADIO
PETER, I DON'T CARE WHAT'S GOING ON WITH YOU AND THAT POOR HOMELESS MAN, BUT HE IS NOT LIVING IN OUR BACKYARD.
DON'T BE STUPID, LOIS. NO ONE'S LIVIN' IN OUR BACKYARD.
THEN WHAT'S THE TENT FOR?

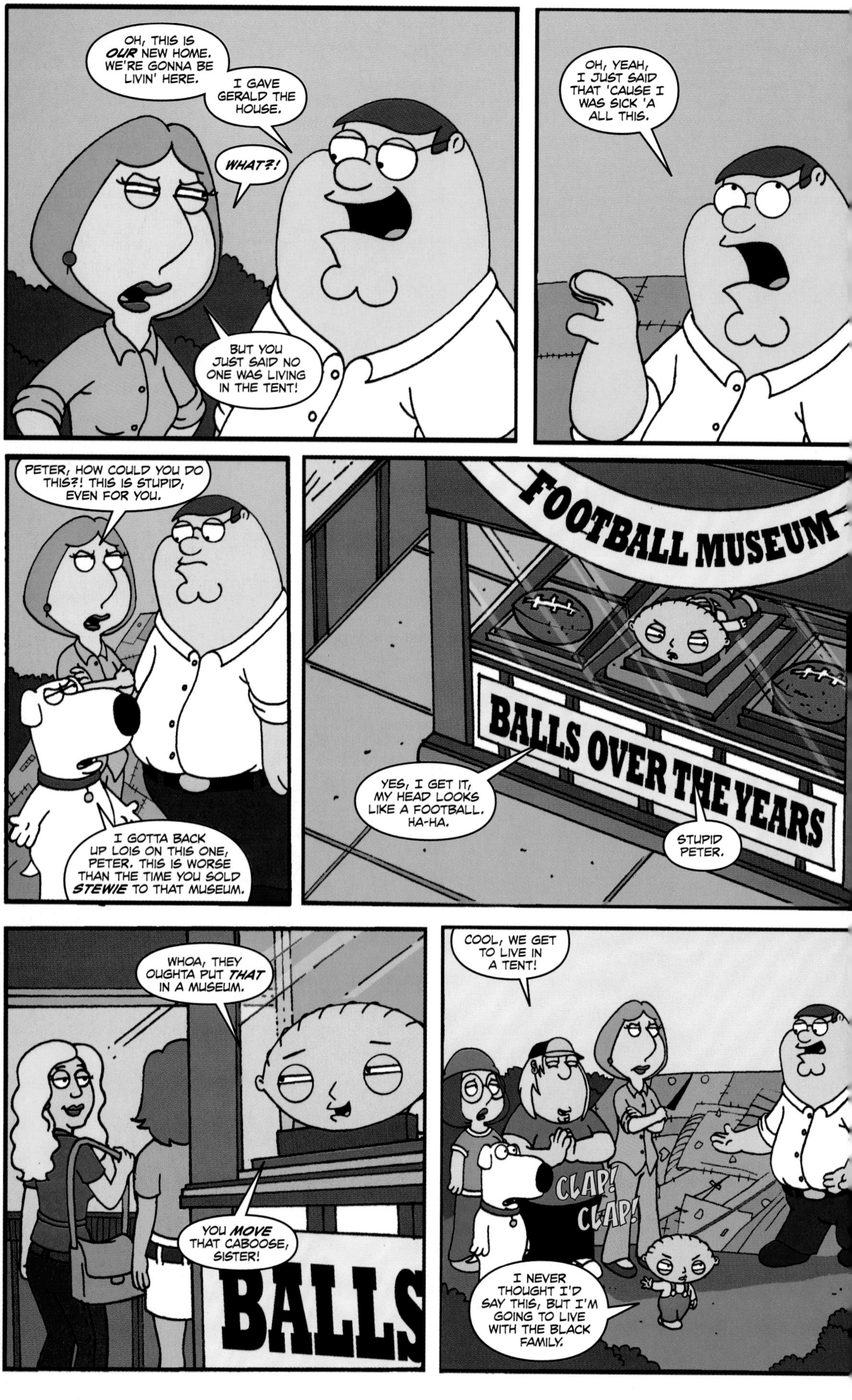
OH, THIS IS OUR NEW HOME. WE'RE GONNA BE LIVIN' HERE.
I GAVE GERALD THE HOUSE.
WHAT?!
BUT YOU JUST SAID NO ONE WAS LIVING IN THE TENT!
OH, YEAH, I JUST SAID THAT 'CAUSE I WAS SICK 'A ALL THIS.
PETER, HOW COULD YOU DO THIS?! THIS IS STUPID, EVEN FOR YOU.
I GOTTA BACK UP LOIS ON THIS ONE, PETER. THIS IS WORSE THAN THE TIME YOU SOLD STEWIE TO THAT MUSEUM.
FOOTBALL MUSEUM
BALLS OVER THE YEARS
YES, I GET IT, MY HEAD LOOKS LIKE A FOOTBALL. HA-HA.
STUPID PETER.
WHOA, THEY OUGHTA PUT THAT IN A MUSEUM.
YOU MOVE THAT CABOOSE, SISTER!
BALLS
COOL, WE GET TO LIVE IN A TENT!
CLAP! CLAP!
I NEVER THOUGHT I'D SAY THIS, BUT I'M GOING TO LIVE WITH THE BLACK FAMILY.

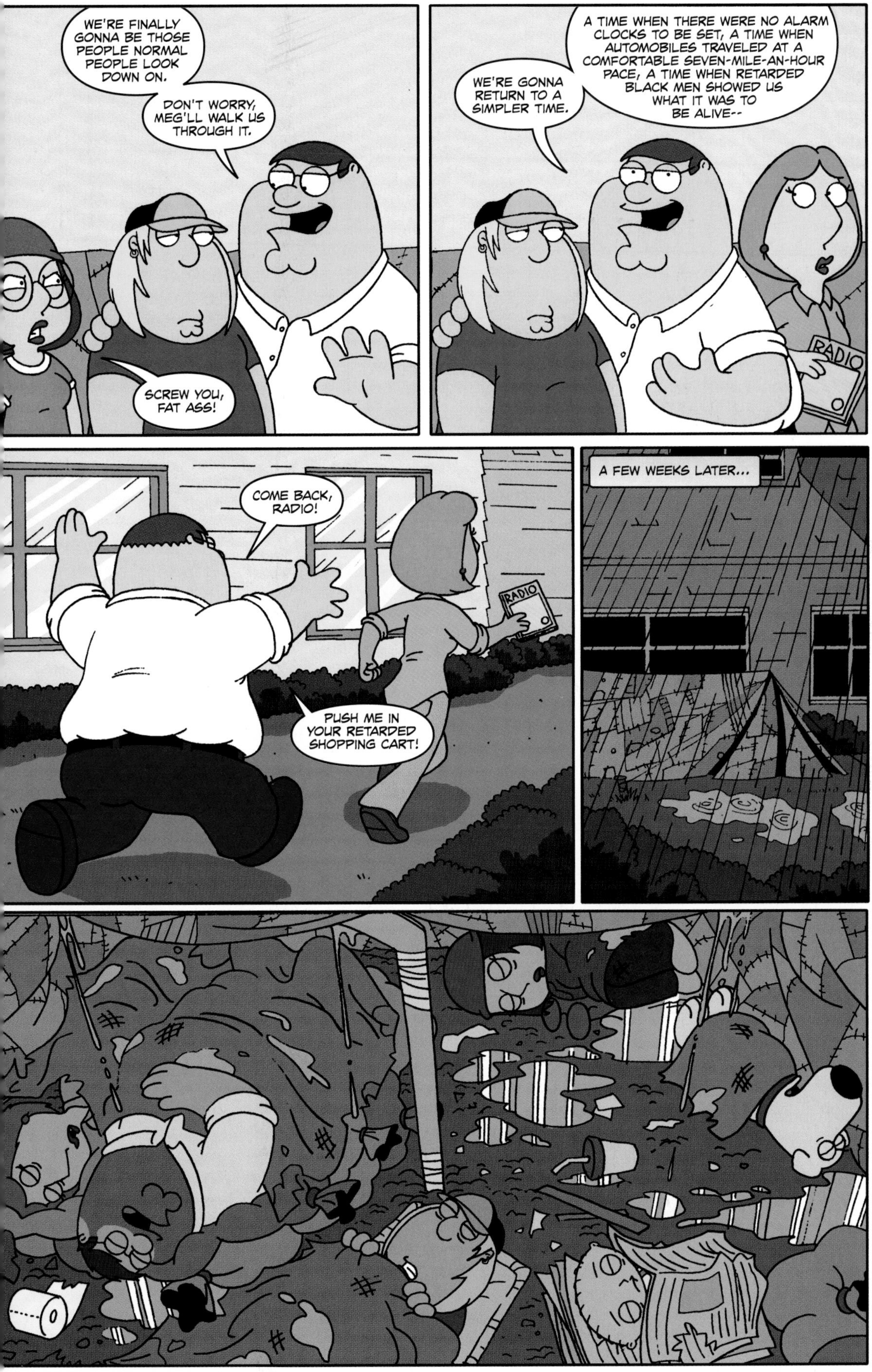
WE'RE FINALLY GONNA BE THOSE PEOPLE NORMAL PEOPLE LOOK DOWN ON.
DON'T WORRY, MEG'LL WALK US THROUGH IT.
SCREW YOU, FAT ASS!
WE'RE GONNA RETURN TO A SIMPLER TIME.
A TIME WHEN THERE WERE NO ALARM CLOCKS TO BE SET, A TIME WHEN AUTOMOBILES TRAVELED AT A COMFORTABLE SEVEN-MILE-AN-HOUR PACE, A TIME WHEN RETARDED BLACK MEN SHOWED US WHAT IT WAS TO BE ALIVE--
RADIO
COME BACK, RADIO!
RADIO
PUSH ME IN YOUR RETARDED SHOPPING CART!
A FEW WEEKS LATER...

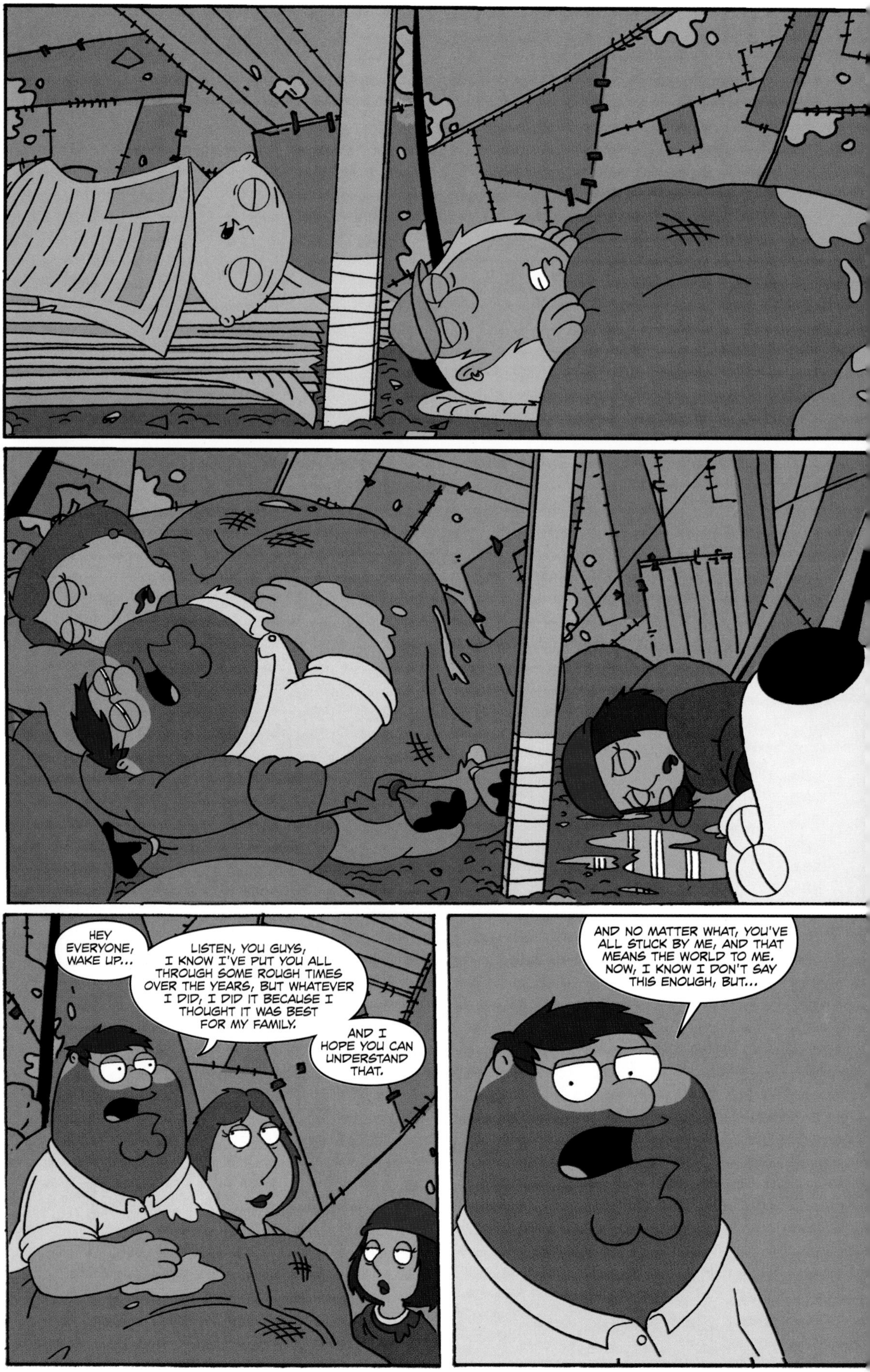
HEY EVERYONE, WAKE UP...
LISTEN, YOU GUYS, I KNOW I'VE PUT YOU ALL THROUGH SOME ROUGH TIMES OVER THE YEARS, BUT WHATEVER I DID, I DID IT BECAUSE I THOUGHT IT WAS BEST FOR MY FAMILY.
AND I HOPE YOU CAN UNDERSTAND THAT.
AND NO MATTER WHAT, YOU'VE ALL STUCK BY ME, AND THAT MEANS THE WORLD TO ME. NOW, I KNOW I DON'T SAY THIS ENOUGH, BUT...

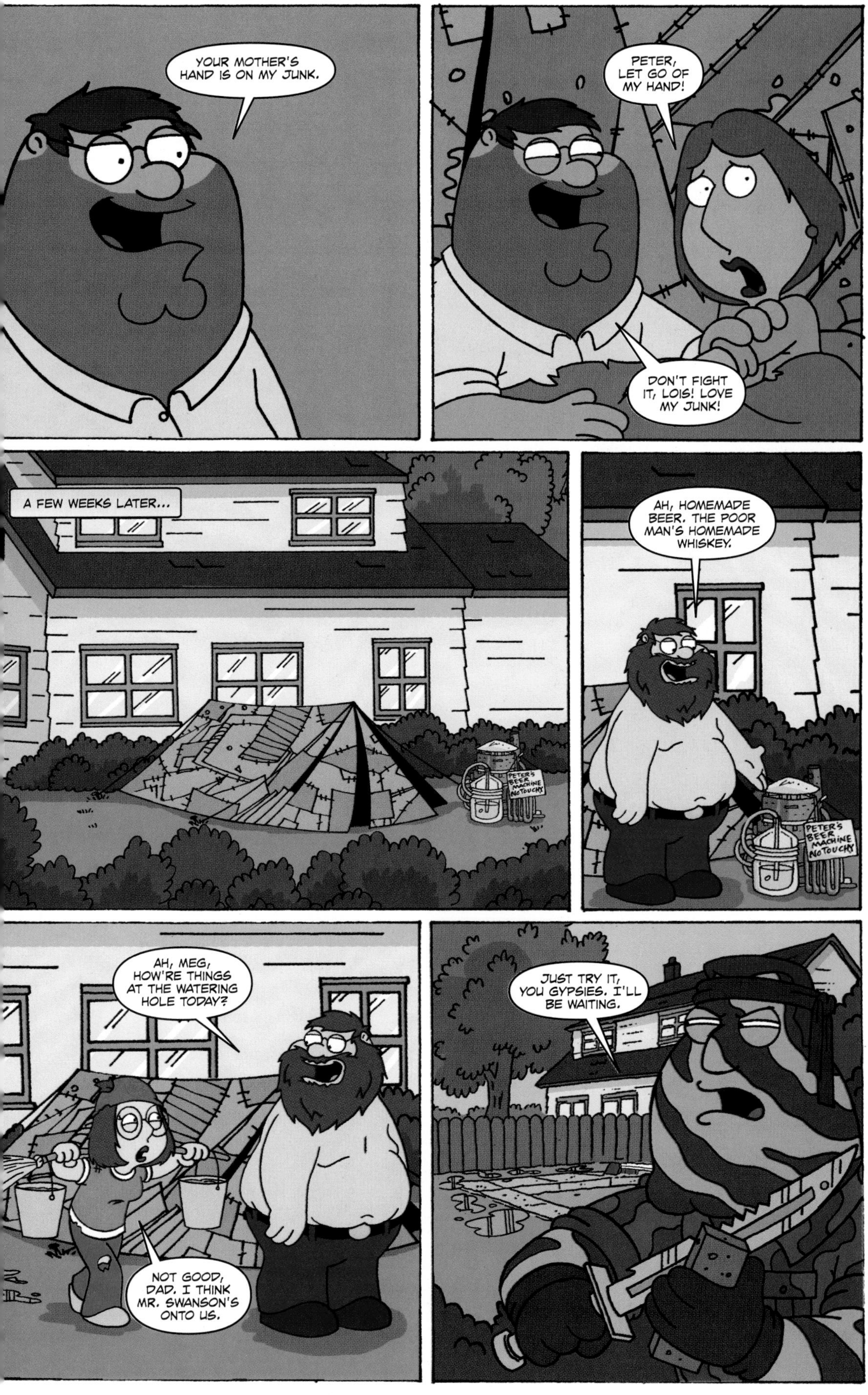
YOUR MOTHER'S HAND IS ON MY JUNK.
PETER, LET GO OF MY HAND!
DON'T FIGHT IT, LOIS! LOVE MY JUNK!
A FEW WEEKS LATER...
PETER'S BEER MACHINE NO TOUCHY
AH, HOMEMADE BEER. THE POOR MAN'S HOMEMADE WHISKEY.
PETER'S BEER MACHINE NO TOUCHY
AH, MEG, HOW'RE THINGS AT THE WATERING HOLE TODAY?
NOT GOOD, DAD. I THINK MR. SWANSON'S ONTO US.
JUST TRY IT, YOU GYPSIES. I'LL BE WAITING.

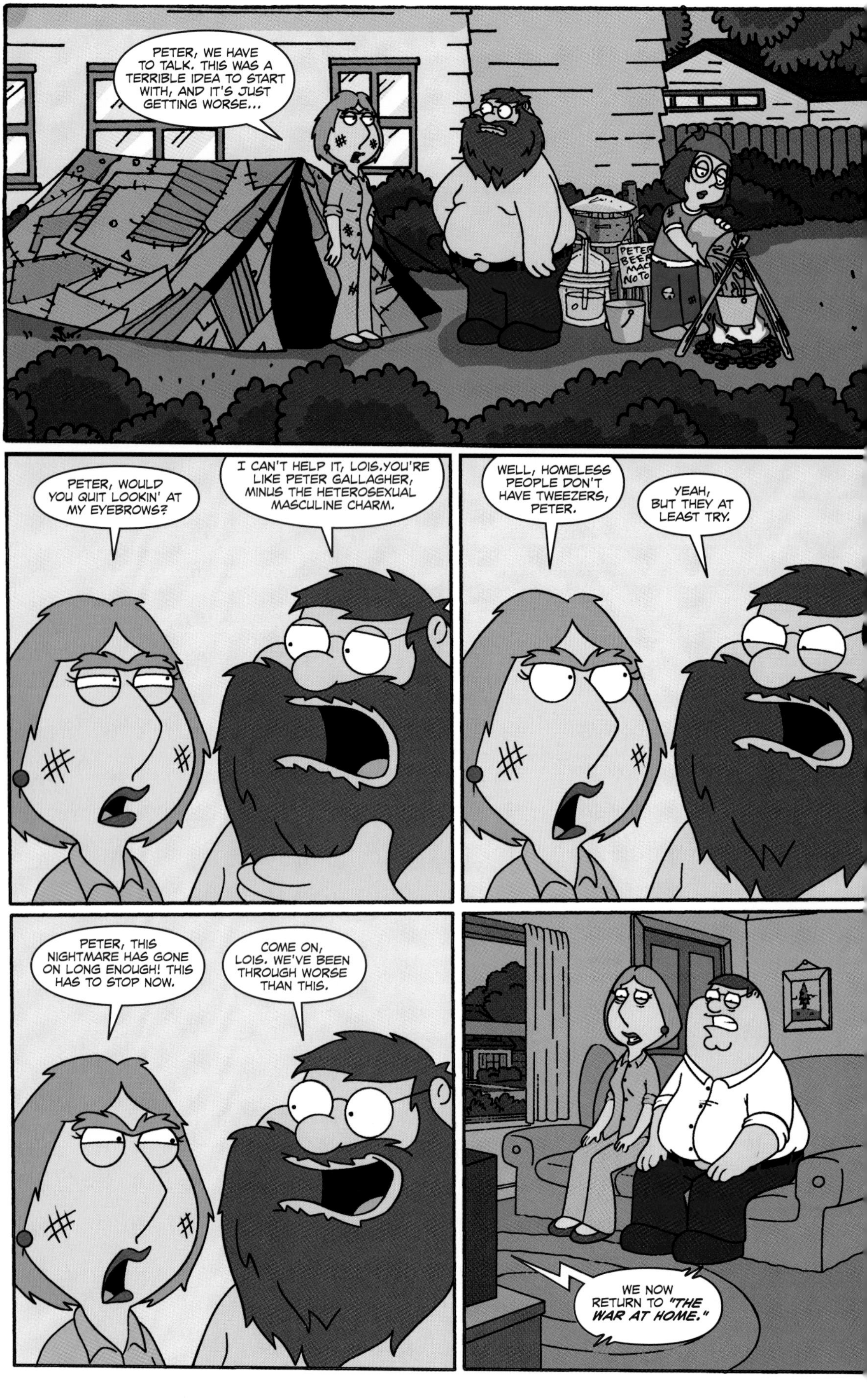

PETER, WE HAVE TO TALK. THIS WAS A TERRIBLE IDEA TO START WITH, AND IT'S JUST GETTING WORSE...
PETER, WOULD YOU QUIT LOOKIN' AT MY EYEBROWS?
I CAN'T HELP IT, LOIS.YOU'RE LIKE PETER GALLAGHER, MINUS THE HETEROSEXUAL MASCULINE CHARM.
WELL, HOMELESS PEOPLE DON'T HAVE TWEEZERS, PETER.
YEAH, BUT THEY AT LEAST TRY.
PETER, THIS NIGHTMARE HAS GONE ON LONG ENOUGH! THIS HAS TO STOP NOW.
COME ON, LOIS. WE'VE BEEN THROUGH WORSE THAN THIS.
WE NOW RETURN TO *"THE WAR AT HOME."*

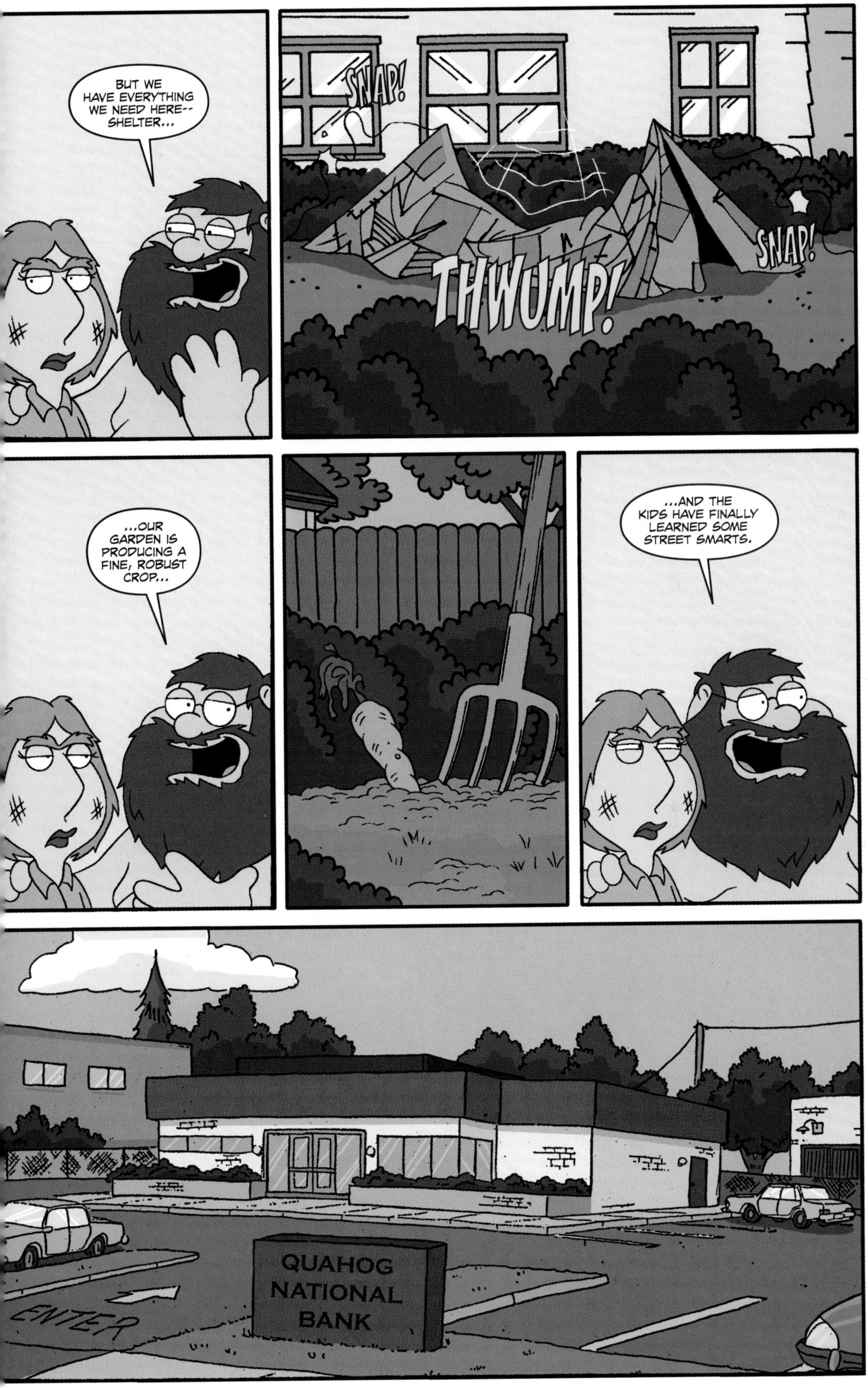

BUT WE HAVE EVERYTHING WE NEED HERE-- SHELTER...
SNAP!
THWUMP!
SNAP!
...OUR GARDEN IS PRODUCING A FINE, ROBUST CROP...
...AND THE KIDS HAVE FINALLY LEARNED SOME STREET SMARTS.
QUAHOG NATIONAL BANK
ENTER

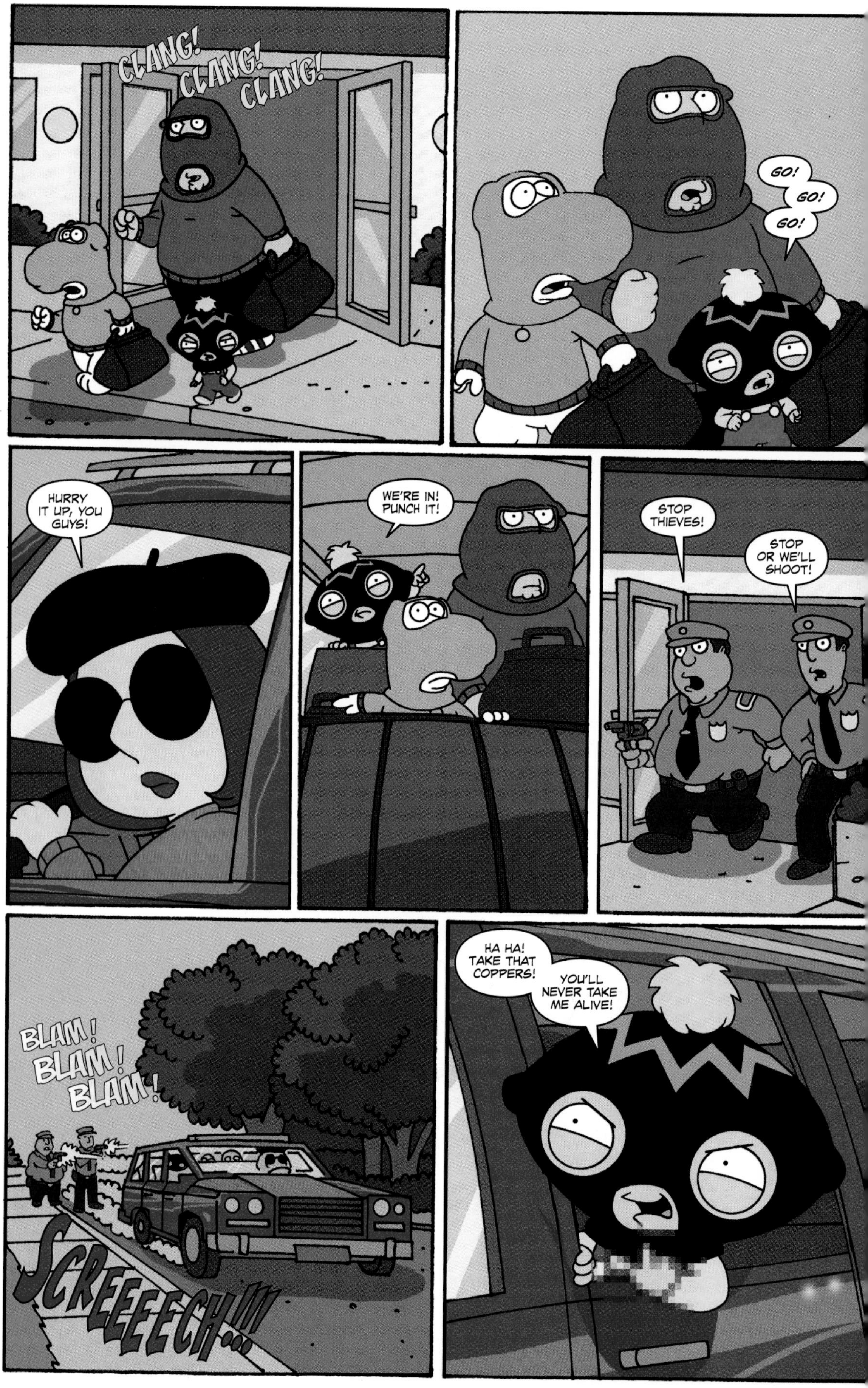
CLANG! CLANG! CLANG!
GO! GO! GO!
HURRY IT UP, YOU GUYS!
WE'RE IN! PUNCH IT!
STOP THIEVES!
STOP OR WE'LL SHOOT!
BLAM! BLAM! BLAM!
SCREEEECH!!!...
HA HA! TAKE THAT COPPERS!
YOU'LL NEVER TAKE ME ALIVE!

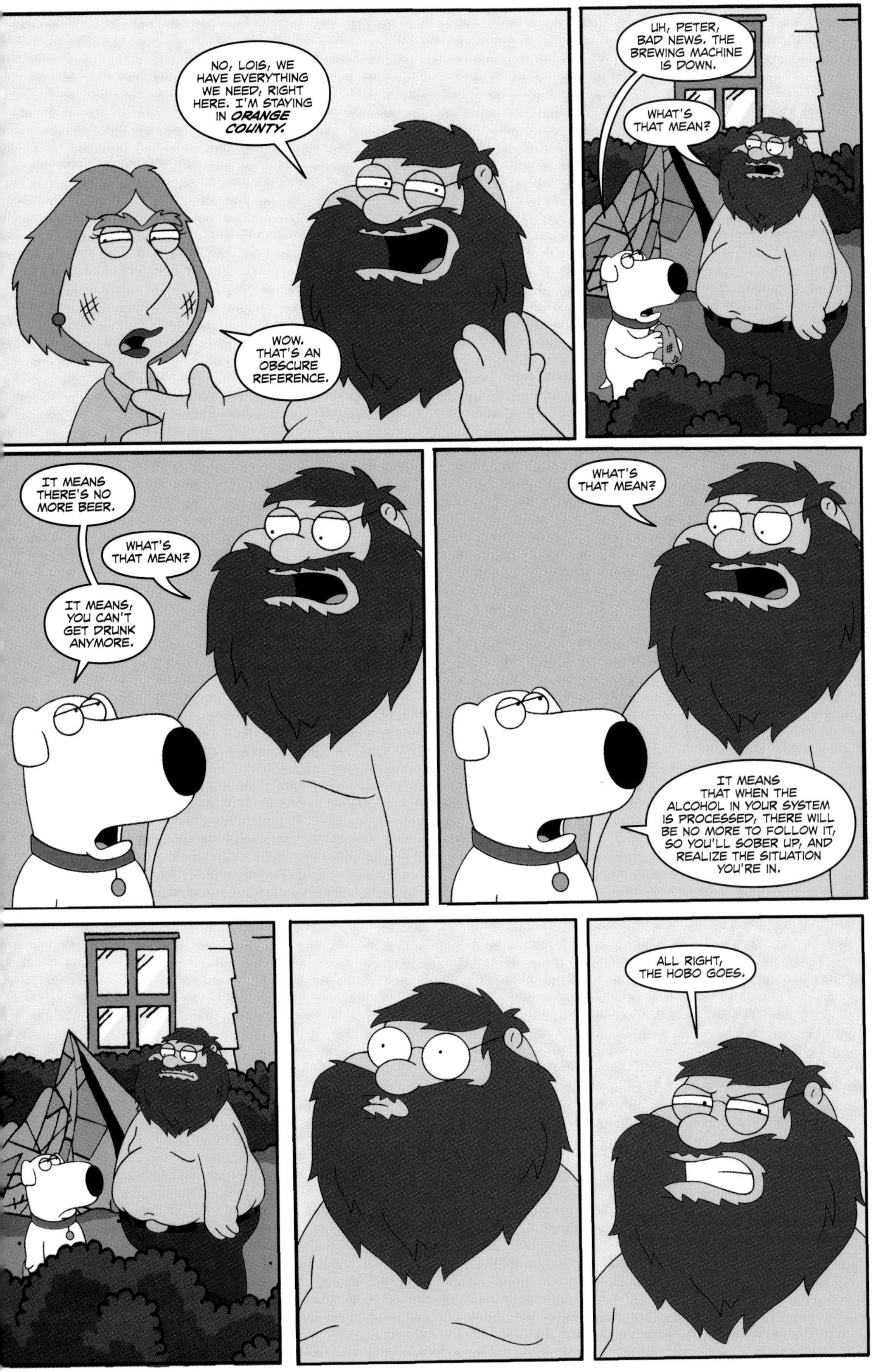

NO, LOIS, WE HAVE EVERYTHING WE NEED, RIGHT HERE. I'M STAYING IN ***ORANGE COUNTY.***
WOW. THAT'S AN OBSCURE REFERENCE.
UH, PETER, BAD NEWS. THE BREWING MACHINE IS DOWN.
WHAT'S THAT MEAN?
IT MEANS THERE'S NO MORE BEER.
WHAT'S THAT MEAN?
IT MEANS, YOU CAN'T GET DRUNK ANYMORE.
WHAT'S THAT MEAN?
IT MEANS THAT WHEN THE ALCOHOL IN YOUR SYSTEM IS PROCESSED, THERE WILL BE NO MORE TO FOLLOW IT, SO YOU'LL SOBER UP, AND REALIZE THE SITUATION YOU'RE IN.
ALL RIGHT, THE HOBO GOES.

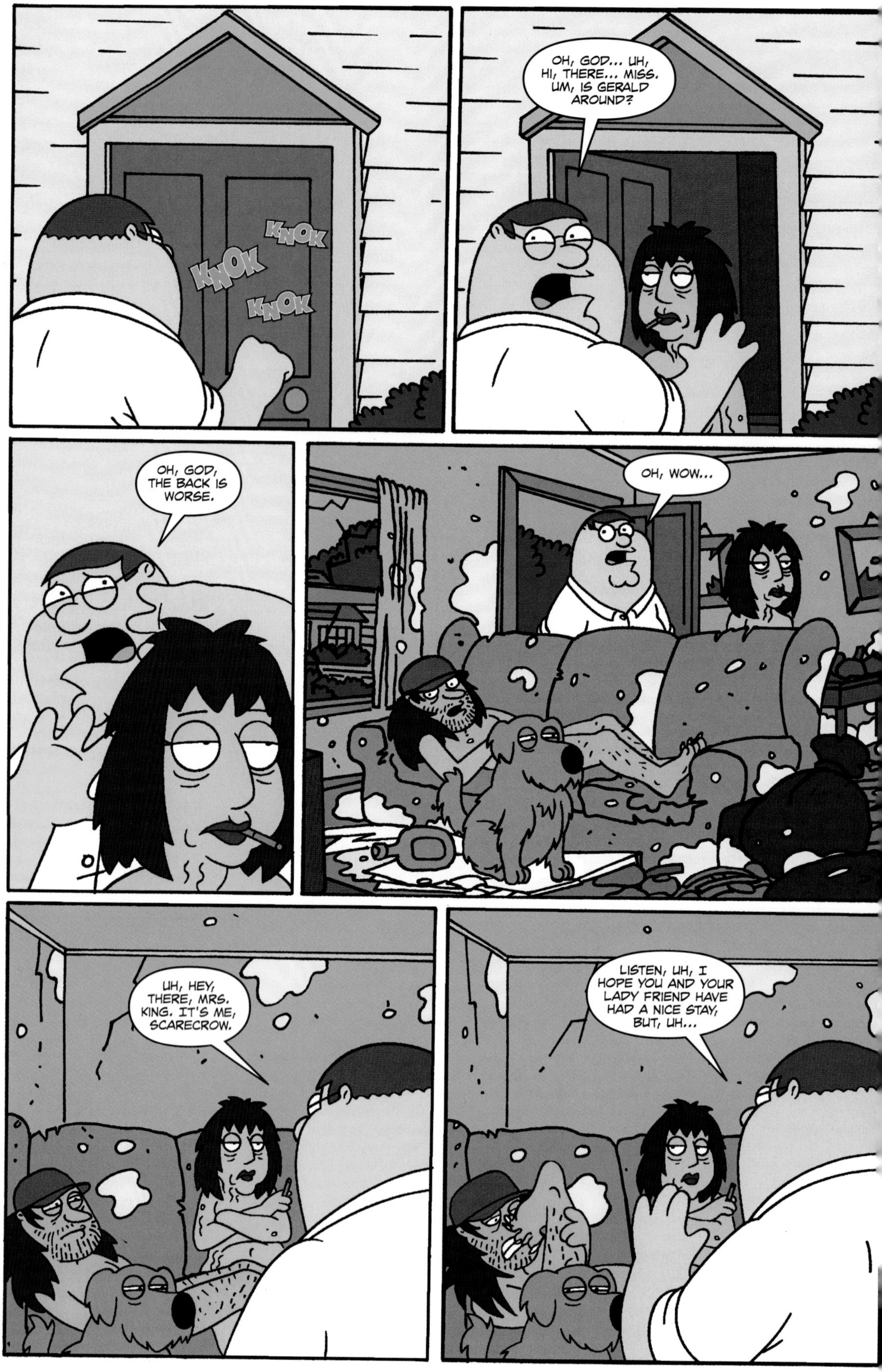
KNOK
KNOK
KNOK
OH, GOD... UH, HI, THERE... MISS. UM, IS GERALD AROUND?
OH, GOD, THE BACK IS WORSE.
OH, WOW...
UH, HEY, THERE, MRS. KING. IT'S ME, SCARECROW.
LISTEN, UH, I HOPE YOU AND YOUR LADY FRIEND HAVE HAD A NICE STAY, BUT, UH...

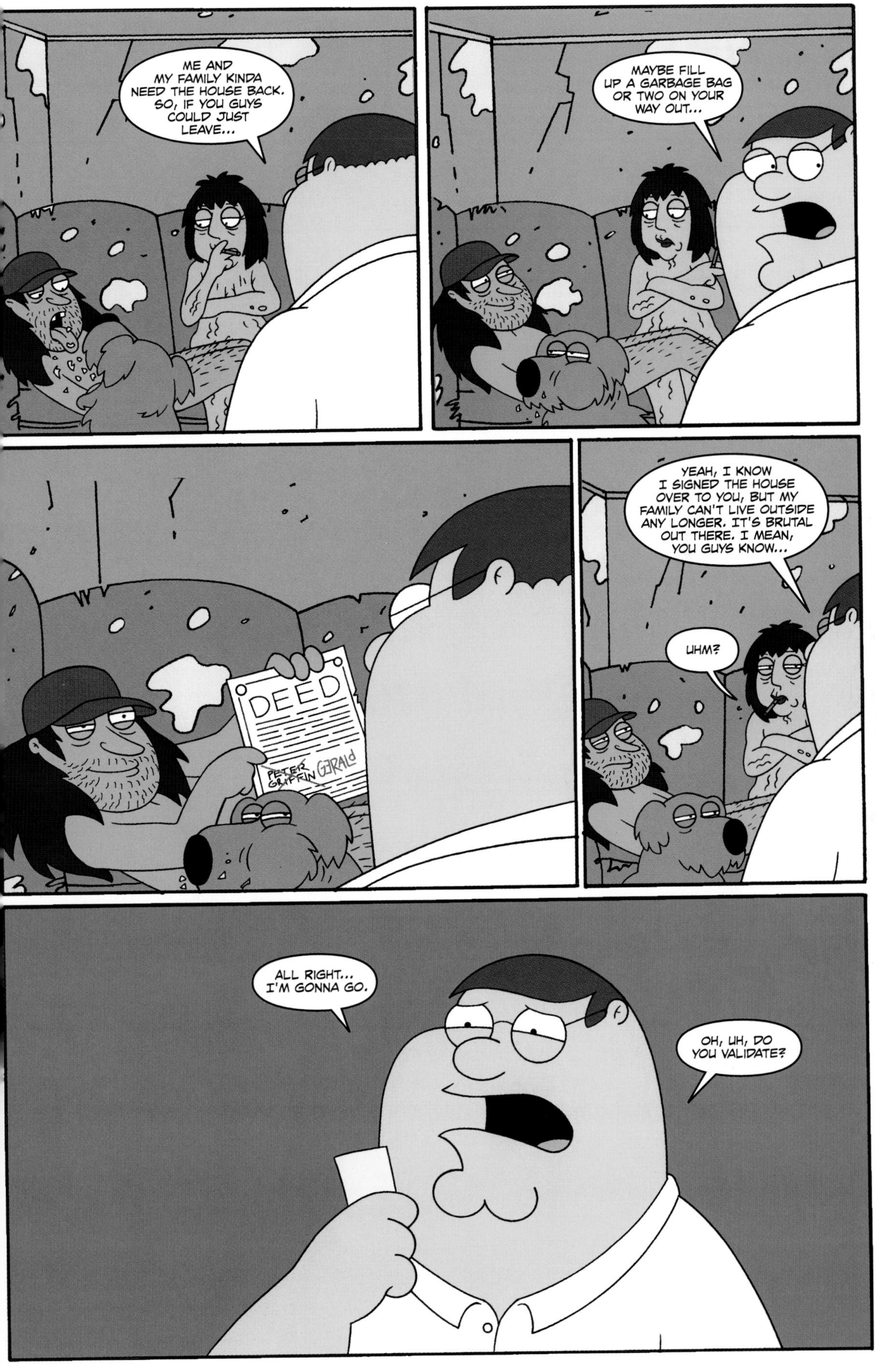
ME AND MY FAMILY KINDA NEED THE HOUSE BACK. SO, IF YOU GUYS COULD JUST LEAVE...
MAYBE FILL UP A GARBAGE BAG OR TWO ON YOUR WAY OUT...
DEED
PETER GRIFFIN GERALD
YEAH, I KNOW I SIGNED THE HOUSE OVER TO YOU, BUT MY FAMILY CAN'T LIVE OUTSIDE ANY LONGER. IT'S BRUTAL OUT THERE. I MEAN, YOU GUYS KNOW...
UHM?
ALL RIGHT... I'M GONNA GO.
OH, UH, DO YOU VALIDATE?

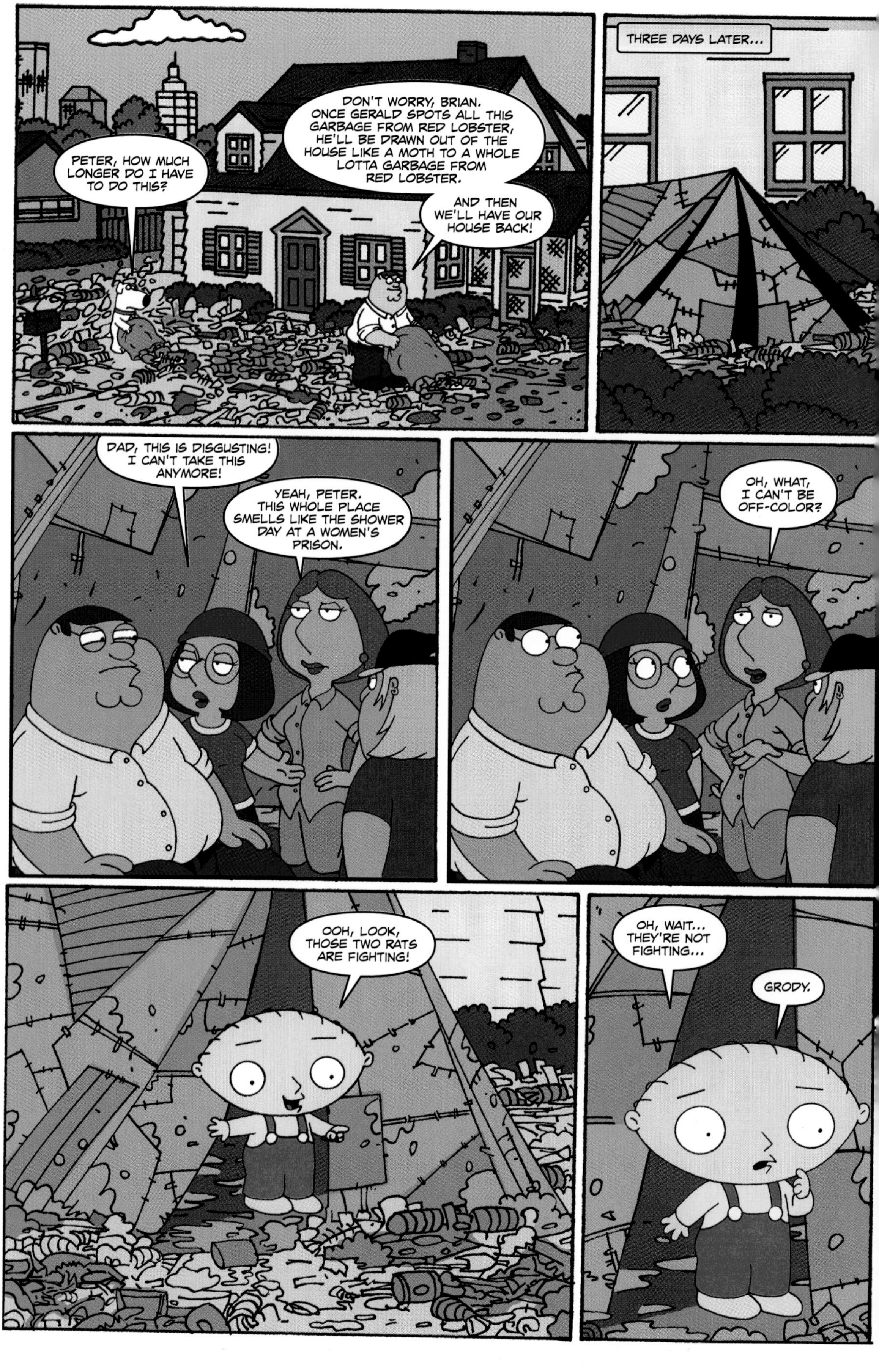
PETER, HOW MUCH LONGER DO I HAVE TO DO THIS?
DON'T WORRY, BRIAN. ONCE GERALD SPOTS ALL THIS GARBAGE FROM RED LOBSTER, HE'LL BE DRAWN OUT OF THE HOUSE LIKE A MOTH TO A WHOLE LOTTA GARBAGE FROM RED LOBSTER.
AND THEN WE'LL HAVE OUR HOUSE BACK!
THREE DAYS LATER...
DAD, THIS IS DISGUSTING! I CAN'T TAKE THIS ANYMORE!
YEAH, PETER. THIS WHOLE PLACE SMELLS LIKE THE SHOWER DAY AT A WOMEN'S PRISON.
OH, WHAT, I CAN'T BE OFF-COLOR?
OOH, LOOK, THOSE TWO RATS ARE FIGHTING!
OH, WAIT... THEY'RE NOT FIGHTING...
GRODY.

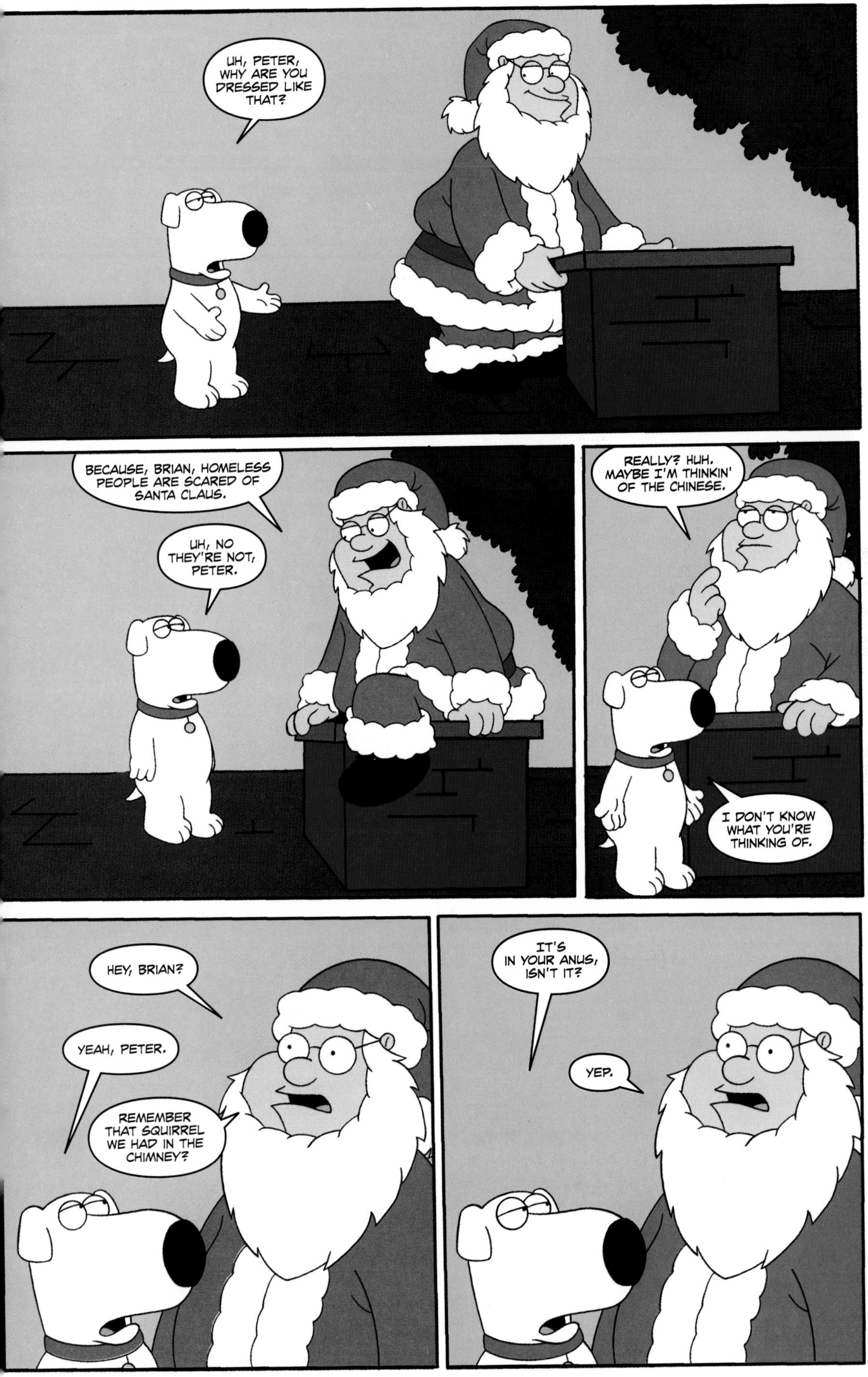
UH, PETER, WHY ARE YOU DRESSED LIKE THAT?
BECAUSE, BRIAN, HOMELESS PEOPLE ARE SCARED OF SANTA CLAUS.
UH, NO THEY'RE NOT, PETER.
REALLY? HUH. MAYBE I'M THINKIN' OF THE CHINESE.
I DON'T KNOW WHAT YOU'RE THINKING OF.
HEY, BRIAN?
YEAH, PETER.
REMEMBER THAT SQUIRREL WE HAD IN THE CHIMNEY?
IT'S IN YOUR ANUS, ISN'T IT?
YEP.

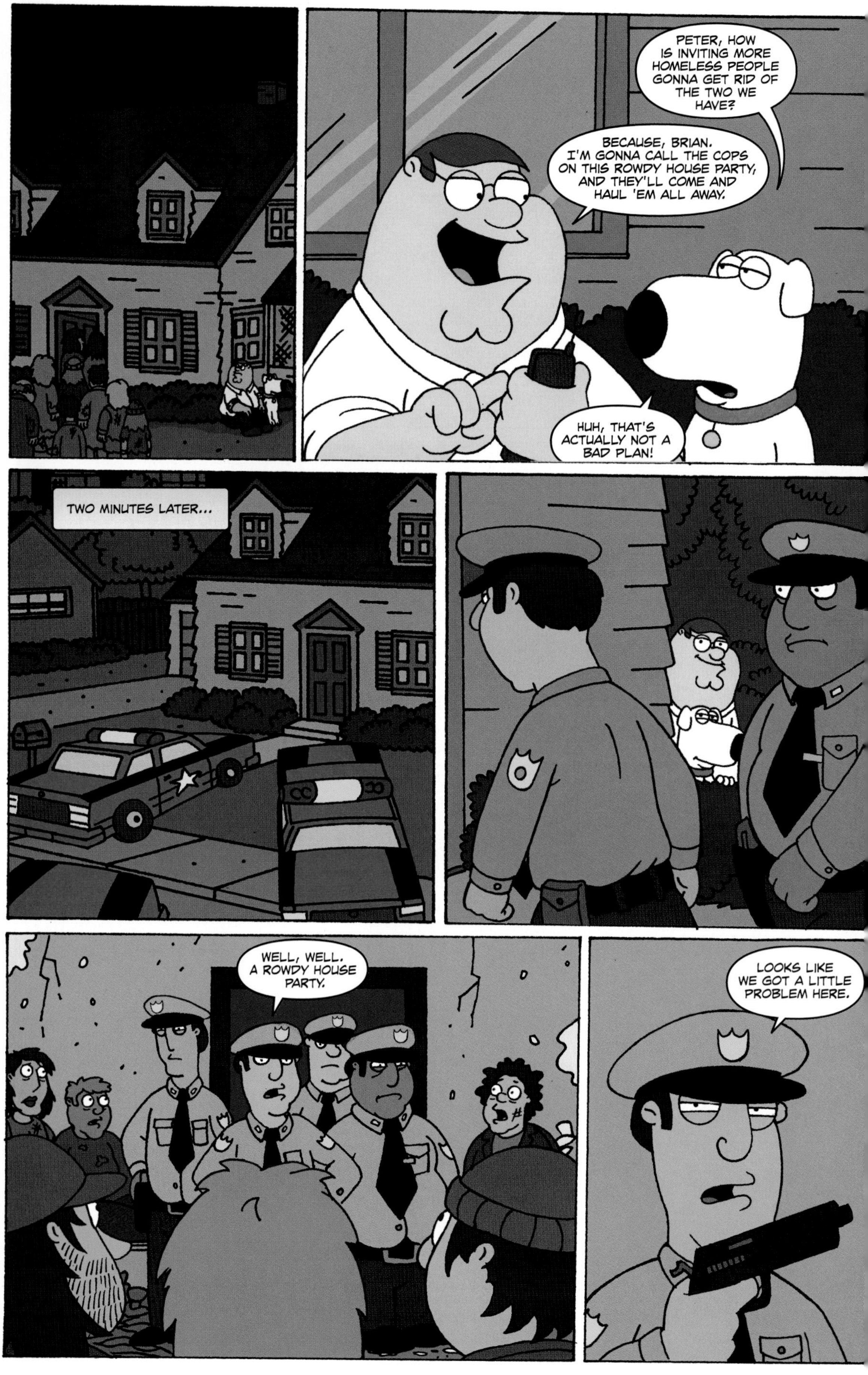
PETER, HOW IS INVITING MORE HOMELESS PEOPLE GONNA GET RID OF THE TWO WE HAVE?
BECAUSE, BRIAN. I'M GONNA CALL THE COPS ON THIS ROWDY HOUSE PARTY, AND THEY'LL COME AND HAUL 'EM ALL AWAY.
HUH, THAT'S ACTUALLY NOT A BAD PLAN!
TWO MINUTES LATER...
WELL, WELL. A ROWDY HOUSE PARTY.
LOOKS LIKE WE GOT A LITTLE PROBLEM HERE.

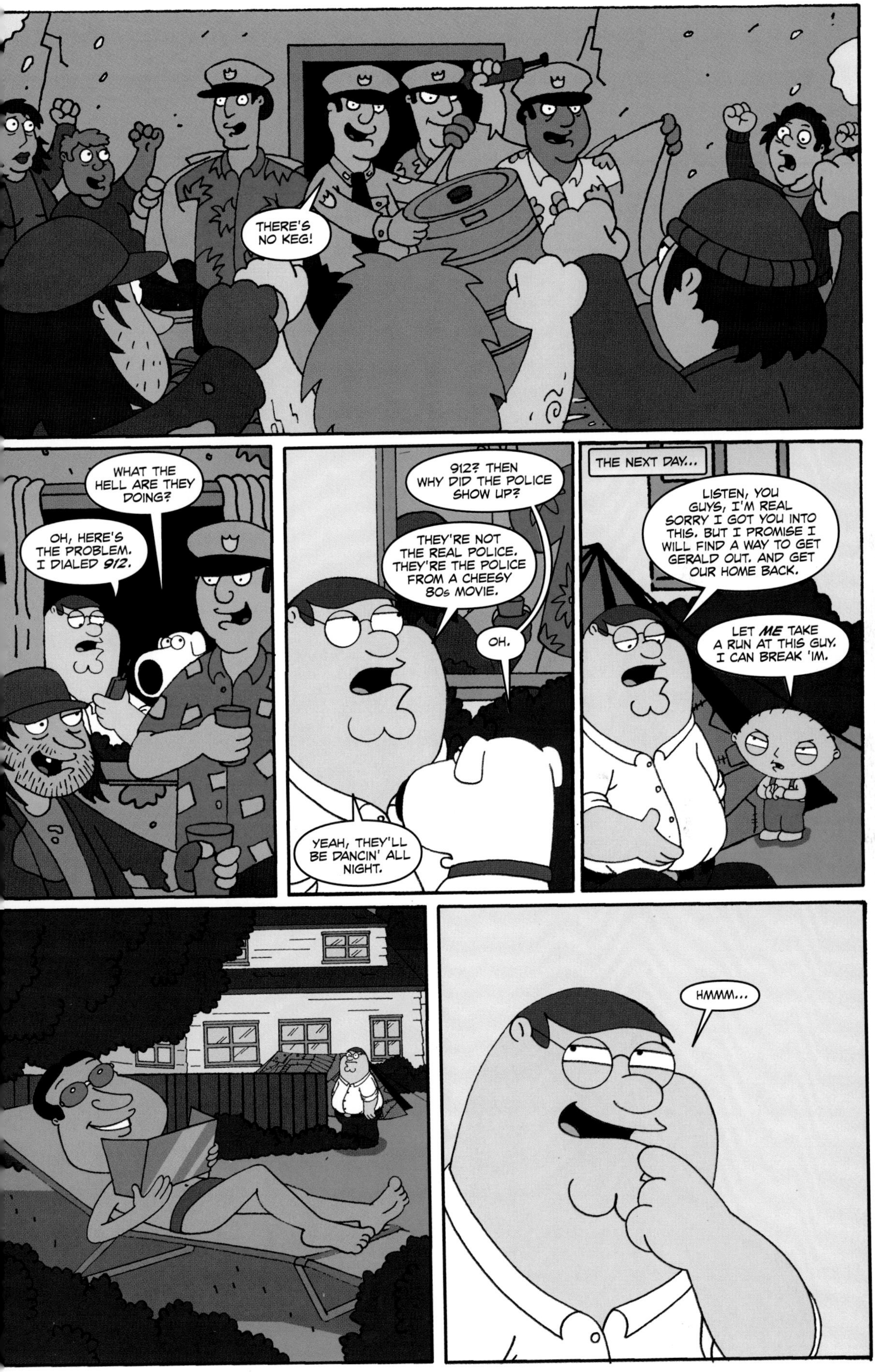
THERE'S NO KEG!
WHAT THE HELL ARE THEY DOING?
OH, HERE'S THE PROBLEM. I DIALED 912.
912? THEN WHY DID THE POLICE SHOW UP?
THEY'RE NOT THE REAL POLICE. THEY'RE THE POLICE FROM A CHEESY 80s MOVIE.
OH.
YEAH, THEY'LL BE DANCIN' ALL NIGHT.
THE NEXT DAY...
LISTEN, YOU GUYS, I'M REAL SORRY I GOT YOU INTO THIS. BUT I PROMISE I WILL FIND A WAY TO GET GERALD OUT. AND GET OUR HOME BACK.
LET ME TAKE A RUN AT THIS GUY. I CAN BREAK 'IM.
HMMM...

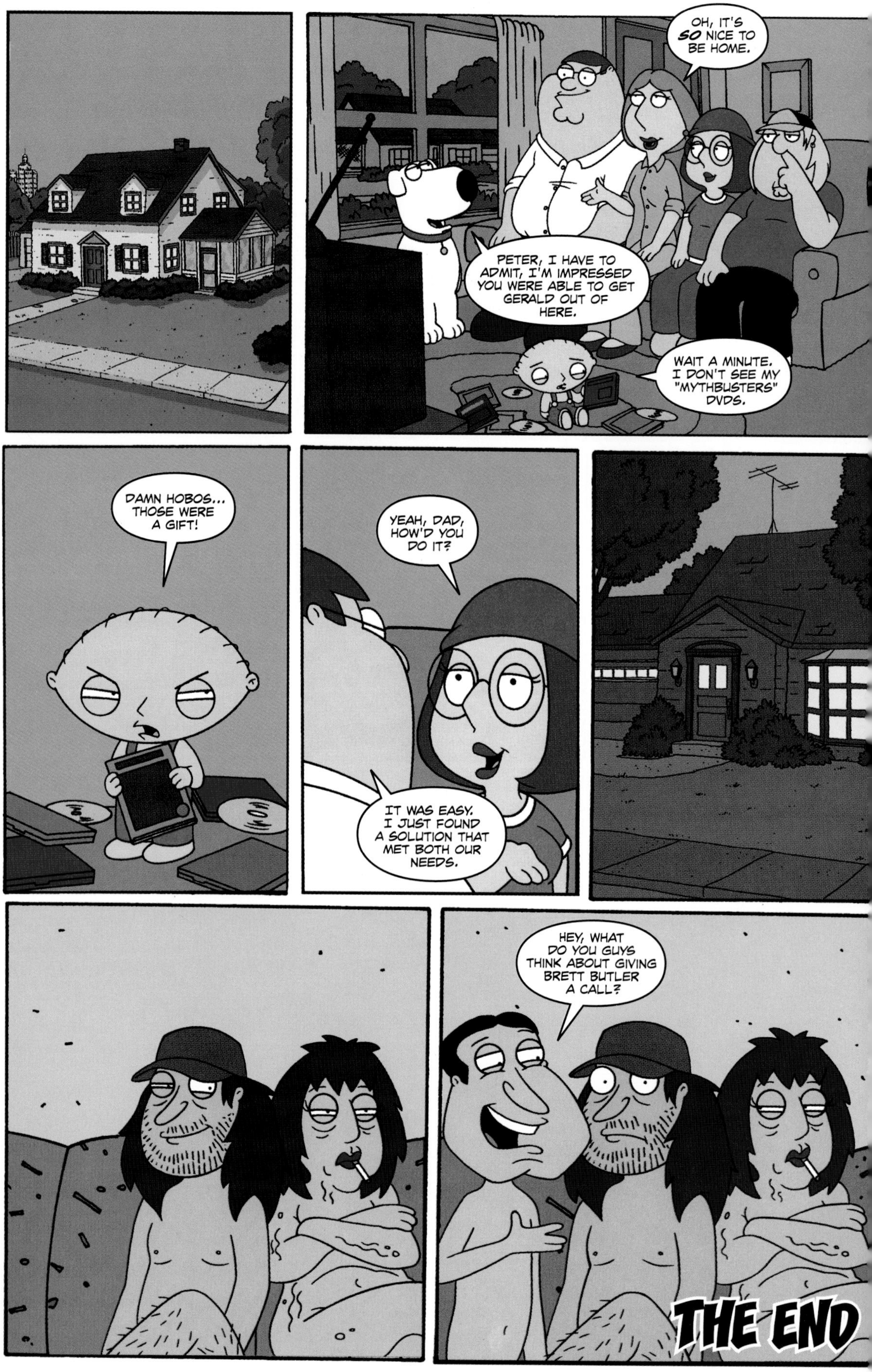
OH, IT'S *SO* NICE TO BE HOME.
PETER, I HAVE TO ADMIT, I'M IMPRESSED YOU WERE ABLE TO GET GERALD OUT OF HERE.
WAIT A MINUTE. I DON'T SEE MY "MYTHBUSTERS" DVDS.
DAMN HOBOS... THOSE WERE A GIFT!
YEAH, DAD, HOW'D YOU DO IT?
IT WAS EASY. I JUST FOUND A SOLUTION THAT MET BOTH OUR NEEDS.
HEY, WHAT DO YOU GUYS THINK ABOUT GIVING BRETT BUTLER A CALL?
THE END

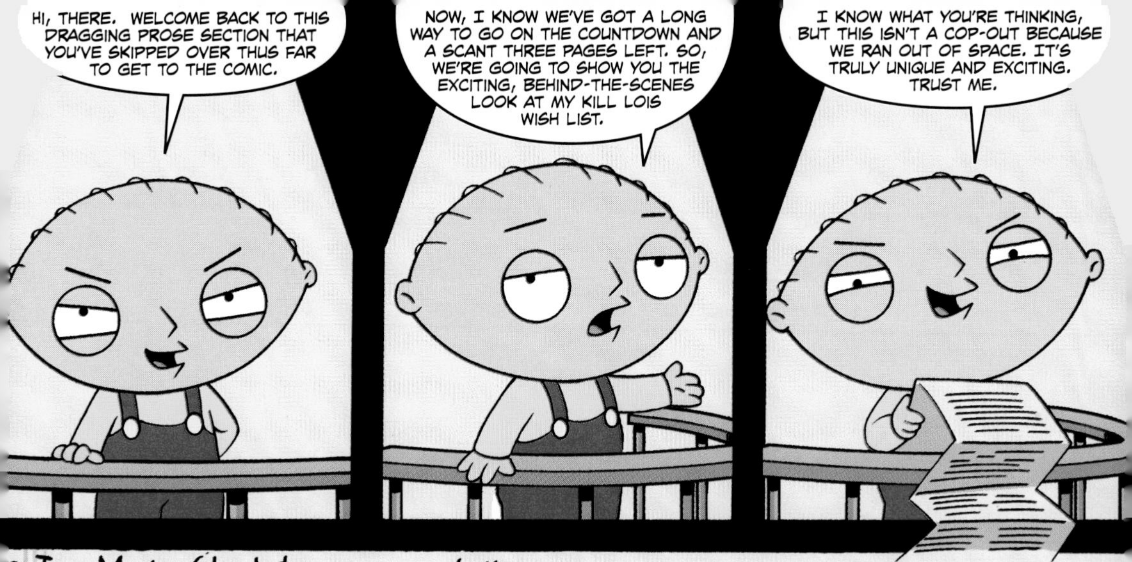

3. Iron Maiden (the torture device, not the kick-ass metal band!)
2. Really big Bee
1. Painful earwig (like in Star Trek)
0. "Tragic" baboon eating at Quahog African Safari
9. Drunken Royal
8. Stabbed in the eye with one of hose cool sword drink stirrers
7. Tied in a sack and thrown off a bridge, like Kramer
6. Hand grenade in her cereal
5. Dance on her chest with rusty golf spikes
4. out of control sleigh ride
3. slam her fat head in the fridge
2. Bleed her out like a deer
1. Hunt her like in "Surviving the Game"
0. Paint her brown and drop her in the suburbs
9. Pissed-off android
8. Set her addicted to crack
7. Shiv in the kidney
6. Lawn mower
5. Aggressive liposuction
4. the ol' Reginald Denny
3. Bear in her Purse

62. Ninja throwing Star to the throat
61. Flame thrower
60. Put in my Vampire teeth and bite her throat (a little icky)
59. Mercury poisoning -- by Tuna! Ha! Take that, Polluters!
58. Death by Evil Genie
57. Mummify with Brawny paper towels - they're Strong!
56. Feed her razors
55. Giant anaconda
54. Enlist her in the Marines
53. Make her star in a movie opposite Martin Lawrence
52. Rake to the head
51. Playground accident
50. Drown in chicken noodle Soup
49. Drive by
48. Bird flu
47. Vat of Nickelodean Slime
46. Wood chipper
45. Ground up and serve to poor Thai Children
44. Bowling accident
43. Dutch Oven
42. The other kind of Dutch Oven

41. Eject her from really, really fast car
40. Tie her to train tracks
39. Axe to the throat
38. A thresher
37. Sarlak Pit-- My favorite
36. Trampled by herd of gnu.
35. Turned into an iced mocha
34. Bed of nails
33. Make her into a nice Vegetable stew
32. Go "Shining" on her
31. Natural gas explosion
30. Drain-O smoothie
29. The Noid
28. Bush in '08
27. That weird bug that crawls into your pee stream
26. Defenistration
25. Suffocation
24. Burned at the stake
23. Dress her as Dutch Immigration Minister Rita Verdonk and ship her to Tehran.
22. Get her head stuck in an Elephant's ass
21. Hot beef injection--literally
20. Gnarly car crash
19. Any form of erotic asphyxiation
18. Declare her a witch and toss her off a cliff
17. Eaten by angry pigs
16. Shark tank
15. "Dr. 90210" marathon
14. Get her within a hundred yards of Dick Cheney
13. Stuff her into garbage disposal
12. Starvation
11. Replace birth control with flesh eating virus
10. Bull fight
9. Lock her in a room and put a block of ice in the window to keep it open and then shoot her from a building across the way, and then when the cops show up, they see there's no way anyone could have gotten in and the only clue they have is the puddle of water by the window, like in that cool brain teaser.
8. Take Oprah off the air-Ha! Take that, you lazy skank!
7. Make her wait another year for "Sopranos"
6. Dunk her in pod of acid, like the Joker
5. Guillotine
4. Make her fall for the "wrong kind of boy" who'll get her into trouble
3. Stick an eel in her bottom
2. Drown her in one of those ponds of cow feces

And finally...

1. Sit tight and wait for the impending Nuclear Holocaust

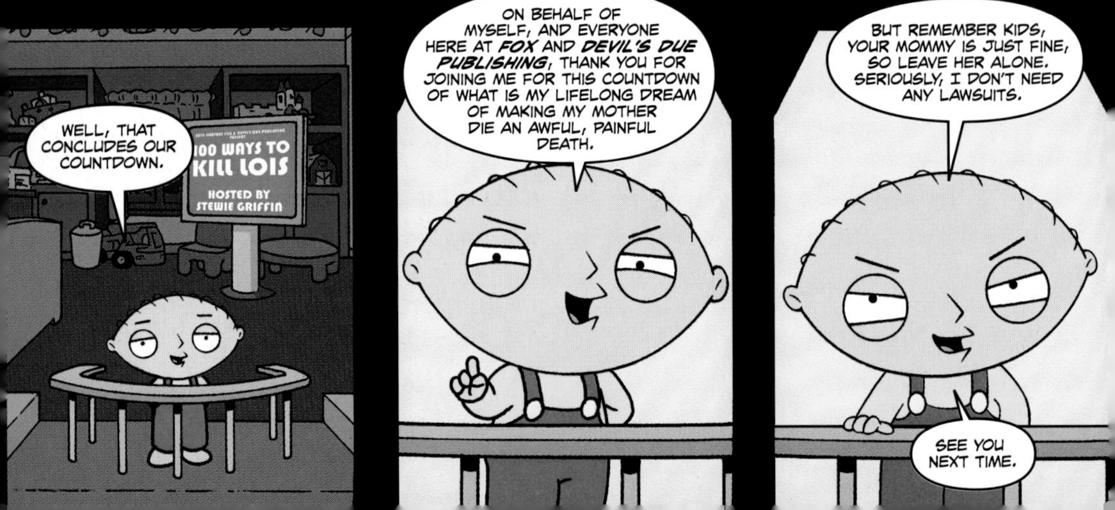

WELL, THAT CONCLUDES OUR COUNTDOWN.
100 WAYS TO KILL LOIS
HOSTED BY STEWIE GRIFFIN
ON BEHALF OF MYSELF, AND EVERYONE HERE AT FOX AND DEVIL'S DUE PUBLISHING, THANK YOU FOR JOINING ME FOR THIS COUNTDOWN OF WHAT IS MY LIFELONG DREAM OF MAKING MY MOTHER DIE AN AWFUL, PAINFUL DEATH.
BUT REMEMBER KIDS, YOUR MOMMY IS JUST FINE, SO LEAVE HER ALONE. SERIOUSLY, I DON'T NEED ANY LAWSUITS.
SEE YOU NEXT TIME.

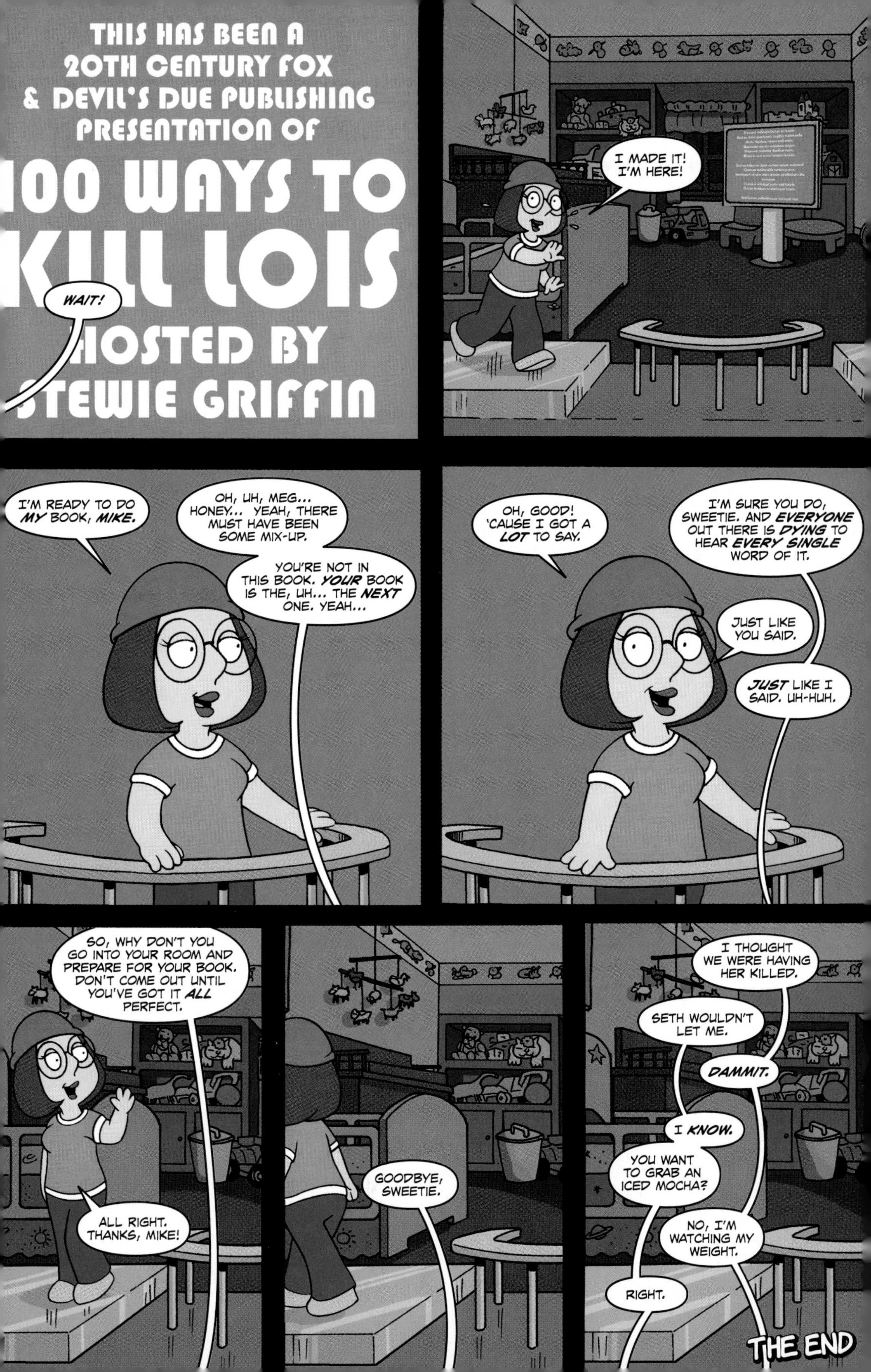
THIS HAS BEEN A 20TH CENTURY FOX & DEVIL'S DUE PUBLISHING PRESENTATION OF
100 WAYS TO KILL LOIS
WAIT!
HOSTED BY STEWIE GRIFFIN
I MADE IT! I'M HERE!
I'M READY TO DO MY BOOK, MIKE.
OH, UH, MEG... HONEY... YEAH, THERE MUST HAVE BEEN SOME MIX-UP.
YOU'RE NOT IN THIS BOOK. YOUR BOOK IS THE, UH... THE NEXT ONE. YEAH...
OH, GOOD! 'CAUSE I GOT A LOT TO SAY.
I'M SURE YOU DO, SWEETIE. AND EVERYONE OUT THERE IS DYING TO HEAR EVERY SINGLE WORD OF IT.
JUST LIKE YOU SAID.
JUST LIKE I SAID. UH-HUH.
SO, WHY DON'T YOU GO INTO YOUR ROOM AND PREPARE FOR YOUR BOOK. DON'T COME OUT UNTIL YOU'VE GOT IT ALL PERFECT.
ALL RIGHT. THANKS, MIKE!
GOODBYE, SWEETIE.
I THOUGHT WE WERE HAVING HER KILLED.
SETH WOULDN'T LET ME.
DAMMIT.
I KNOW.
YOU WANT TO GRAB AN ICED MOCHA?
NO, I'M WATCHING MY WEIGHT.
RIGHT.
THE END

FAMILY GUY™

AS SEEN ON TV

PETER GRIFFIN'S GUIDE TO PARENTING

FAMILY COMES FIRST (RIGHT AFTER TV)

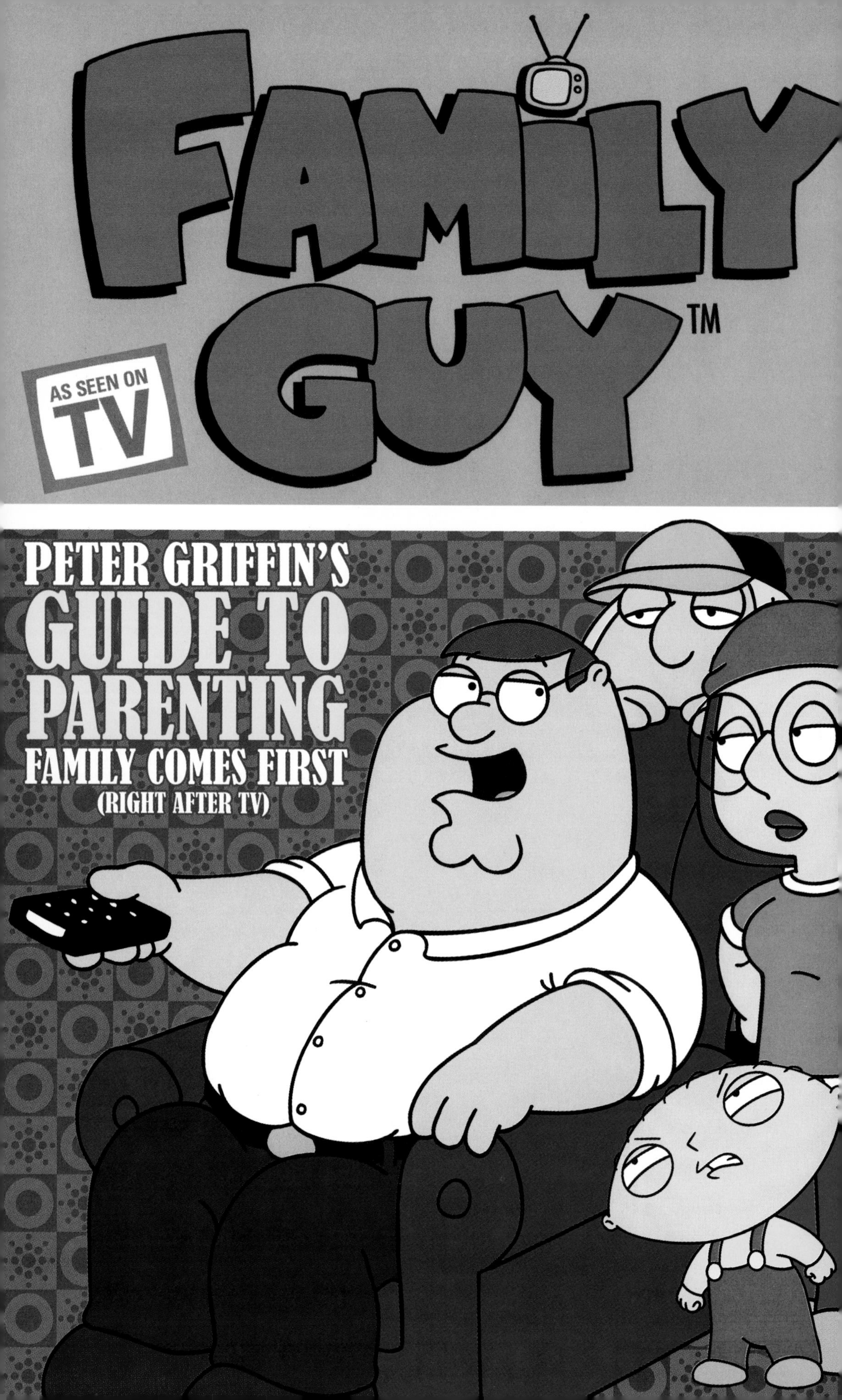

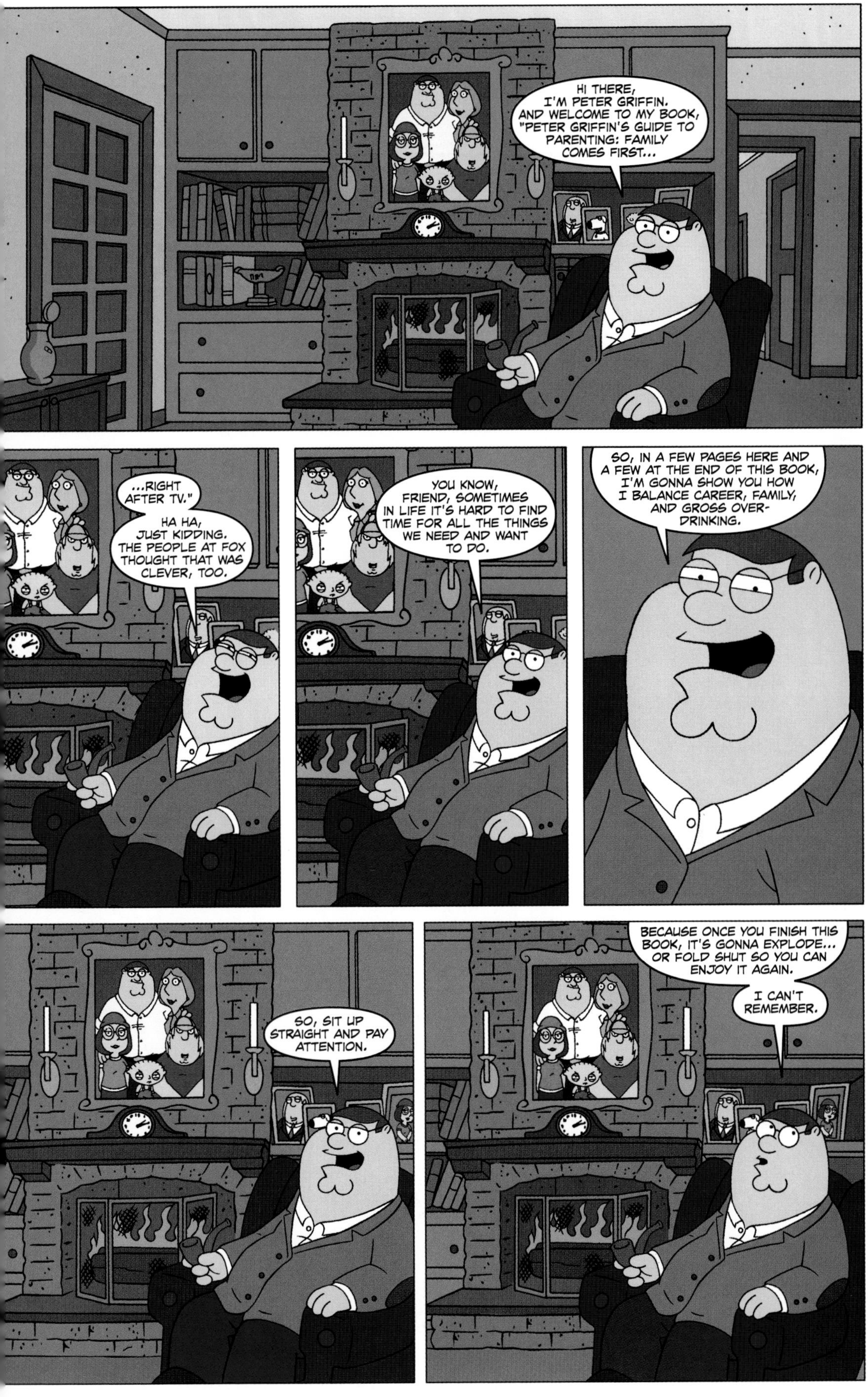
HI THERE, I'M PETER GRIFFIN. AND WELCOME TO MY BOOK, "PETER GRIFFIN'S GUIDE TO PARENTING: FAMILY COMES FIRST...
...RIGHT AFTER TV."
HA HA, JUST KIDDING. THE PEOPLE AT FOX THOUGHT THAT WAS CLEVER, TOO.
YOU KNOW, FRIEND, SOMETIMES IN LIFE IT'S HARD TO FIND TIME FOR ALL THE THINGS WE NEED AND WANT TO DO.
SO, IN A FEW PAGES HERE AND A FEW AT THE END OF THIS BOOK, I'M GONNA SHOW YOU HOW I BALANCE CAREER, FAMILY, AND GROSS OVER-DRINKING.
SO, SIT UP STRAIGHT AND PAY ATTENTION.
BECAUSE ONCE YOU FINISH THIS BOOK, IT'S GONNA EXPLODE... OR FOLD SHUT SO YOU CAN ENJOY IT AGAIN.
I CAN'T REMEMBER.

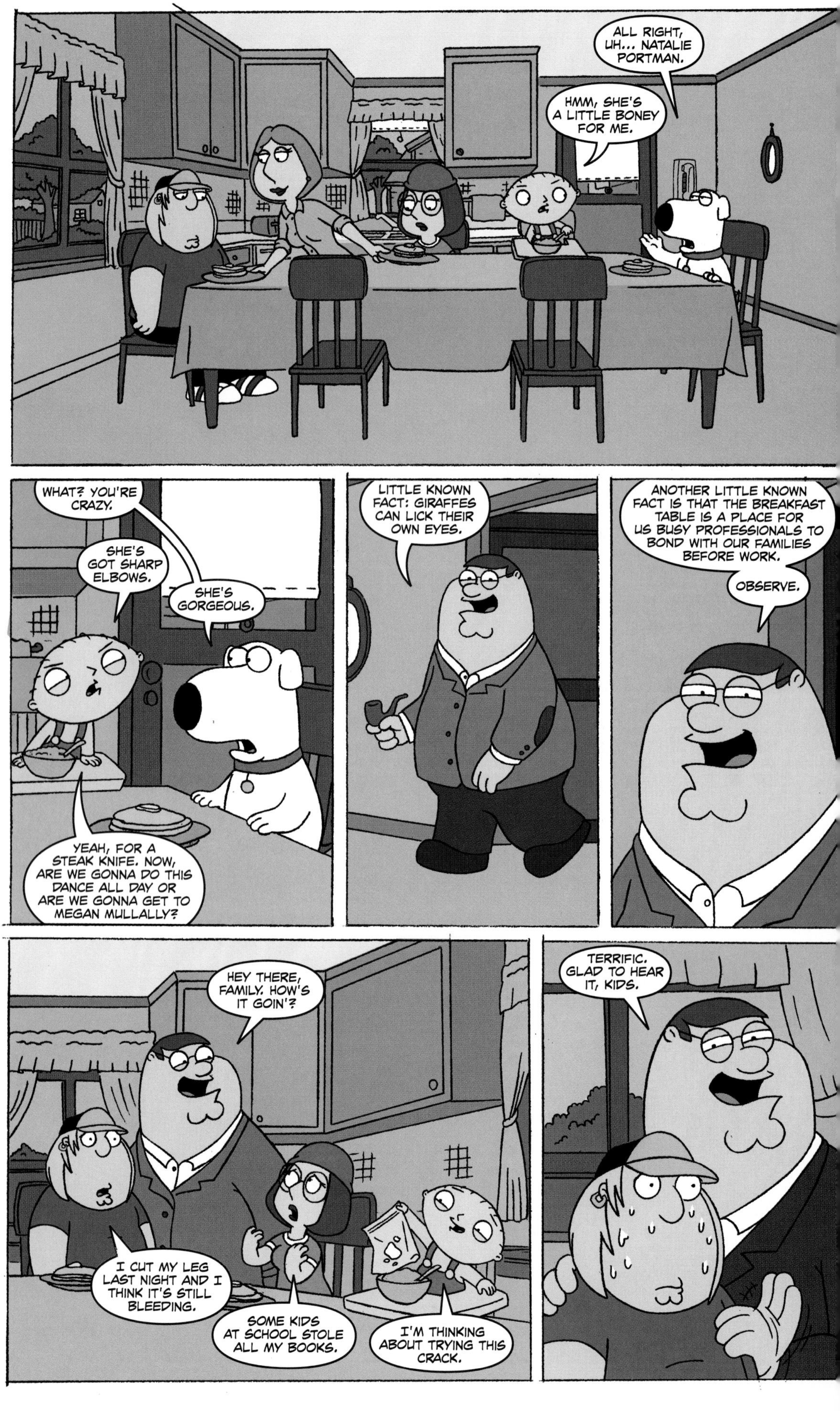
ALL RIGHT, UH... NATALIE PORTMAN.
HMM, SHE'S A LITTLE BONEY FOR ME.
WHAT? YOU'RE CRAZY.
SHE'S GOT SHARP ELBOWS.
SHE'S GORGEOUS.
YEAH, FOR A STEAK KNIFE. NOW, ARE WE GONNA DO THIS DANCE ALL DAY OR ARE WE GONNA GET TO MEGAN MULLALLY?
LITTLE KNOWN FACT: GIRAFFES CAN LICK THEIR OWN EYES.
ANOTHER LITTLE KNOWN FACT IS THAT THE BREAKFAST TABLE IS A PLACE FOR US BUSY PROFESSIONALS TO BOND WITH OUR FAMILIES BEFORE WORK.
OBSERVE.
HEY THERE, FAMILY. HOW'S IT GOIN'?
I CUT MY LEG LAST NIGHT AND I THINK IT'S STILL BLEEDING.
SOME KIDS AT SCHOOL STOLE ALL MY BOOKS.
I'M THINKING ABOUT TRYING THIS CRACK.
TERRIFIC. GLAD TO HEAR IT, KIDS.

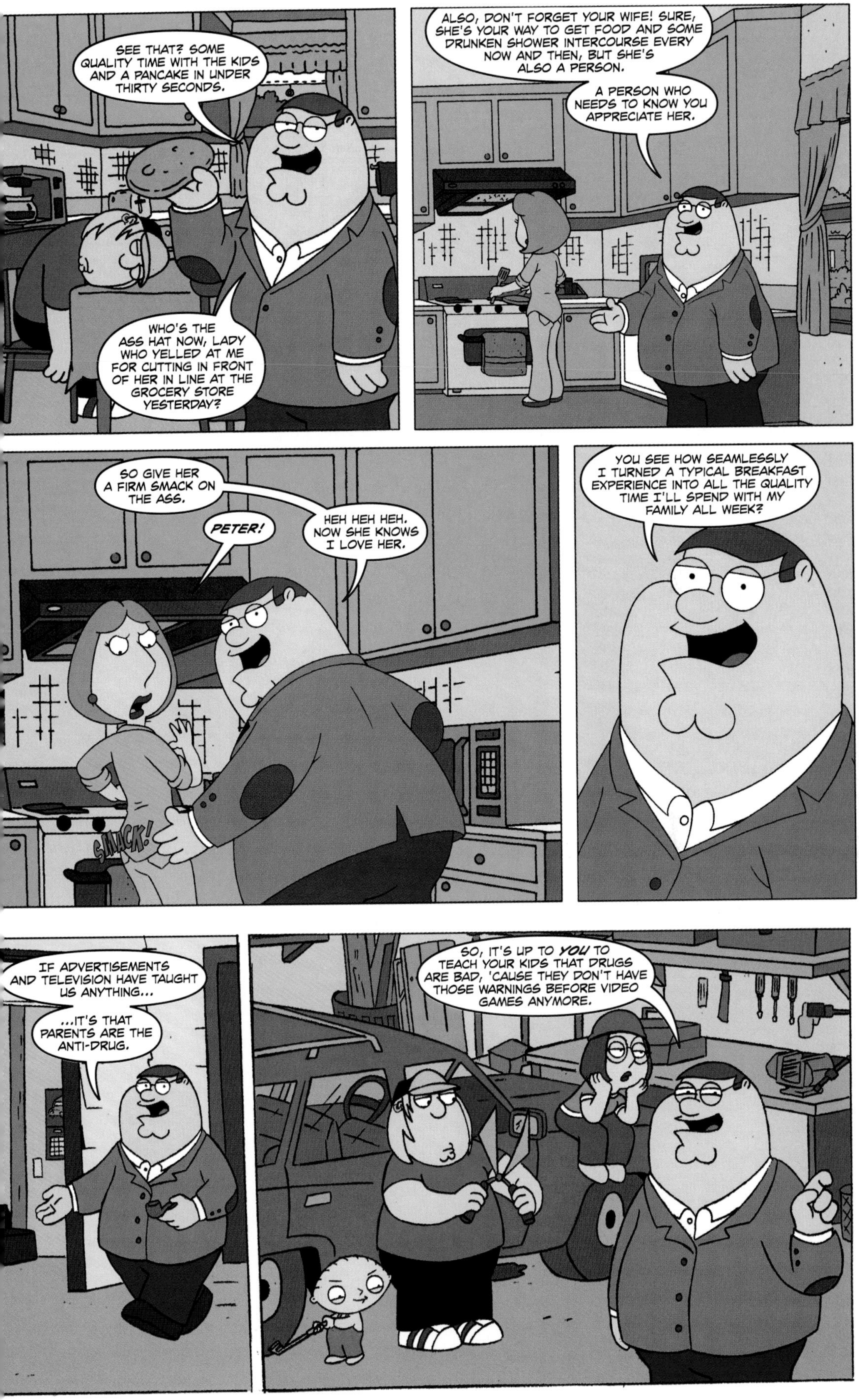
SEE THAT? SOME QUALITY TIME WITH THE KIDS AND A PANCAKE IN UNDER THIRTY SECONDS.
WHO'S THE ASS HAT NOW, LADY WHO YELLED AT ME FOR CUTTING IN FRONT OF HER IN LINE AT THE GROCERY STORE YESTERDAY?
ALSO, DON'T FORGET YOUR WIFE! SURE, SHE'S YOUR WAY TO GET FOOD AND SOME DRUNKEN SHOWER INTERCOURSE EVERY NOW AND THEN, BUT SHE'S ALSO A PERSON.
A PERSON WHO NEEDS TO KNOW YOU APPRECIATE HER.
SO GIVE HER A FIRM SMACK ON THE ASS.
PETER!
HEH HEH HEH. NOW SHE KNOWS I LOVE HER.
SMACK!
YOU SEE HOW SEAMLESSLY I TURNED A TYPICAL BREAKFAST EXPERIENCE INTO ALL THE QUALITY TIME I'LL SPEND WITH MY FAMILY ALL WEEK?
IF ADVERTISEMENTS AND TELEVISION HAVE TAUGHT US ANYTHING...
...IT'S THAT PARENTS ARE THE ANTI-DRUG.
SO, IT'S UP TO YOU TO TEACH YOUR KIDS THAT DRUGS ARE BAD, 'CAUSE THEY DON'T HAVE THOSE WARNINGS BEFORE VIDEO GAMES ANYMORE.

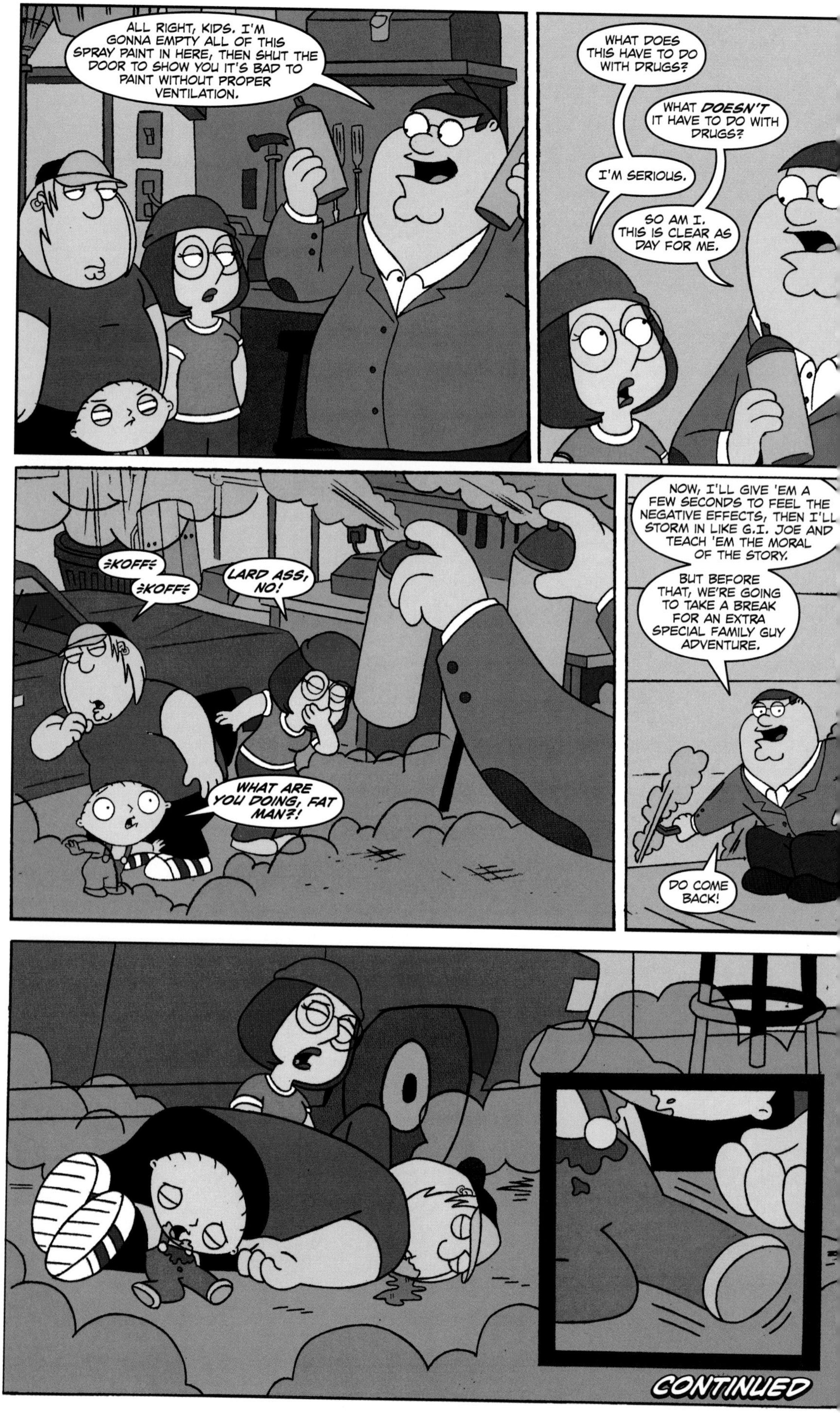
ALL RIGHT, KIDS. I'M GONNA EMPTY ALL OF THIS SPRAY PAINT IN HERE, THEN SHUT THE DOOR TO SHOW YOU IT'S BAD TO PAINT WITHOUT PROPER VENTILATION.
WHAT DOES THIS HAVE TO DO WITH DRUGS?
WHAT *DOESN'T* IT HAVE TO DO WITH DRUGS?
I'M SERIOUS.
SO AM I. THIS IS CLEAR AS DAY FOR ME.
KOFF
KOFF
LARD ASS, NO!
WHAT ARE YOU DOING, FAT MAN?!
NOW, I'LL GIVE 'EM A FEW SECONDS TO FEEL THE NEGATIVE EFFECTS, THEN I'LL STORM IN LIKE G.I. JOE AND TEACH 'EM THE MORAL OF THE STORY.
BUT BEFORE THAT, WE'RE GOING TO TAKE A BREAK FOR AN EXTRA SPECIAL FAMILY GUY ADVENTURE.
DO COME BACK!
CONTINUED

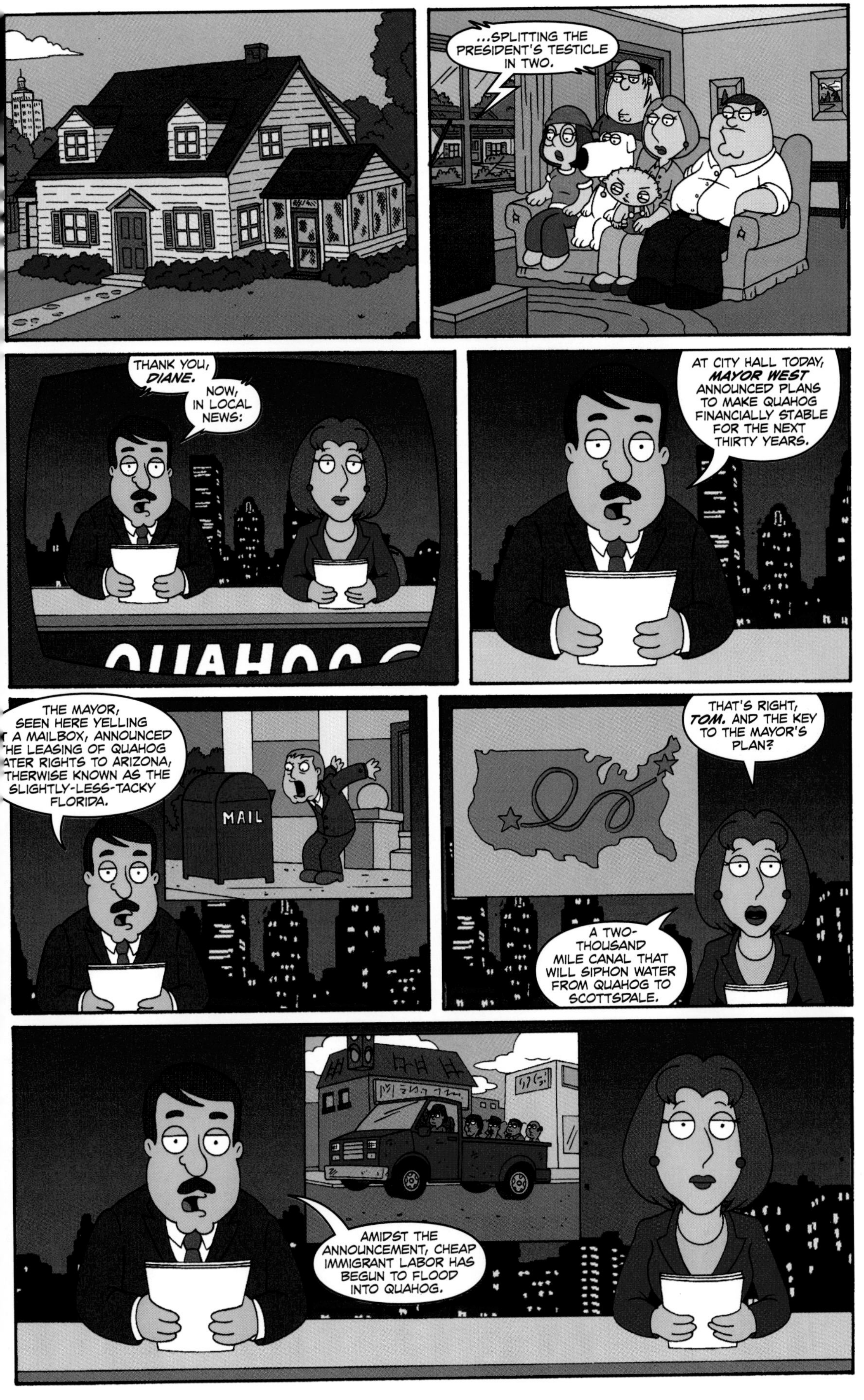
...SPLITTING THE PRESIDENT'S TESTICLE IN TWO.
THANK YOU, *DIANE.*
NOW, IN LOCAL NEWS:
AT CITY HALL TODAY, *MAYOR WEST* ANNOUNCED PLANS TO MAKE QUAHOG FINANCIALLY STABLE FOR THE NEXT THIRTY YEARS.
THE MAYOR, SEEN HERE YELLING T A MAILBOX, ANNOUNCED HE LEASING OF QUAHOG ATER RIGHTS TO ARIZONA, THERWISE KNOWN AS THE SLIGHTLY-LESS-TACKY FLORIDA.
MAIL
THAT'S RIGHT, *TOM.* AND THE KEY TO THE MAYOR'S PLAN?
A TWO-THOUSAND MILE CANAL THAT WILL SIPHON WATER FROM QUAHOG TO SCOTTSDALE.
AMIDST THE ANNOUNCEMENT, CHEAP IMMIGRANT LABOR HAS BEGUN TO FLOOD INTO QUAHOG.

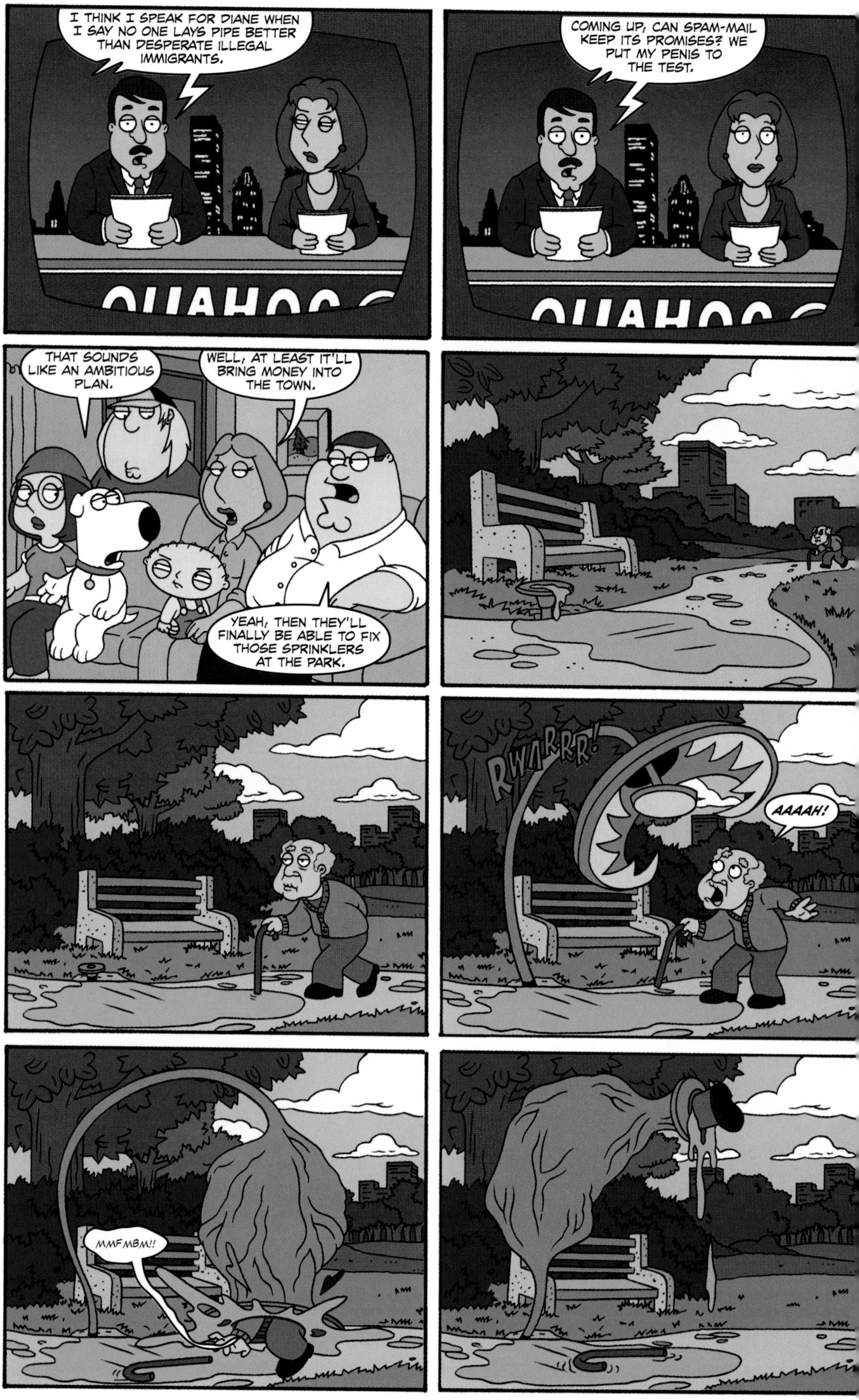
I THINK I SPEAK FOR DIANE WHEN I SAY NO ONE LAYS PIPE BETTER THAN DESPERATE ILLEGAL IMMIGRANTS.
QUAHOG
COMING UP, CAN SPAM-MAIL KEEP ITS PROMISES? WE PUT MY PENIS TO THE TEST.
QUAHOG
THAT SOUNDS LIKE AN AMBITIOUS PLAN.
WELL, AT LEAST IT'LL BRING MONEY INTO THE TOWN.
YEAH, THEN THEY'LL FINALLY BE ABLE TO FIX THOSE SPRINKLERS AT THE PARK.
RWARRRR!
AAAAH!
MMFMBM!!

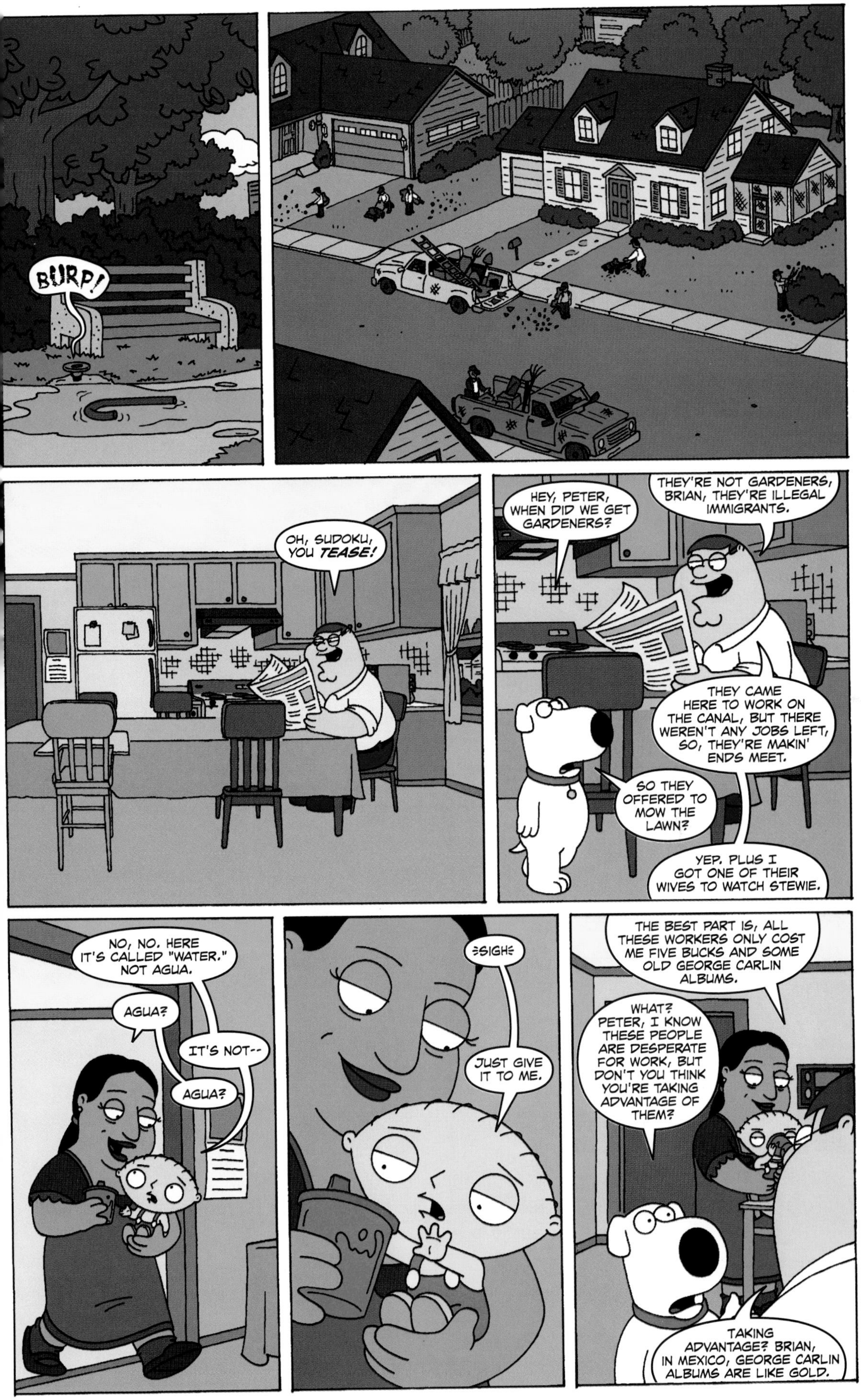
BURP!
OH, SUDOKU, YOU *TEASE!*
HEY, PETER, WHEN DID WE GET GARDENERS?
THEY'RE NOT GARDENERS, BRIAN, THEY'RE ILLEGAL IMMIGRANTS.
THEY CAME HERE TO WORK ON THE CANAL, BUT THERE WEREN'T ANY JOBS LEFT, SO, THEY'RE MAKIN' ENDS MEET.
SO THEY OFFERED TO MOW THE LAWN?
YEP. PLUS I GOT ONE OF THEIR WIVES TO WATCH STEWIE.
NO, NO. HERE IT'S CALLED "WATER." NOT AGUA.
AGUA?
IT'S NOT--
AGUA?
SIGH
JUST GIVE IT TO ME.
THE BEST PART IS, ALL THESE WORKERS ONLY COST ME FIVE BUCKS AND SOME OLD GEORGE CARLIN ALBUMS.
WHAT? PETER, I KNOW THESE PEOPLE ARE DESPERATE FOR WORK, BUT DON'T YOU THINK YOU'RE TAKING ADVANTAGE OF THEM?
TAKING ADVANTAGE? BRIAN, IN MEXICO, GEORGE CARLIN ALBUMS ARE LIKE GOLD.

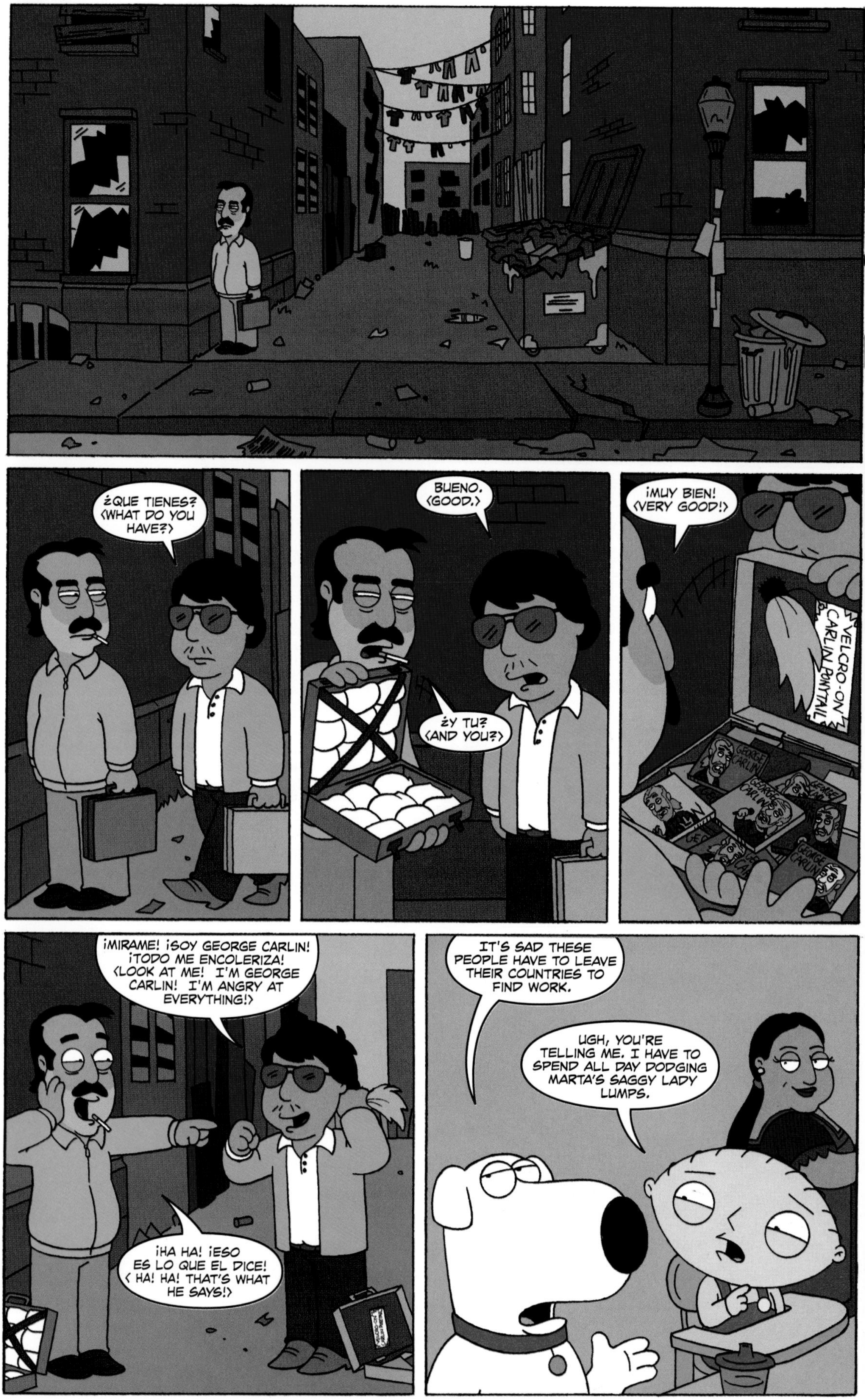
¿QUE TIENES? (WHAT DO YOU HAVE?)
BUENO. (GOOD.)
¿Y TU? (AND YOU?)
¡MUY BIEN! (VERY GOOD!)
VELCRO-ON CARLIN PONYTAIL
GEORGE CARLIN
¡MIRAME! ¡SOY GEORGE CARLIN! ¡TODO ME ENCOLERIZA! (LOOK AT ME! I'M GEORGE CARLIN! I'M ANGRY AT EVERYTHING!)
¡HA HA! ¡ESO ES LO QUE EL DICE! (HA! HA! THAT'S WHAT HE SAYS!)
IT'S SAD THESE PEOPLE HAVE TO LEAVE THEIR COUNTRIES TO FIND WORK.
UGH, YOU'RE TELLING ME. I HAVE TO SPEND ALL DAY DODGING MARTA'S SAGGY LADY LUMPS.

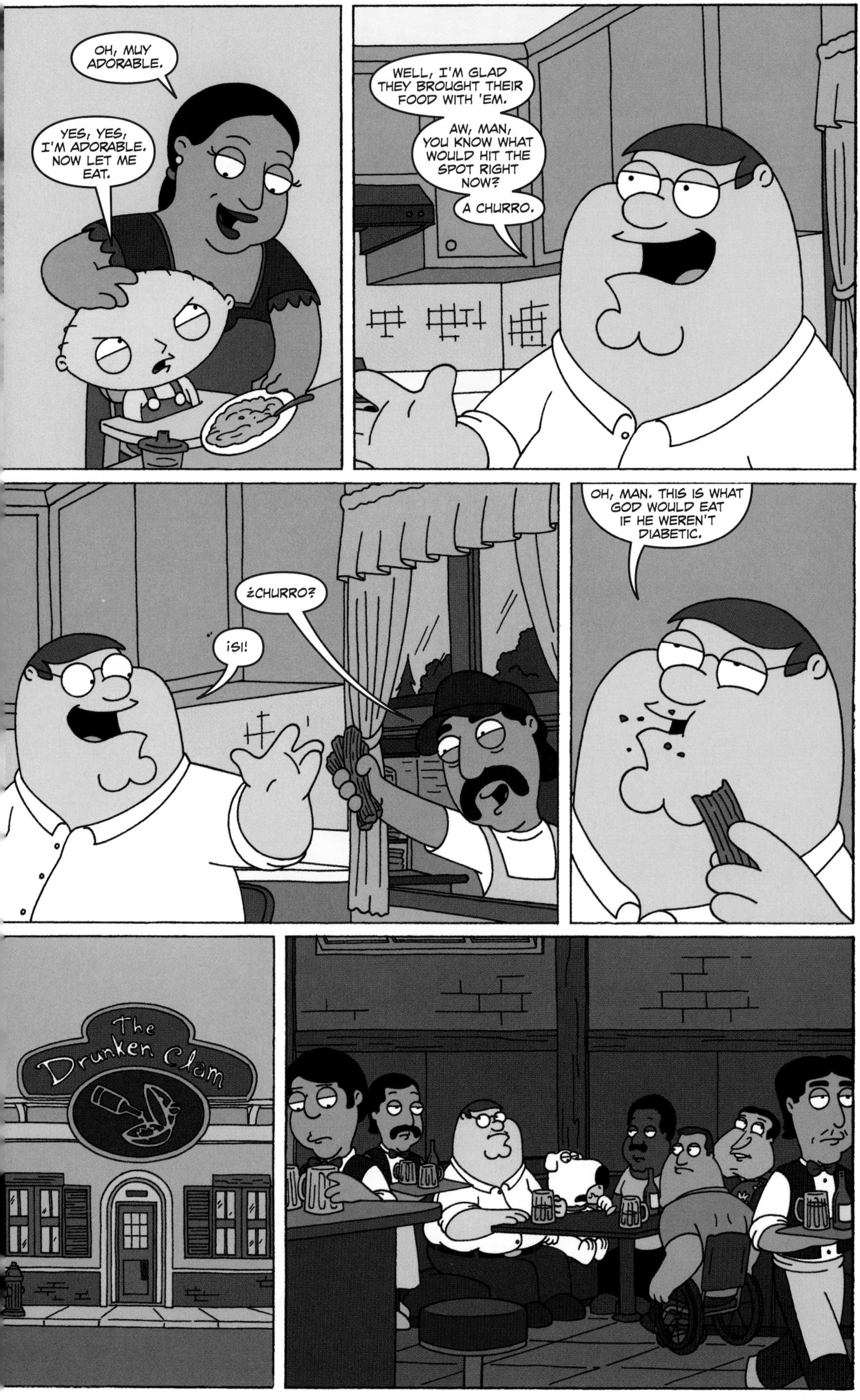
OH, MUY ADORABLE.
YES, YES, I'M ADORABLE. NOW LET ME EAT.
WELL, I'M GLAD THEY BROUGHT THEIR FOOD WITH 'EM.
AW, MAN, YOU KNOW WHAT WOULD HIT THE SPOT RIGHT NOW?
A CHURRO.
¿CHURRO?
¡SI!
OH, MAN. THIS IS WHAT GOD WOULD EAT IF HE WEREN'T DIABETIC.
The Drunken Clam

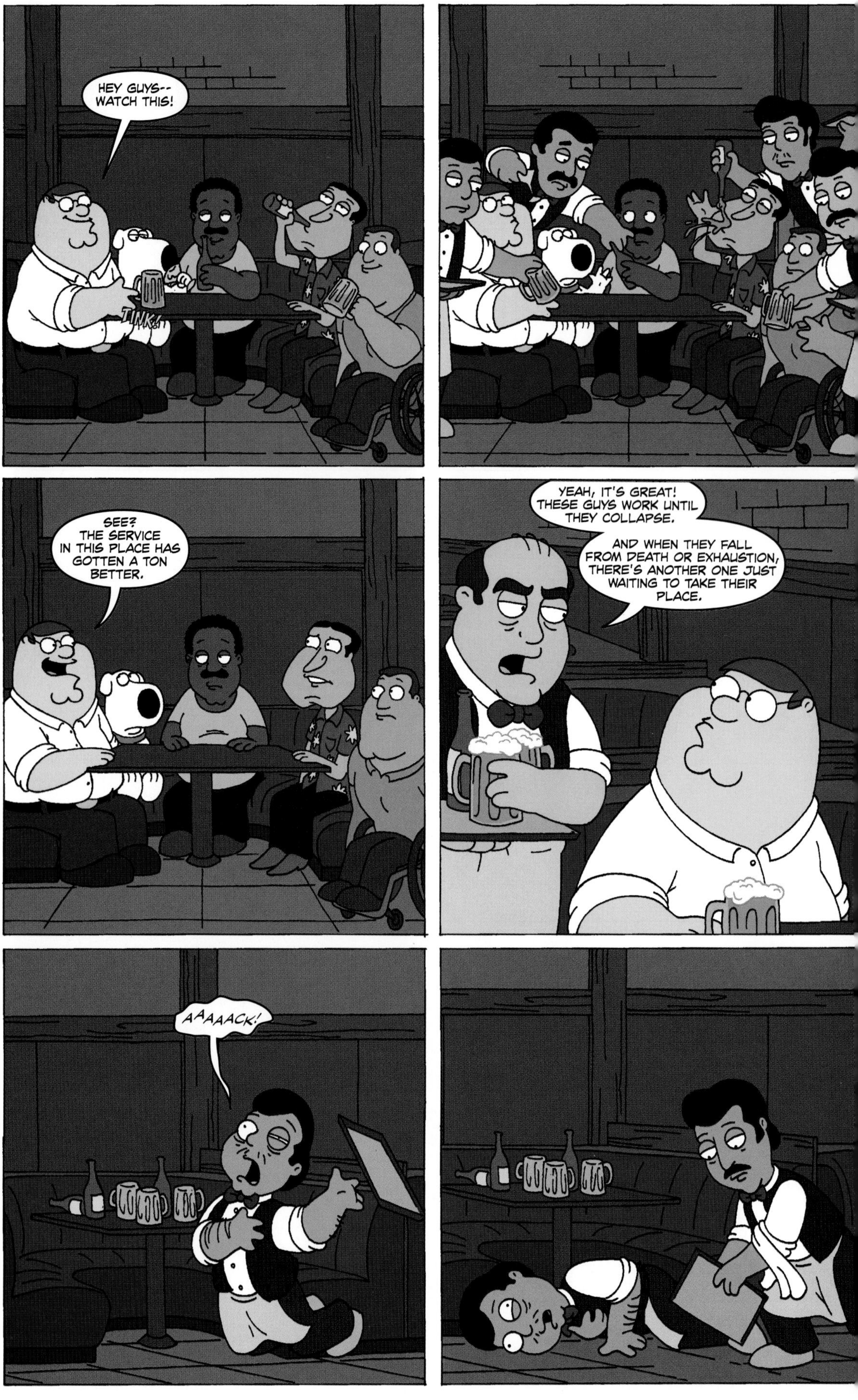
HEY GUYS--
WATCH THIS!
TINK!
SEE?
THE SERVICE
IN THIS PLACE HAS
GOTTEN A TON
BETTER.
YEAH, IT'S GREAT!
THESE GUYS WORK UNTIL
THEY COLLAPSE.
AND WHEN THEY FALL
FROM DEATH OR EXHAUSTION,
THERE'S ANOTHER ONE JUST
WAITING TO TAKE THEIR
PLACE.
AAAAACK!

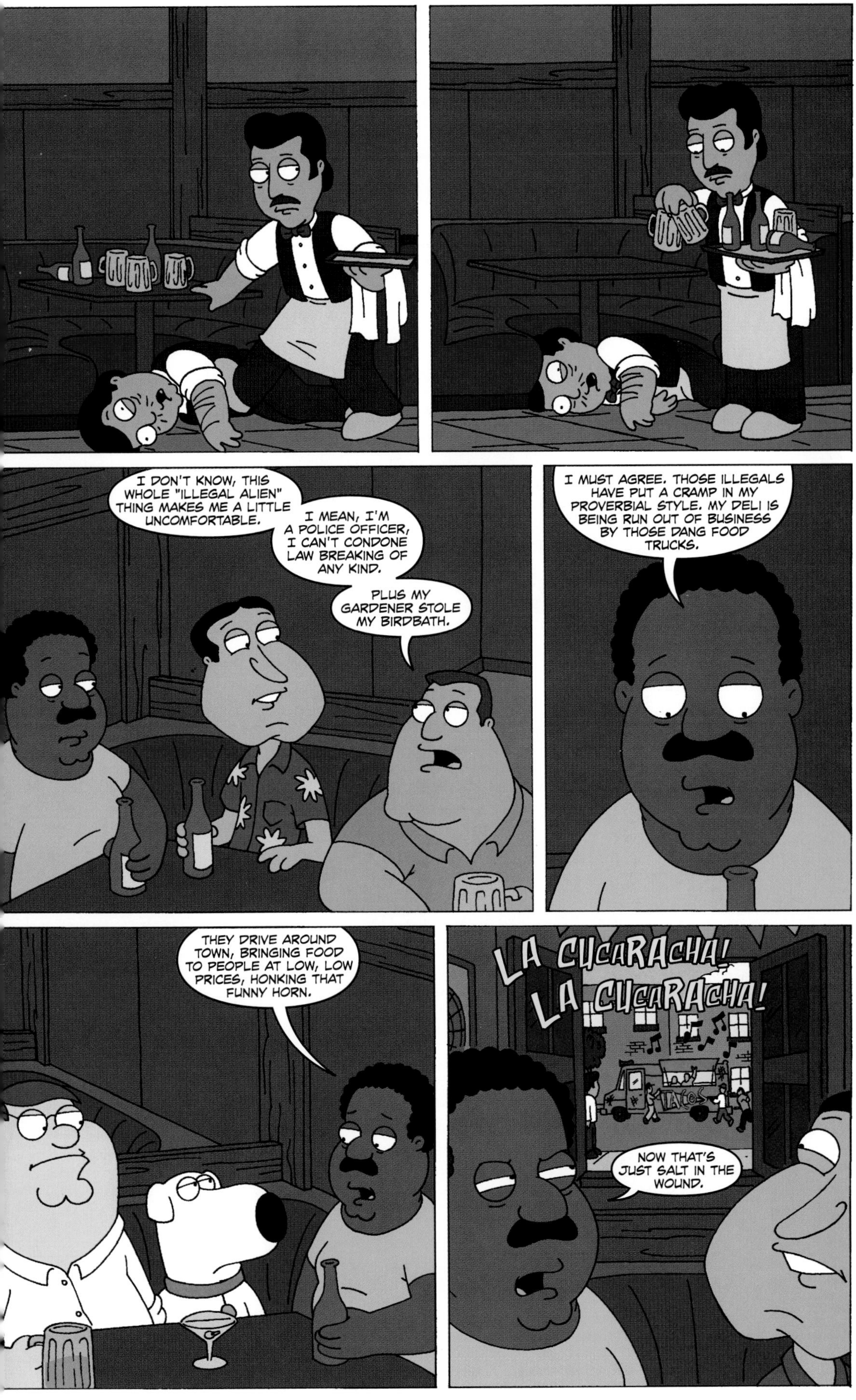
I DON'T KNOW, THIS WHOLE "ILLEGAL ALIEN" THING MAKES ME A LITTLE UNCOMFORTABLE.
I MEAN, I'M A POLICE OFFICER, I CAN'T CONDONE LAW BREAKING OF ANY KIND.
PLUS MY GARDENER STOLE MY BIRDBATH.
I MUST AGREE. THOSE ILLEGALS HAVE PUT A CRAMP IN MY PROVERBIAL STYLE. MY DELI IS BEING RUN OUT OF BUSINESS BY THOSE DANG FOOD TRUCKS.
THEY DRIVE AROUND TOWN, BRINGING FOOD TO PEOPLE AT LOW, LOW PRICES, HONKING THAT FUNNY HORN.
LA CUCARACHA!
LA CUCARACHA!
TACOS
NOW THAT'S JUST SALT IN THE WOUND.

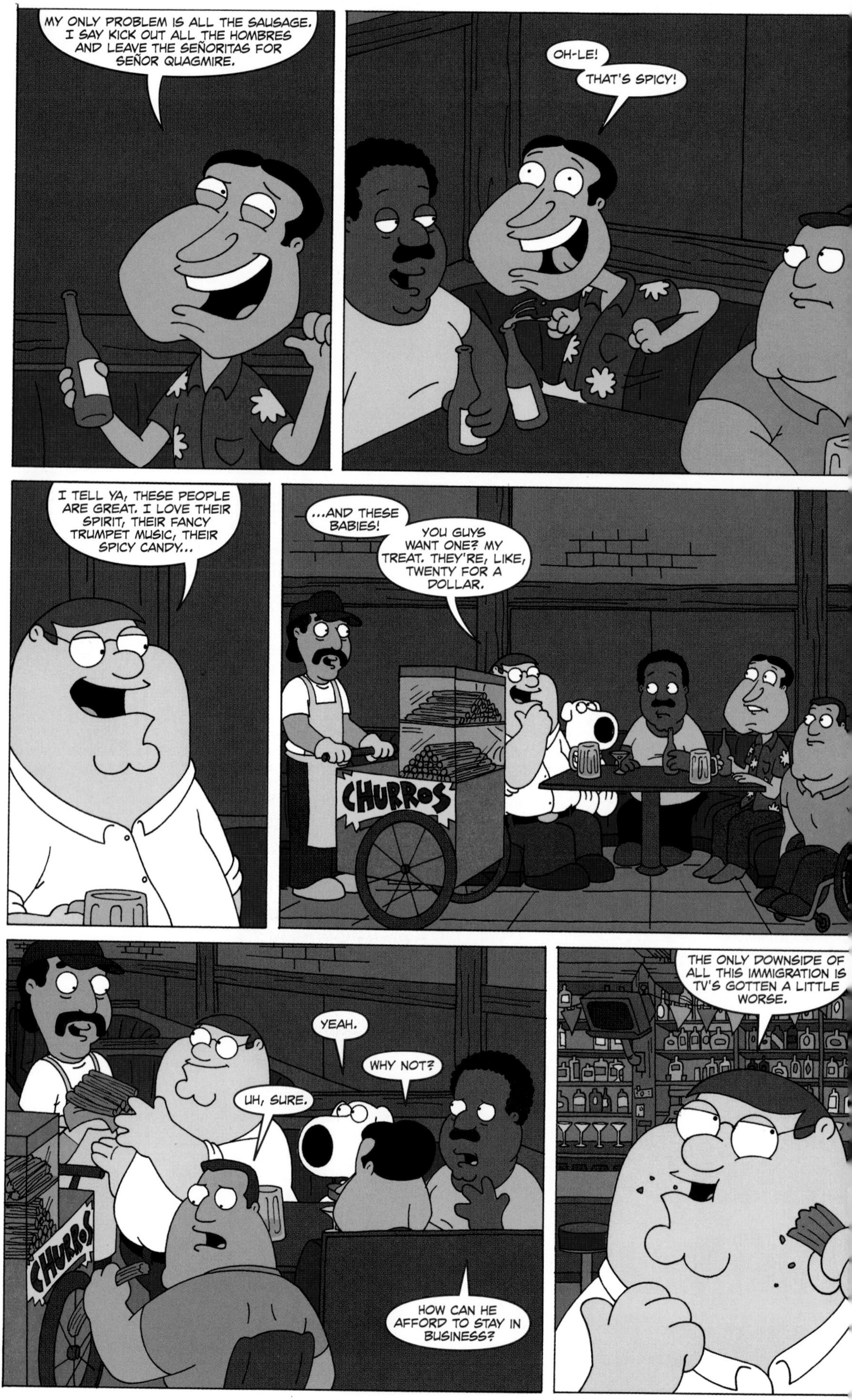
MY ONLY PROBLEM IS ALL THE SAUSAGE. I SAY KICK OUT ALL THE HOMBRES AND LEAVE THE SEÑORITAS FOR SEÑOR QUAGMIRE.
OH-LE!
THAT'S SPICY!
I TELL YA, THESE PEOPLE ARE GREAT. I LOVE THEIR SPIRIT, THEIR FANCY TRUMPET MUSIC, THEIR SPICY CANDY...
...AND THESE BABIES!
YOU GUYS WANT ONE? MY TREAT. THEY'RE, LIKE, TWENTY FOR A DOLLAR.
CHURROS
YEAH.
WHY NOT?
UH, SURE.
CHURROS
HOW CAN HE AFFORD TO STAY IN BUSINESS?
THE ONLY DOWNSIDE OF ALL THIS IMMIGRATION IS TV'S GOTTEN A LITTLE WORSE.

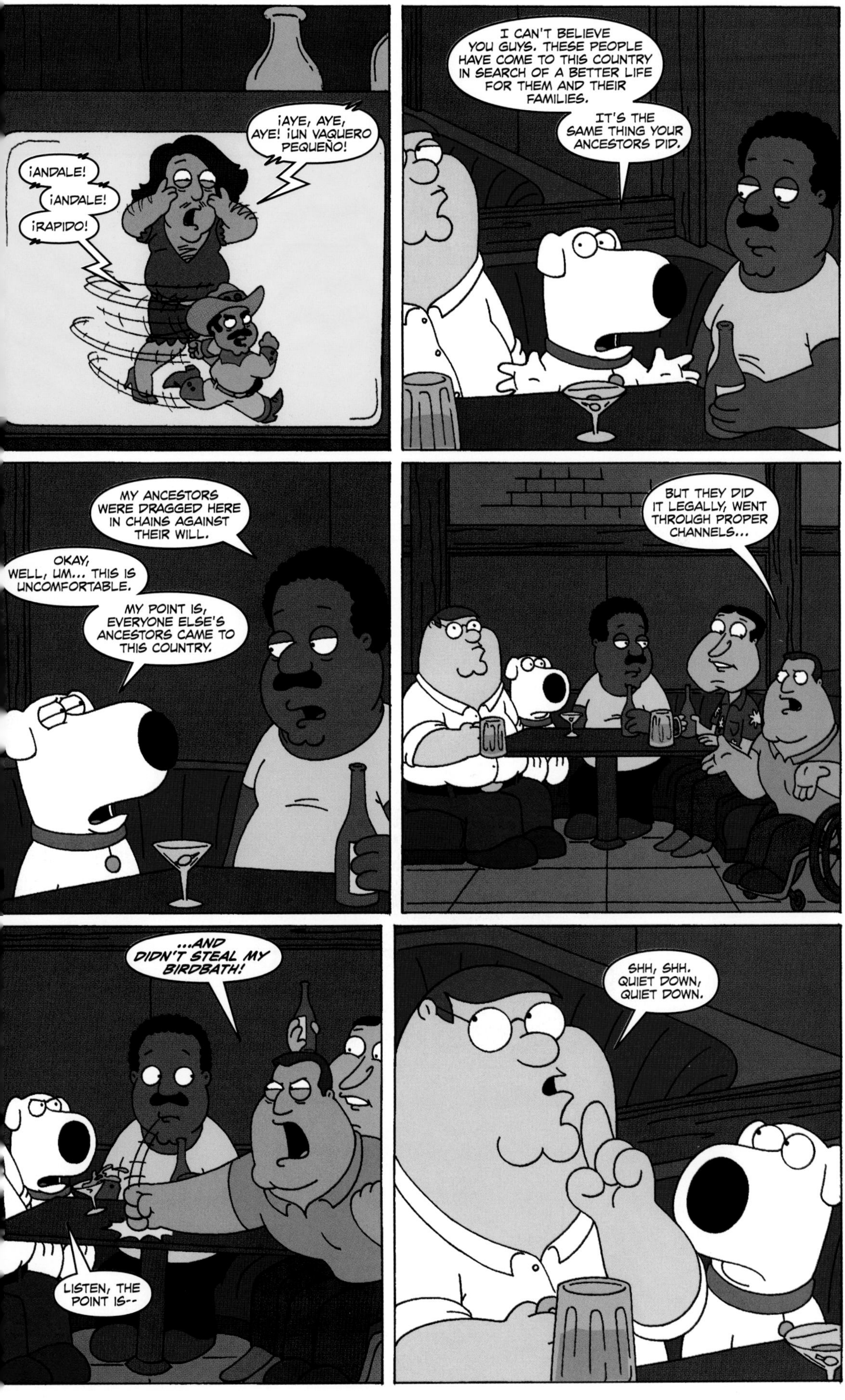
¡AYE, AYE, AYE! ¡UN VAQUERO PEQUEÑO!
¡ANDALE!
¡ANDALE!
¡RAPIDO!
I CAN'T BELIEVE YOU GUYS. THESE PEOPLE HAVE COME TO THIS COUNTRY IN SEARCH OF A BETTER LIFE FOR THEM AND THEIR FAMILIES.
IT'S THE SAME THING YOUR ANCESTORS DID.
MY ANCESTORS WERE DRAGGED HERE IN CHAINS AGAINST THEIR WILL.
OKAY, WELL, UM... THIS IS UNCOMFORTABLE.
MY POINT IS, EVERYONE ELSE'S ANCESTORS CAME TO THIS COUNTRY.
BUT THEY DID IT LEGALLY, WENT THROUGH PROPER CHANNELS...
...AND DIDN'T STEAL MY BIRDBATH!
LISTEN, THE POINT IS--
SHH, SHH. QUIET DOWN, QUIET DOWN.

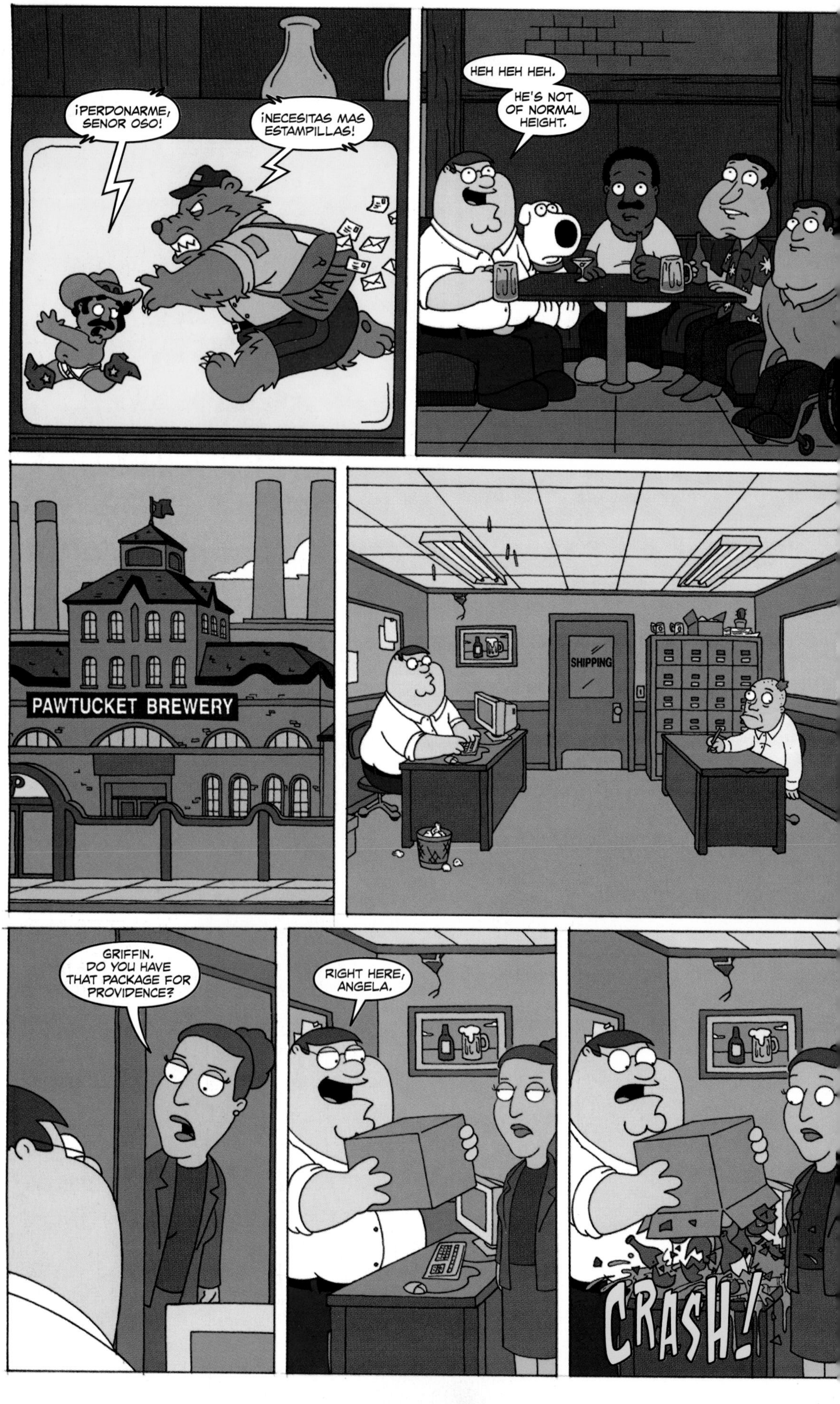

¡PERDONARME, SENOR OSO!
¡NECESITAS MAS ESTAMPILLAS!
HEH HEH HEH.
HE'S NOT OF NORMAL HEIGHT.
PAWTUCKET BREWERY
SHIPPING
GRIFFIN. DO YOU HAVE THAT PACKAGE FOR PROVIDENCE?
RIGHT HERE, ANGELA.
CRASH!

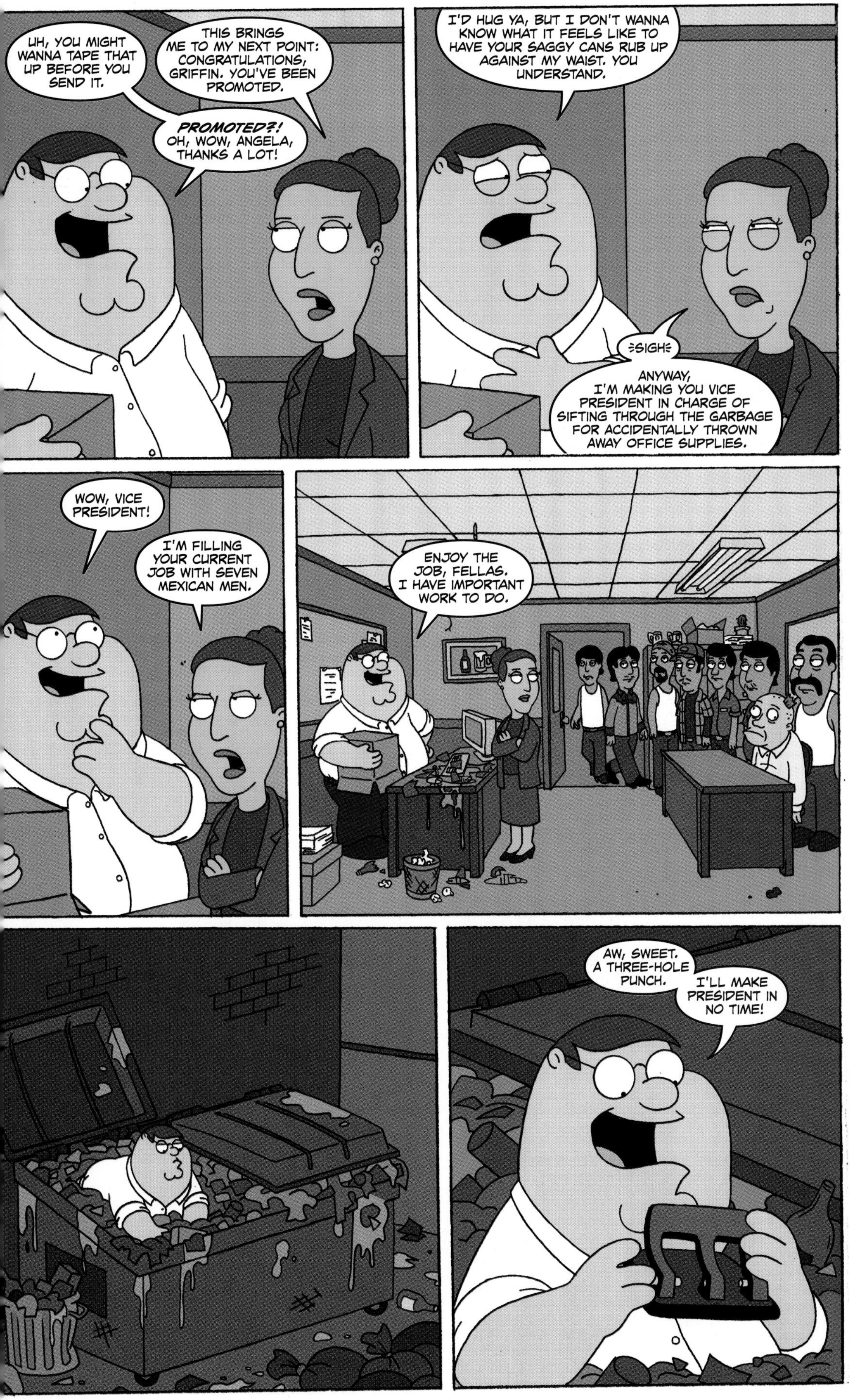

UH, YOU MIGHT WANNA TAPE THAT UP BEFORE YOU SEND IT.
THIS BRINGS ME TO MY NEXT POINT: CONGRATULATIONS, GRIFFIN. YOU'VE BEEN PROMOTED.
PROMOTED?! OH, WOW, ANGELA, THANKS A LOT!
I'D HUG YA, BUT I DON'T WANNA KNOW WHAT IT FEELS LIKE TO HAVE YOUR SAGGY CANS RUB UP AGAINST MY WAIST. YOU UNDERSTAND.
SIGH
ANYWAY, I'M MAKING YOU VICE PRESIDENT IN CHARGE OF SIFTING THROUGH THE GARBAGE FOR ACCIDENTALLY THROWN AWAY OFFICE SUPPLIES.
WOW, VICE PRESIDENT!
I'M FILLING YOUR CURRENT JOB WITH SEVEN MEXICAN MEN.
ENJOY THE JOB, FELLAS. I HAVE IMPORTANT WORK TO DO.
AW, SWEET. A THREE-HOLE PUNCH.
I'LL MAKE PRESIDENT IN NO TIME!

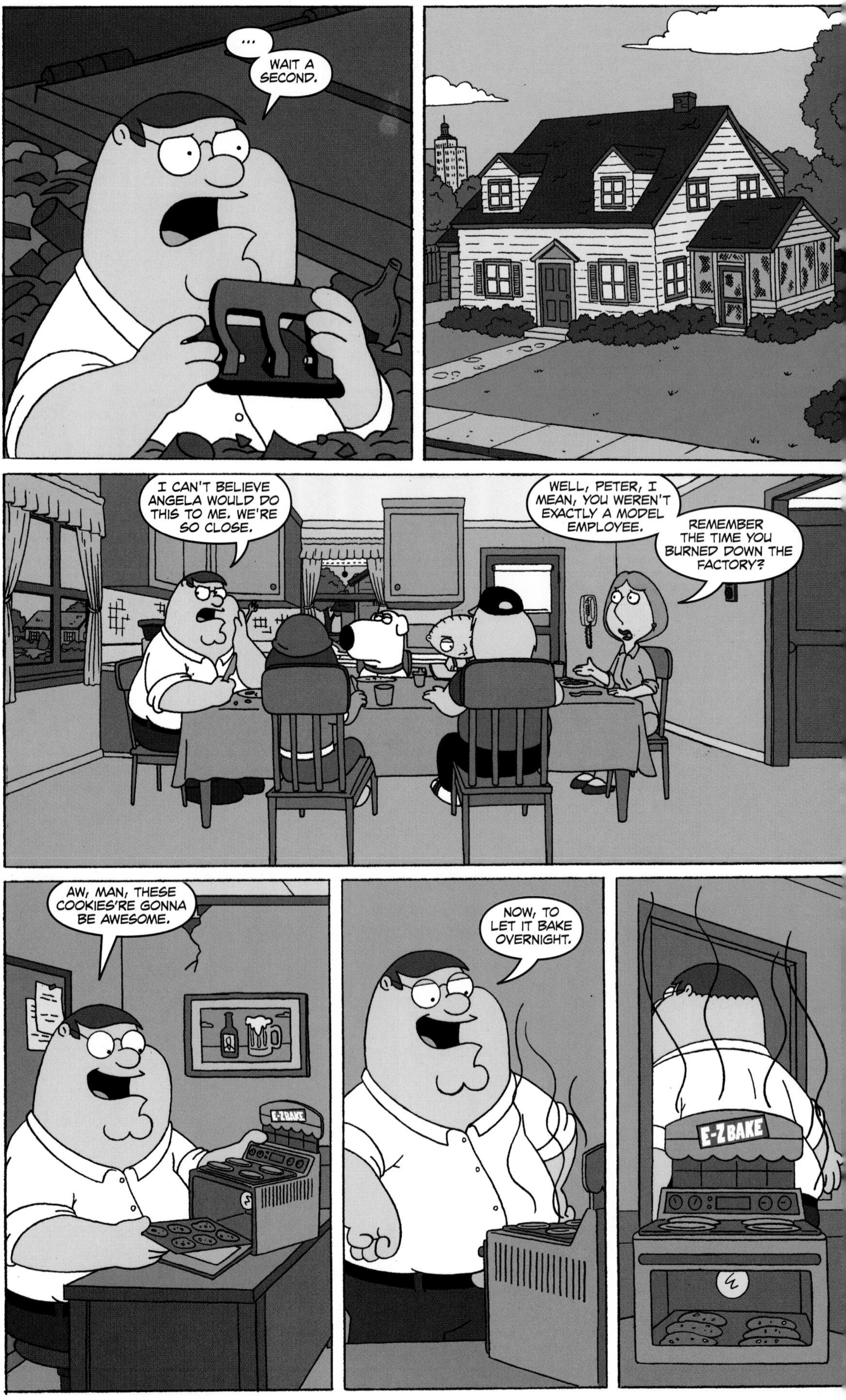
...
WAIT A SECOND.
I CAN'T BELIEVE ANGELA WOULD DO THIS TO ME. WE'RE SO CLOSE.
WELL, PETER, I MEAN, YOU WEREN'T EXACTLY A MODEL EMPLOYEE.
REMEMBER THE TIME YOU BURNED DOWN THE FACTORY?
AW, MAN, THESE COOKIES'RE GONNA BE AWESOME.
E-Z BAKE
NOW, TO LET IT BAKE OVERNIGHT.
E-Z BAKE

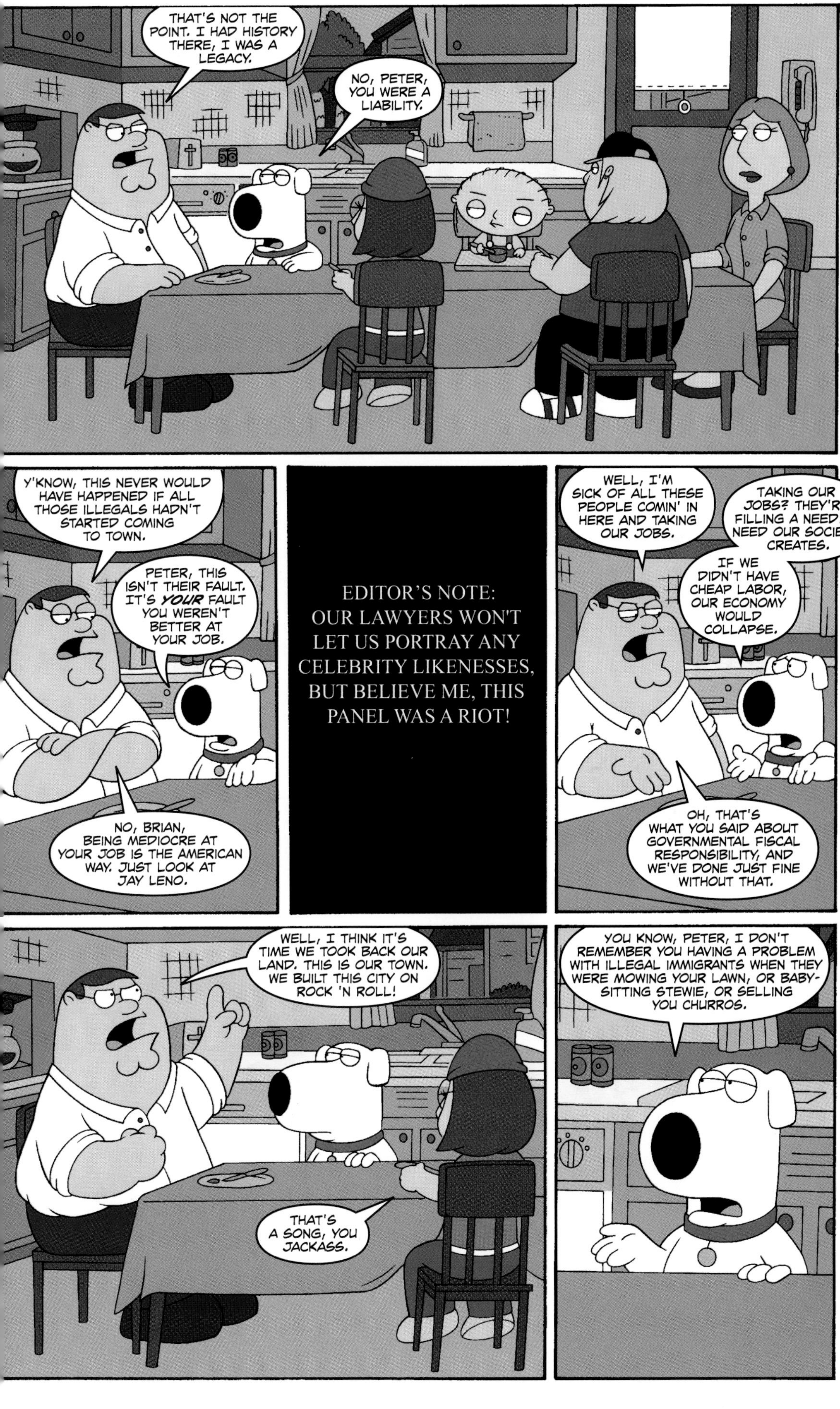
THAT'S NOT THE POINT. I HAD HISTORY THERE, I WAS A LEGACY.
NO, PETER, YOU WERE A LIABILITY.
Y'KNOW, THIS NEVER WOULD HAVE HAPPENED IF ALL THOSE ILLEGALS HADN'T STARTED COMING TO TOWN.
PETER, THIS ISN'T THEIR FAULT. IT'S *YOUR* FAULT YOU WEREN'T BETTER AT YOUR JOB.
NO, BRIAN, BEING MEDIOCRE AT YOUR JOB IS THE AMERICAN WAY. JUST LOOK AT JAY LENO.
EDITOR'S NOTE: OUR LAWYERS WON'T LET US PORTRAY ANY CELEBRITY LIKENESSES, BUT BELIEVE ME, THIS PANEL WAS A RIOT!
WELL, I'M SICK OF ALL THESE PEOPLE COMIN' IN HERE AND TAKING OUR JOBS.
TAKING OUR JOBS? THEY'RE FILLING A NEED! A NEED OUR SOCIETY CREATES.
IF WE DIDN'T HAVE CHEAP LABOR, OUR ECONOMY WOULD COLLAPSE.
OH, THAT'S WHAT YOU SAID ABOUT GOVERNMENTAL FISCAL RESPONSIBILITY, AND WE'VE DONE JUST FINE WITHOUT THAT.
WELL, I THINK IT'S TIME WE TOOK BACK OUR LAND. THIS IS OUR TOWN. WE BUILT THIS CITY ON ROCK 'N ROLL!
THAT'S A SONG, YOU JACKASS.
YOU KNOW, PETER, I DON'T REMEMBER YOU HAVING A PROBLEM WITH ILLEGAL IMMIGRANTS WHEN THEY WERE MOWING YOUR LAWN, OR BABY-SITTING STEWIE, OR SELLING YOU CHURROS.

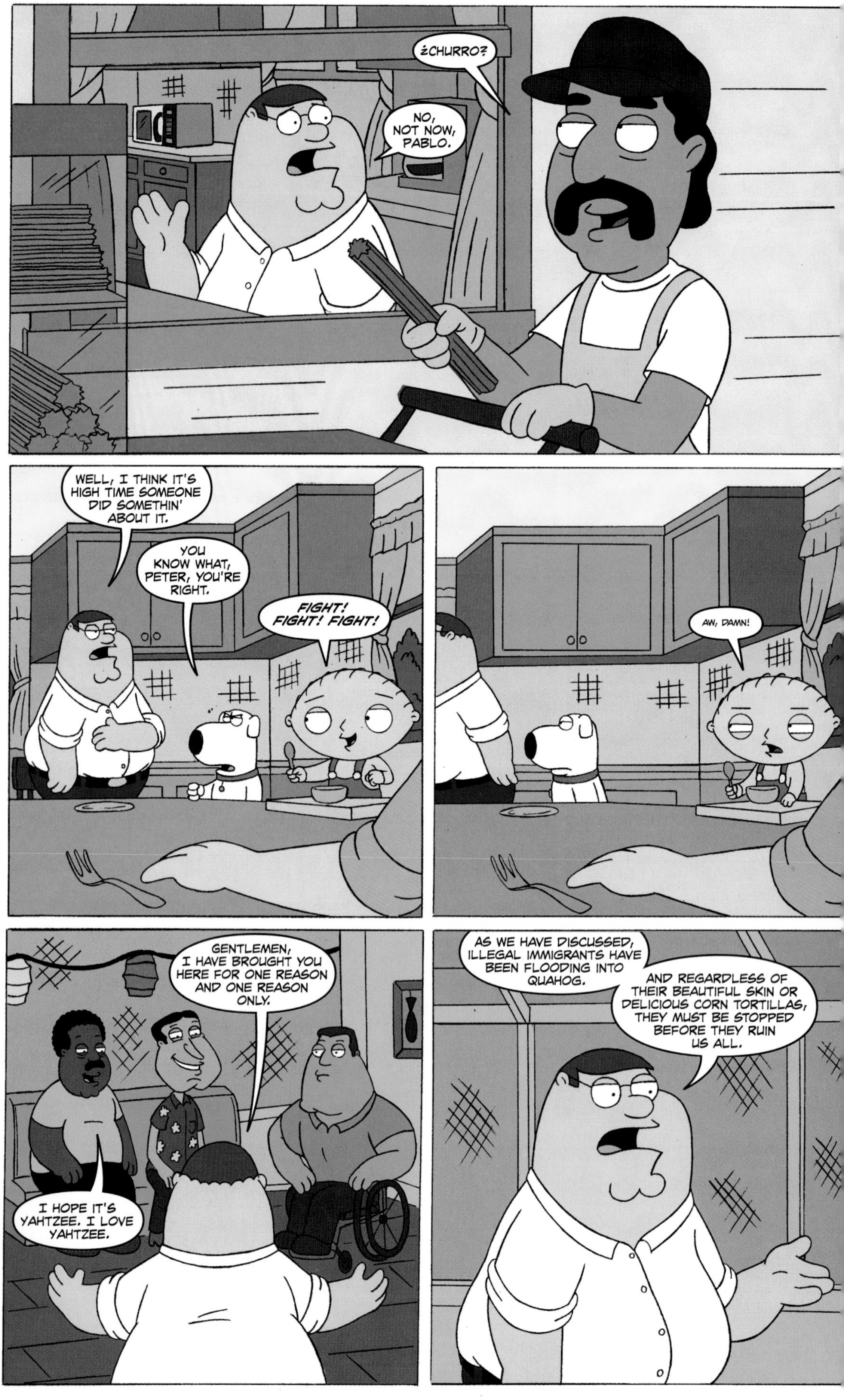
¿CHURRO?
NO, NOT NOW, PABLO.
WELL, I THINK IT'S HIGH TIME SOMEONE DID SOMETHIN' ABOUT IT.
YOU KNOW WHAT, PETER, YOU'RE RIGHT.
FIGHT! FIGHT! FIGHT!
AW, DAMN!
GENTLEMEN, I HAVE BROUGHT YOU HERE FOR ONE REASON AND ONE REASON ONLY.
I HOPE IT'S YAHTZEE. I LOVE YAHTZEE.
AS WE HAVE DISCUSSED, ILLEGAL IMMIGRANTS HAVE BEEN FLOODING INTO QUAHOG.
AND REGARDLESS OF THEIR BEAUTIFUL SKIN OR DELICIOUS CORN TORTILLAS, THEY MUST BE STOPPED BEFORE THEY RUIN US ALL.

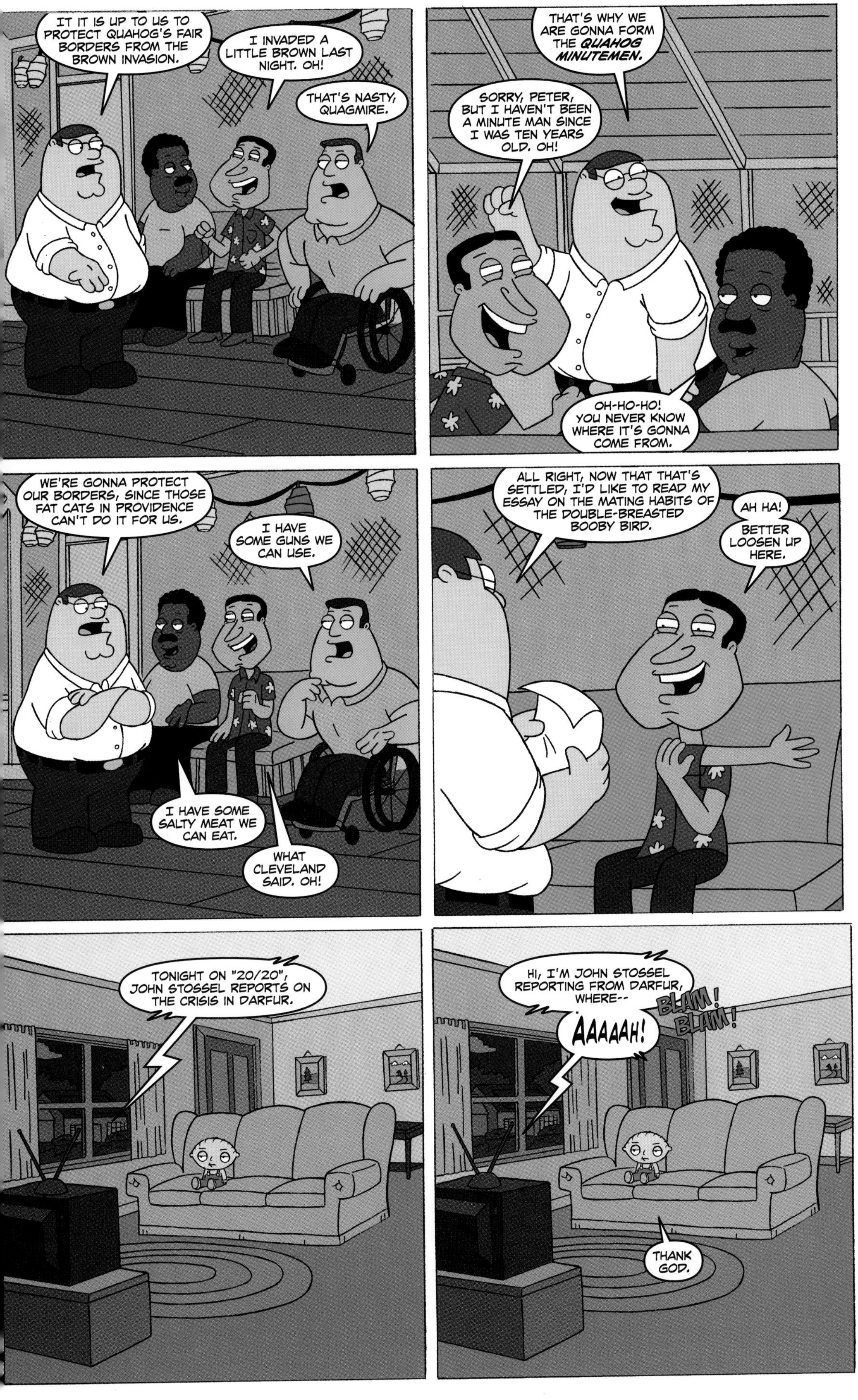
IT IT IS UP TO US TO PROTECT QUAHOG'S FAIR BORDERS FROM THE BROWN INVASION.
I INVADED A LITTLE BROWN LAST NIGHT. OH!
THAT'S NASTY, QUAGMIRE.
THAT'S WHY WE ARE GONNA FORM THE QUAHOG MINUTEMEN.
SORRY, PETER, BUT I HAVEN'T BEEN A MINUTE MAN SINCE I WAS TEN YEARS OLD. OH!
OH-HO-HO! YOU NEVER KNOW WHERE IT'S GONNA COME FROM.
WE'RE GONNA PROTECT OUR BORDERS, SINCE THOSE FAT CATS IN PROVIDENCE CAN'T DO IT FOR US.
I HAVE SOME GUNS WE CAN USE.
I HAVE SOME SALTY MEAT WE CAN EAT.
WHAT CLEVELAND SAID. OH!
ALL RIGHT, NOW THAT THAT'S SETTLED, I'D LIKE TO READ MY ESSAY ON THE MATING HABITS OF THE DOUBLE-BREASTED BOOBY BIRD.
AH HA! BETTER LOOSEN UP HERE.
TONIGHT ON "20/20", JOHN STOSSEL REPORTS ON THE CRISIS IN DARFUR.
HI, I'M JOHN STOSSEL REPORTING FROM DARFUR, WHERE--
AAAAAH!
BLAM! BLAM!
THANK GOD.

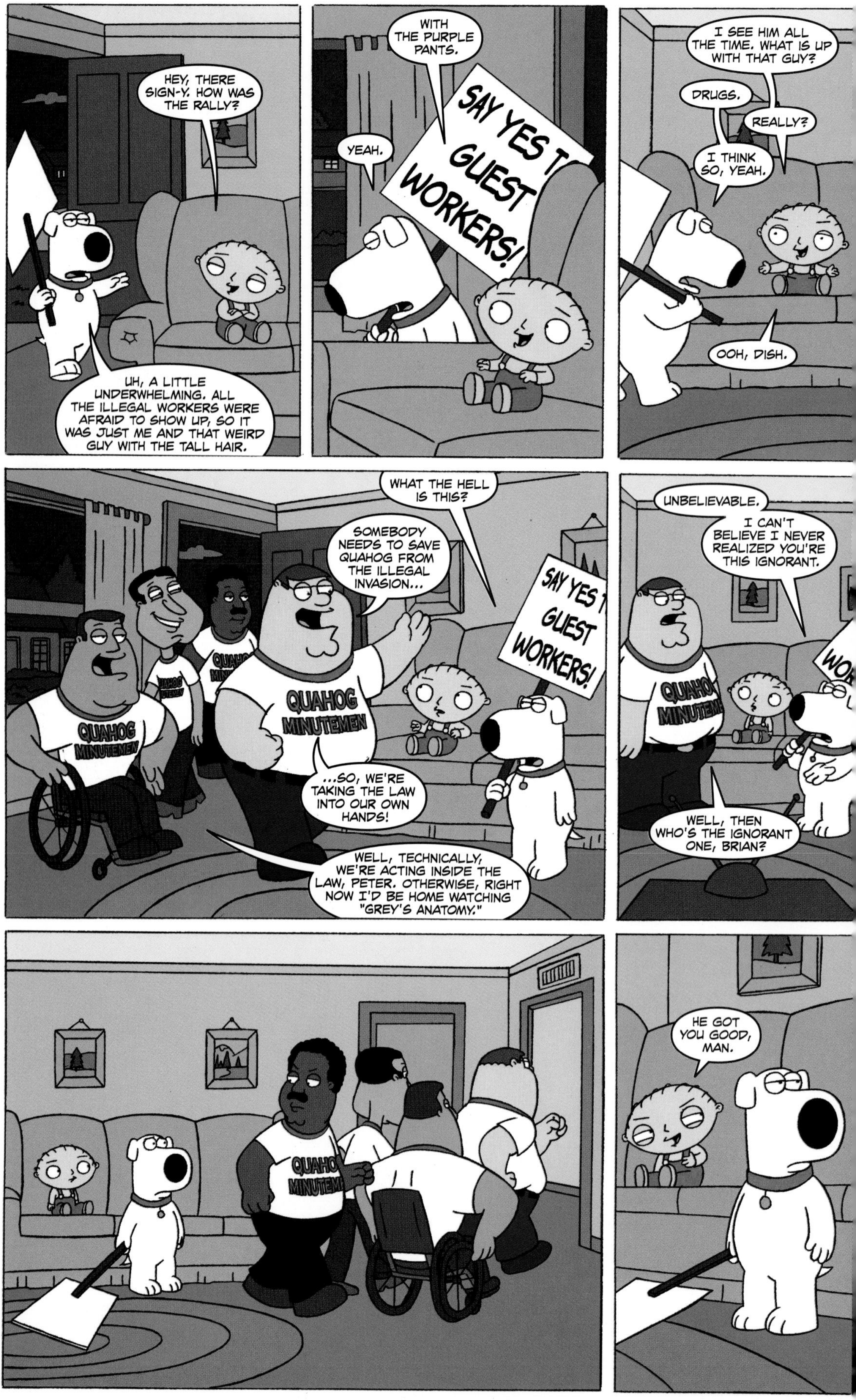
HEY, THERE SIGN-Y. HOW WAS THE RALLY?
UH, A LITTLE UNDERWHELMING. ALL THE ILLEGAL WORKERS WERE AFRAID TO SHOW UP, SO IT WAS JUST ME AND THAT WEIRD GUY WITH THE TALL HAIR.
WITH THE PURPLE PANTS.
YEAH.
SAY YES T GUEST WORKERS!
I SEE HIM ALL THE TIME. WHAT IS UP WITH THAT GUY?
DRUGS.
REALLY?
I THINK SO, YEAH.
OOH, DISH.
WHAT THE HELL IS THIS?
SOMEBODY NEEDS TO SAVE QUAHOG FROM THE ILLEGAL INVASION...
...SO, WE'RE TAKING THE LAW INTO OUR OWN HANDS!
WELL, TECHNICALLY, WE'RE ACTING INSIDE THE LAW, PETER. OTHERWISE, RIGHT NOW I'D BE HOME WATCHING "GREY'S ANATOMY."
QUAHOG MINUTEMEN
SAY YES T GUEST WORKERS!
UNBELIEVABLE.
I CAN'T BELIEVE I NEVER REALIZED YOU'RE THIS IGNORANT.
WELL, THEN WHO'S THE IGNORANT ONE, BRIAN?
HE GOT YOU GOOD, MAN.

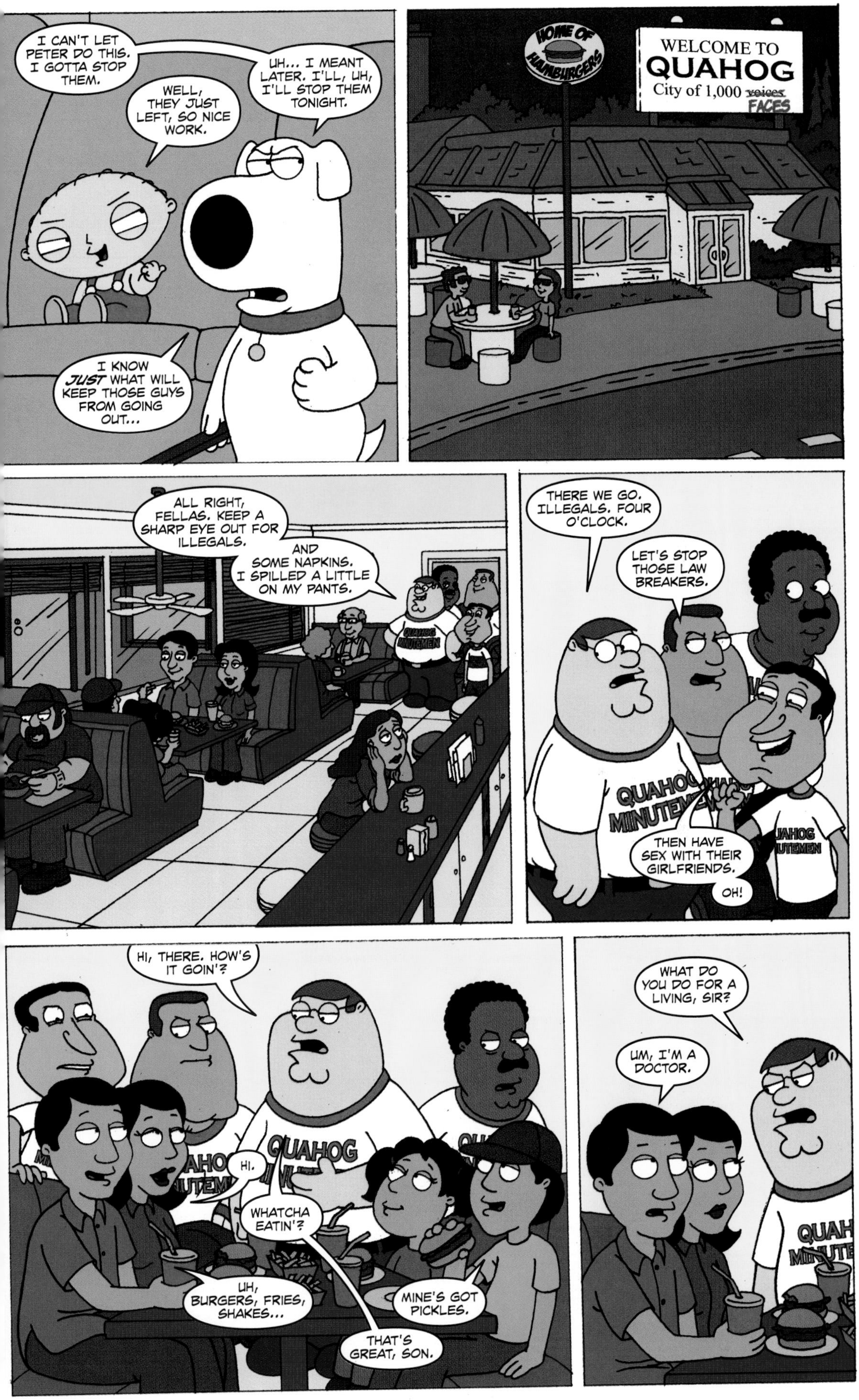
I CAN'T LET PETER DO THIS. I GOTTA STOP THEM.
WELL, THEY JUST LEFT, SO NICE WORK.
UH... I MEANT LATER. I'LL, UH, I'LL STOP THEM TONIGHT.
I KNOW *JUST* WHAT WILL KEEP THOSE GUYS FROM GOING OUT...
HOME OF HAMBURGERS
WELCOME TO QUAHOG City of 1,000 ~~voices~~ FACES
ALL RIGHT, FELLAS. KEEP A SHARP EYE OUT FOR ILLEGALS.
AND SOME NAPKINS. I SPILLED A LITTLE ON MY PANTS.
QUAHOG MINUTEMEN
THERE WE GO. ILLEGALS. FOUR O'CLOCK.
LET'S STOP THOSE LAW BREAKERS.
QUAHOG MINUTEMEN
THEN HAVE SEX WITH THEIR GIRLFRIENDS.
OH!
HI, THERE. HOW'S IT GOIN'?
QUAHOG
HI.
WHATCHA EATIN'?
UH, BURGERS, FRIES, SHAKES...
MINE'S GOT PICKLES.
THAT'S GREAT, SON.
WHAT DO YOU DO FOR A LIVING, SIR?
UM, I'M A DOCTOR.

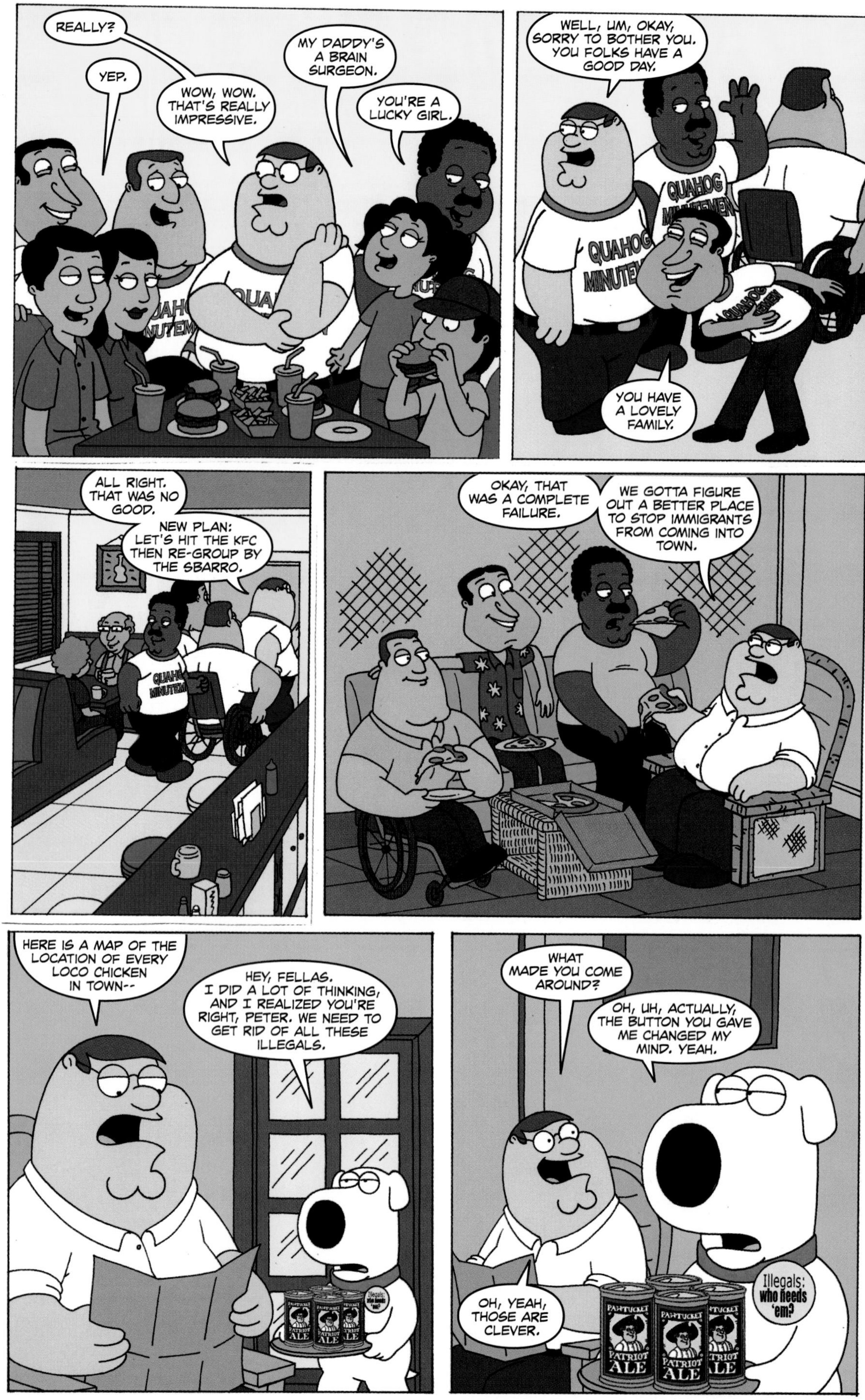

REALLY?
YEP.
WOW, WOW. THAT'S REALLY IMPRESSIVE.
MY DADDY'S A BRAIN SURGEON.
YOU'RE A LUCKY GIRL.
QUAHOG MINUTEMEN
WELL, UM, OKAY, SORRY TO BOTHER YOU. YOU FOLKS HAVE A GOOD DAY.
QUAHOG MINUTEMEN
YOU HAVE A LOVELY FAMILY.
ALL RIGHT. THAT WAS NO GOOD.
NEW PLAN: LET'S HIT THE KFC THEN RE-GROUP BY THE SBARRO.
QUAHOG MINUTEMEN
OKAY, THAT WAS A COMPLETE FAILURE.
WE GOTTA FIGURE OUT A BETTER PLACE TO STOP IMMIGRANTS FROM COMING INTO TOWN.
HERE IS A MAP OF THE LOCATION OF EVERY LOCO CHICKEN IN TOWN--
HEY, FELLAS. I DID A LOT OF THINKING, AND I REALIZED YOU'RE RIGHT, PETER. WE NEED TO GET RID OF ALL THESE ILLEGALS.
WHAT MADE YOU COME AROUND?
OH, UH, ACTUALLY, THE BUTTON YOU GAVE ME CHANGED MY MIND. YEAH.
OH, YEAH, THOSE ARE CLEVER.
PAWTUCKET PATRIOT ALE
Illegals: who needs 'em?

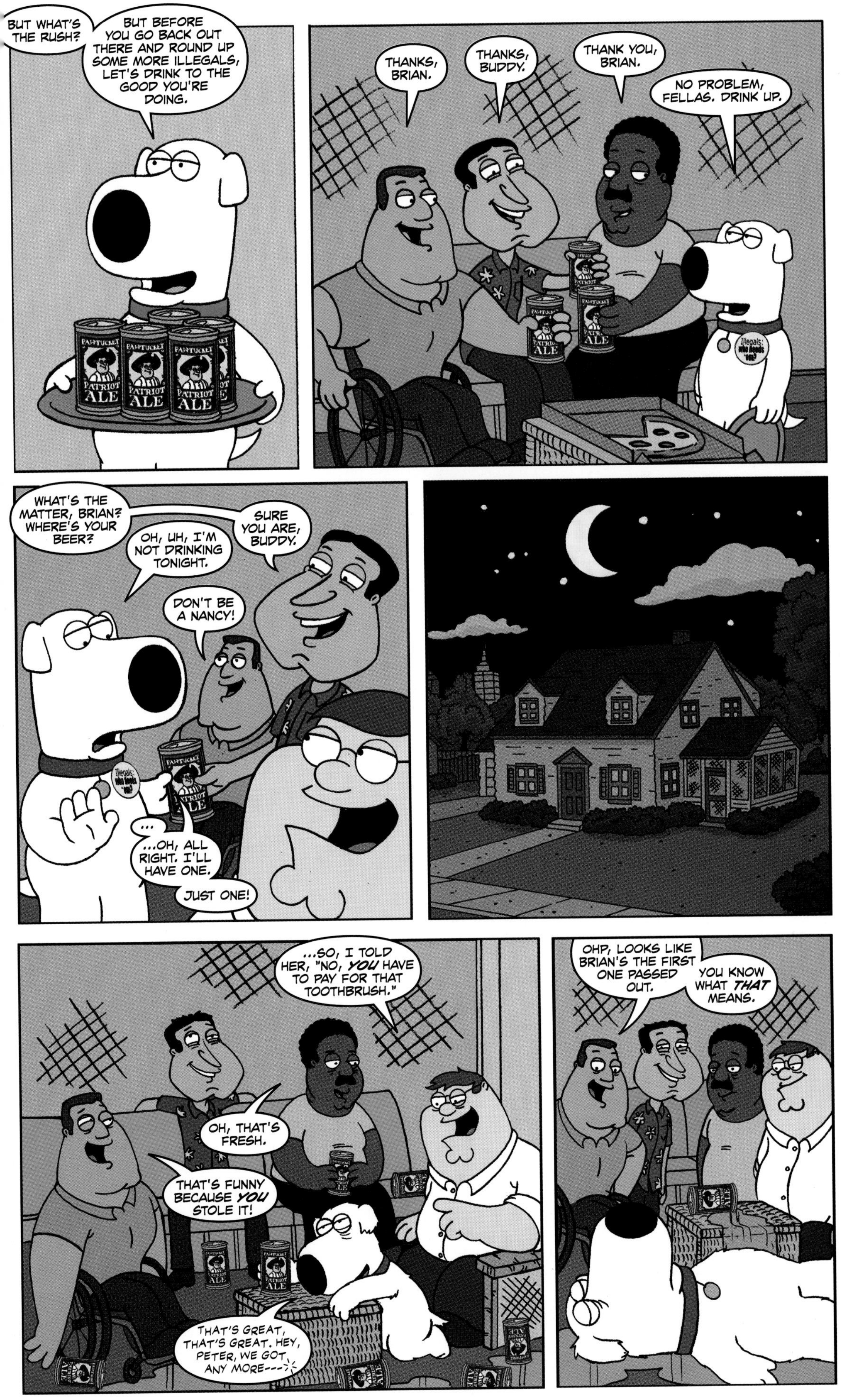
BUT WHAT'S THE RUSH?
BUT BEFORE YOU GO BACK OUT THERE AND ROUND UP SOME MORE ILLEGALS, LET'S DRINK TO THE GOOD YOU'RE DOING.
PAWTUCKET PATRIOT ALE
THANKS, BRIAN.
THANKS, BUDDY.
THANK YOU, BRIAN.
NO PROBLEM, FELLAS. DRINK UP.
Illegals: who needs 'em?
WHAT'S THE MATTER, BRIAN? WHERE'S YOUR BEER?
SURE YOU ARE, BUDDY.
OH, UH, I'M NOT DRINKING TONIGHT.
DON'T BE A NANCY!
...
...OH, ALL RIGHT. I'LL HAVE ONE.
JUST ONE!
...SO, I TOLD HER, "NO, YOU HAVE TO PAY FOR THAT TOOTHBRUSH."
OH, THAT'S FRESH.
THAT'S FUNNY BECAUSE YOU STOLE IT!
THAT'S GREAT, THAT'S GREAT. HEY, PETER, WE GOT ANY MORE---
OHP, LOOKS LIKE BRIAN'S THE FIRST ONE PASSED OUT.
YOU KNOW WHAT THAT MEANS.

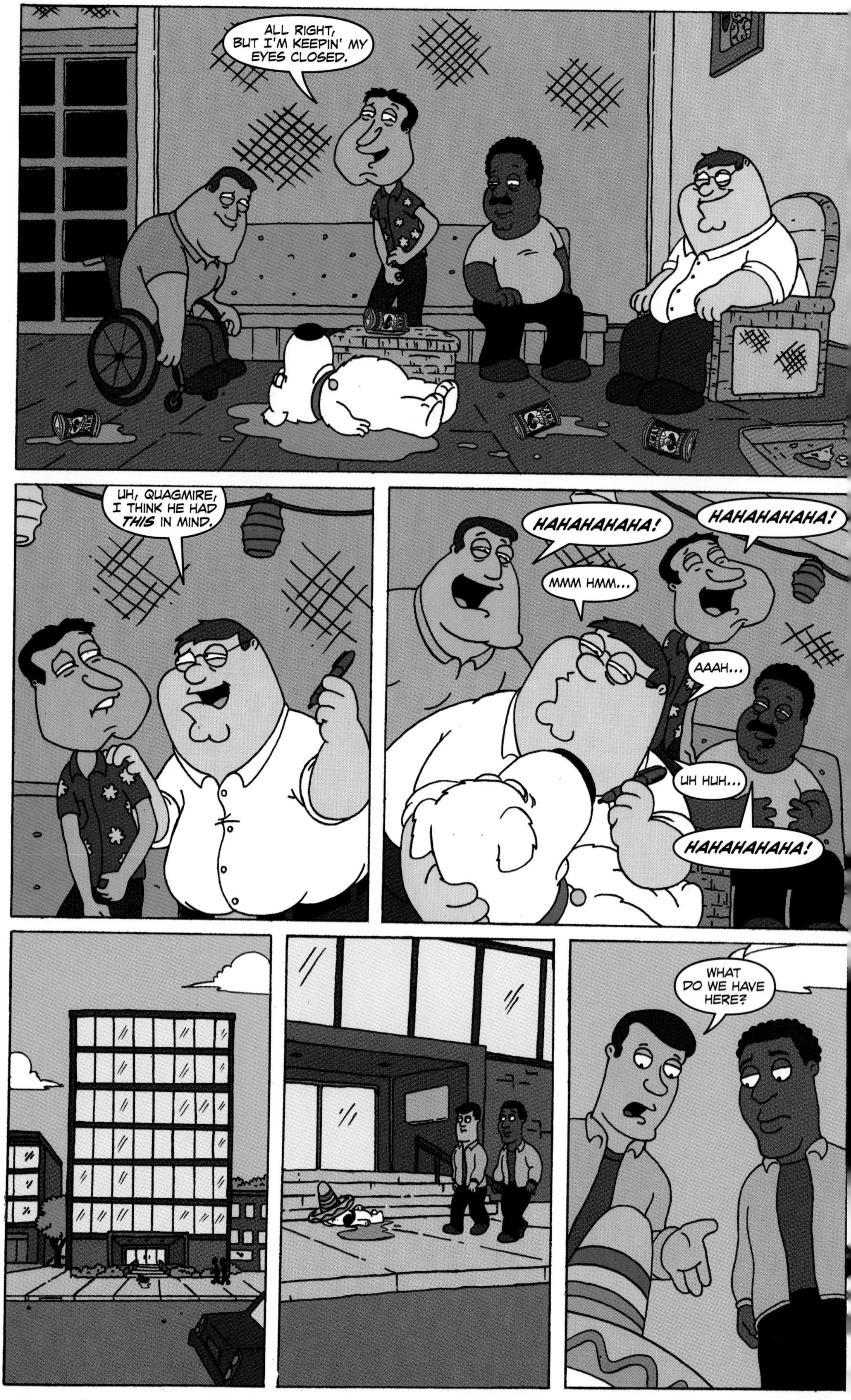
ALL RIGHT, BUT I'M KEEPIN' MY EYES CLOSED.
UH, QUAGMIRE, I THINK HE HAD *THIS* IN MIND.
HAHAHAHAHA!
HAHAHAHAHA!
MMM HMM...
AAAH...
UH HUH...
HAHAHAHAHA!
WHAT DO WE HAVE HERE?

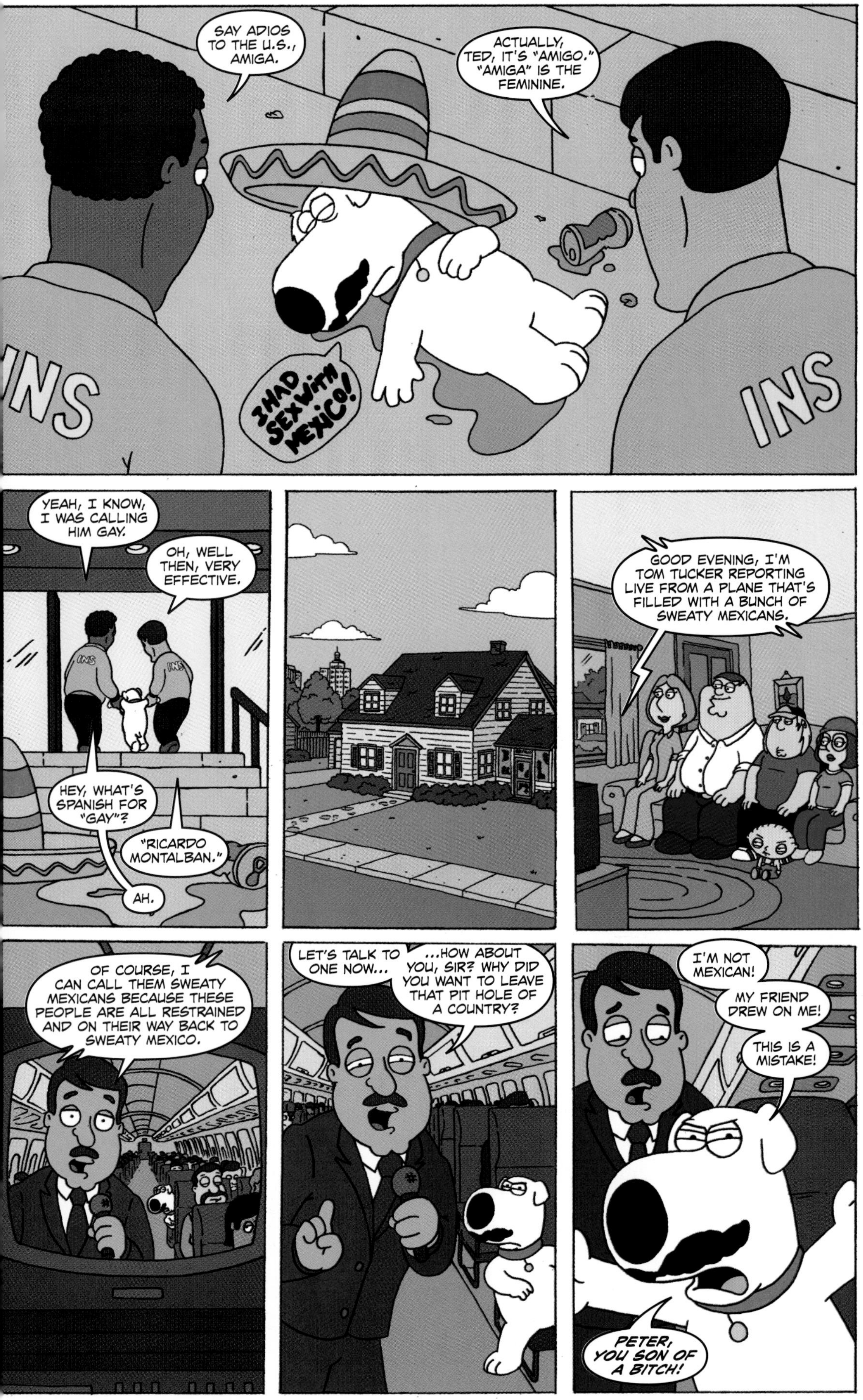
SAY ADIOS TO THE U.S., AMIGA.
ACTUALLY, TED, IT'S "AMIGO." "AMIGA" IS THE FEMININE.
I HAD SEX WITH MEXICO!
INS
INS
YEAH, I KNOW, I WAS CALLING HIM GAY.
OH, WELL THEN, VERY EFFECTIVE.
INS
INS
HEY, WHAT'S SPANISH FOR "GAY"?
"RICARDO MONTALBAN."
AH.
GOOD EVENING, I'M TOM TUCKER REPORTING LIVE FROM A PLANE THAT'S FILLED WITH A BUNCH OF SWEATY MEXICANS.
OF COURSE, I CAN CALL THEM SWEATY MEXICANS BECAUSE THESE PEOPLE ARE ALL RESTRAINED AND ON THEIR WAY BACK TO SWEATY MEXICO.
LET'S TALK TO ONE NOW...
...HOW ABOUT YOU, SIR? WHY DID YOU WANT TO LEAVE THAT PIT HOLE OF A COUNTRY?
I'M NOT MEXICAN!
MY FRIEND DREW ON ME!
THIS IS A MISTAKE!
PETER, YOU SON OF A BITCH!

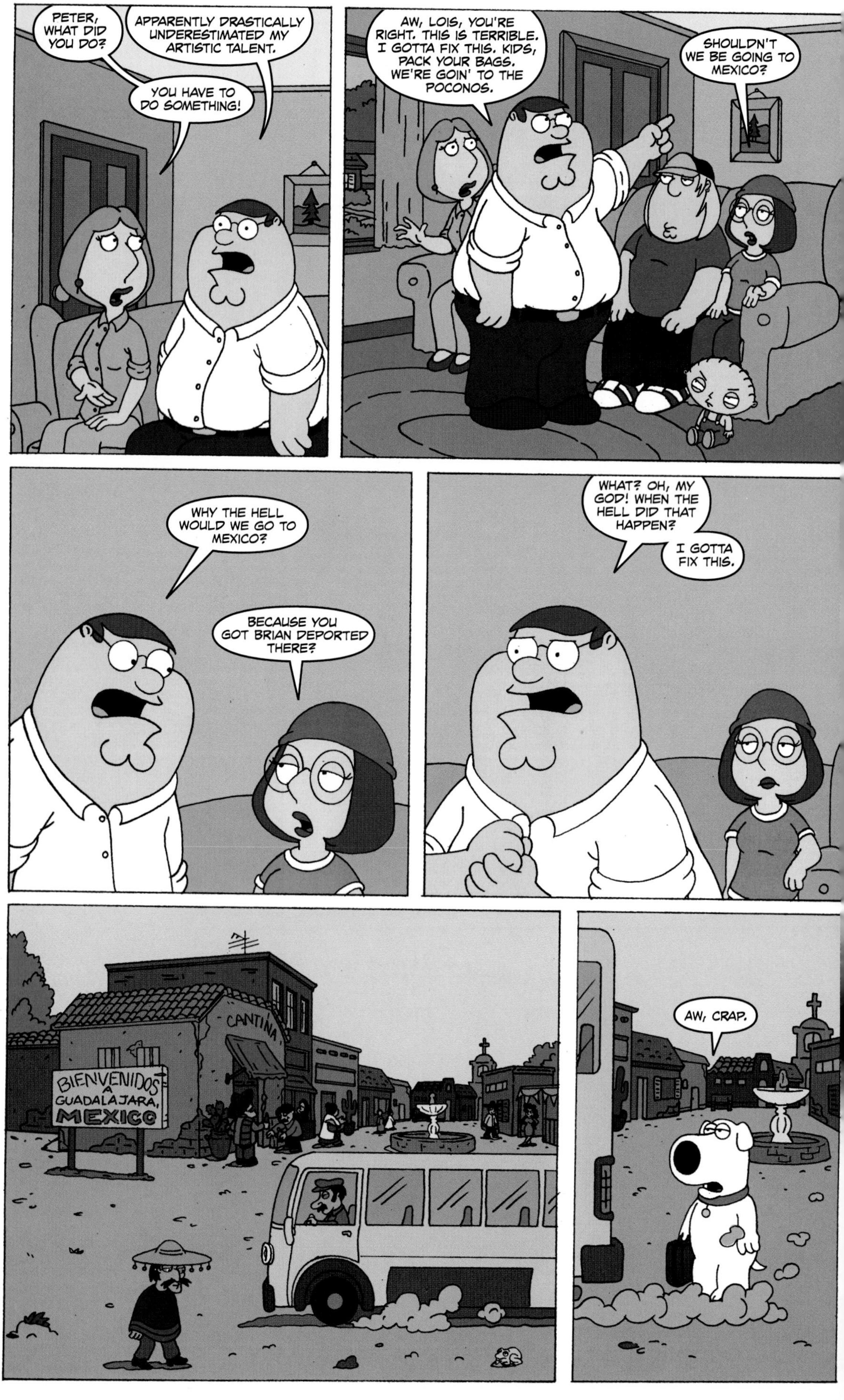
PETER, WHAT DID YOU DO?
APPARENTLY DRASTICALLY UNDERESTIMATED MY ARTISTIC TALENT.
YOU HAVE TO DO SOMETHING!
AW, LOIS, YOU'RE RIGHT. THIS IS TERRIBLE. I GOTTA FIX THIS. KIDS, PACK YOUR BAGS. WE'RE GOIN' TO THE POCONOS.
SHOULDN'T WE BE GOING TO MEXICO?
WHY THE HELL WOULD WE GO TO MEXICO?
BECAUSE YOU GOT BRIAN DEPORTED THERE?
WHAT? OH, MY GOD! WHEN THE HELL DID THAT HAPPEN?
I GOTTA FIX THIS.
CANTINA
BIENVENIDOS A GUADALAJARA, MEXICO
AW, CRAP.

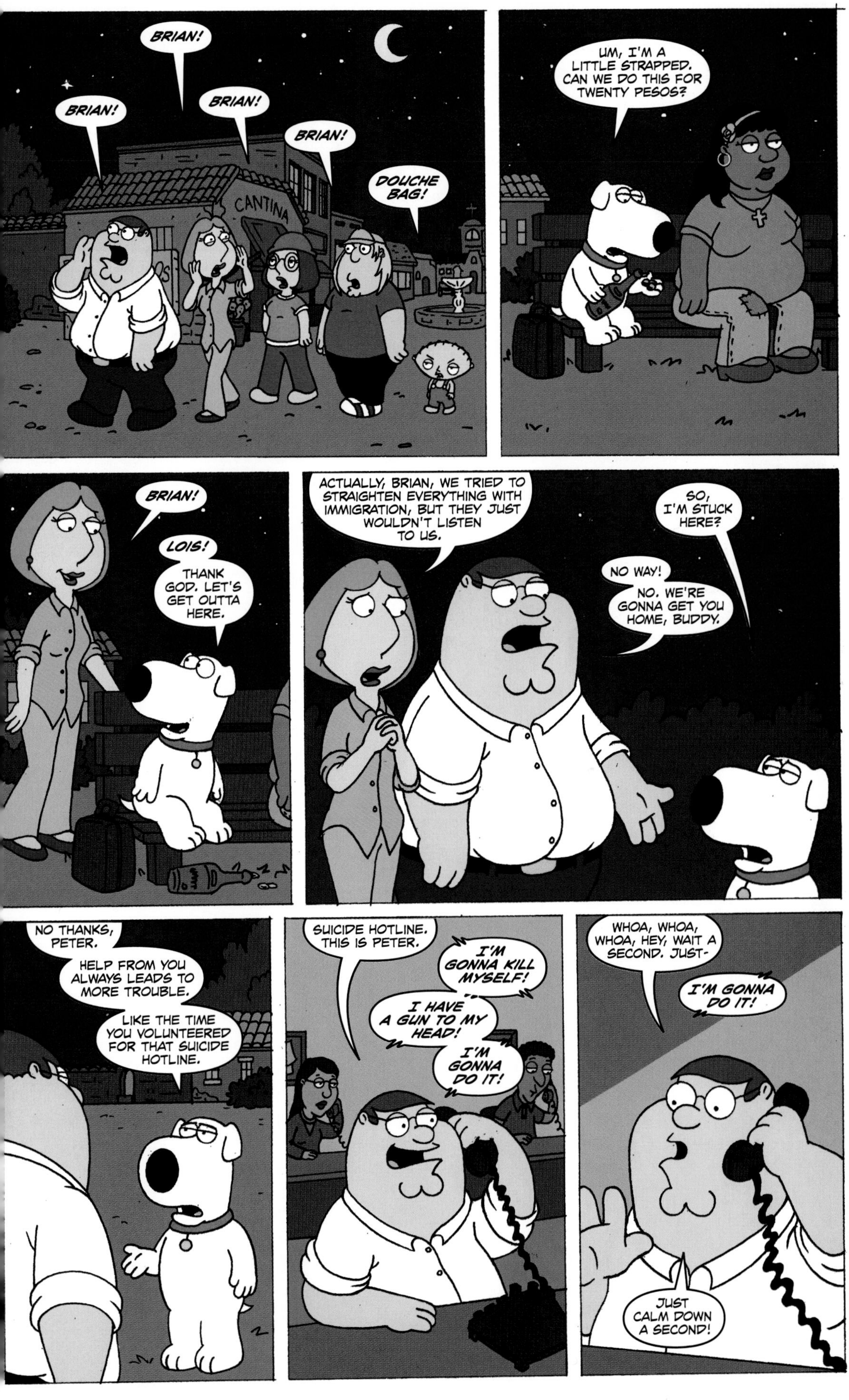
BRIAN!
BRIAN!
BRIAN!
BRIAN!
DOUCHE BAG!
CANTINA
UM, I'M A LITTLE STRAPPED. CAN WE DO THIS FOR TWENTY PESOS?
BRIAN!
LOIS!
THANK GOD. LET'S GET OUTTA HERE.
ACTUALLY, BRIAN, WE TRIED TO STRAIGHTEN EVERYTHING WITH IMMIGRATION, BUT THEY JUST WOULDN'T LISTEN TO US.
SO, I'M STUCK HERE?
NO WAY!
NO. WE'RE GONNA GET YOU HOME, BUDDY.
NO THANKS, PETER.
HELP FROM YOU ALWAYS LEADS TO MORE TROUBLE.
LIKE THE TIME YOU VOLUNTEERED FOR THAT SUICIDE HOTLINE.
SUICIDE HOTLINE. THIS IS PETER.
I'M GONNA KILL MYSELF!
I HAVE A GUN TO MY HEAD!
I'M GONNA DO IT!
WHOA, WHOA, WHOA, HEY, WAIT A SECOND. JUST-
I'M GONNA DO IT!
JUST CALM DOWN A SECOND!

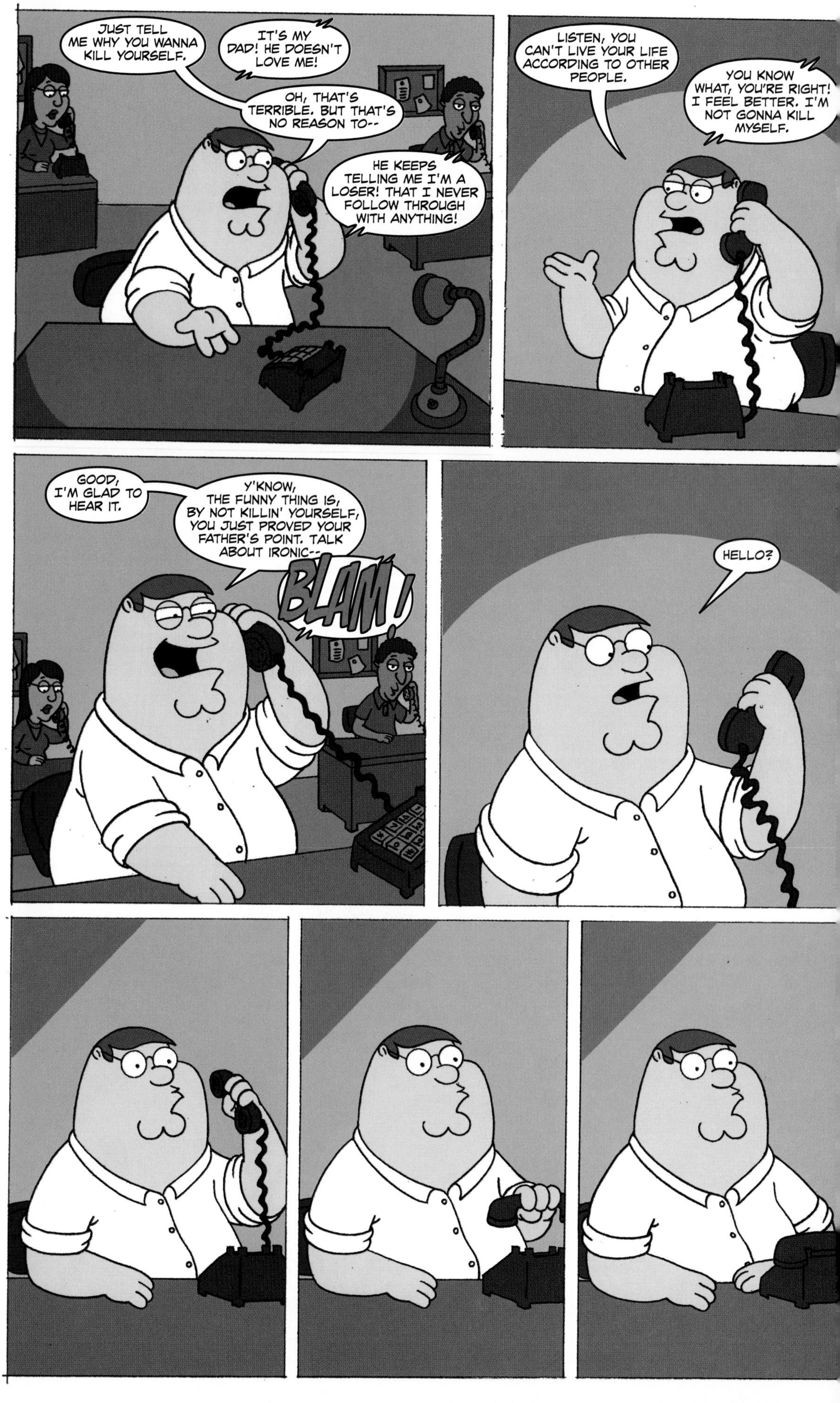
JUST TELL ME WHY YOU WANNA KILL YOURSELF.
IT'S MY DAD! HE DOESN'T LOVE ME!
OH, THAT'S TERRIBLE. BUT THAT'S NO REASON TO--
HE KEEPS TELLING ME I'M A LOSER! THAT I NEVER FOLLOW THROUGH WITH ANYTHING!
LISTEN, YOU CAN'T LIVE YOUR LIFE ACCORDING TO OTHER PEOPLE.
YOU KNOW WHAT, YOU'RE RIGHT! I FEEL BETTER. I'M NOT GONNA KILL MYSELF.
GOOD, I'M GLAD TO HEAR IT.
Y'KNOW, THE FUNNY THING IS, BY NOT KILLIN' YOURSELF, YOU JUST PROVED YOUR FATHER'S POINT. TALK ABOUT IRONIC--
BLAM!
HELLO?

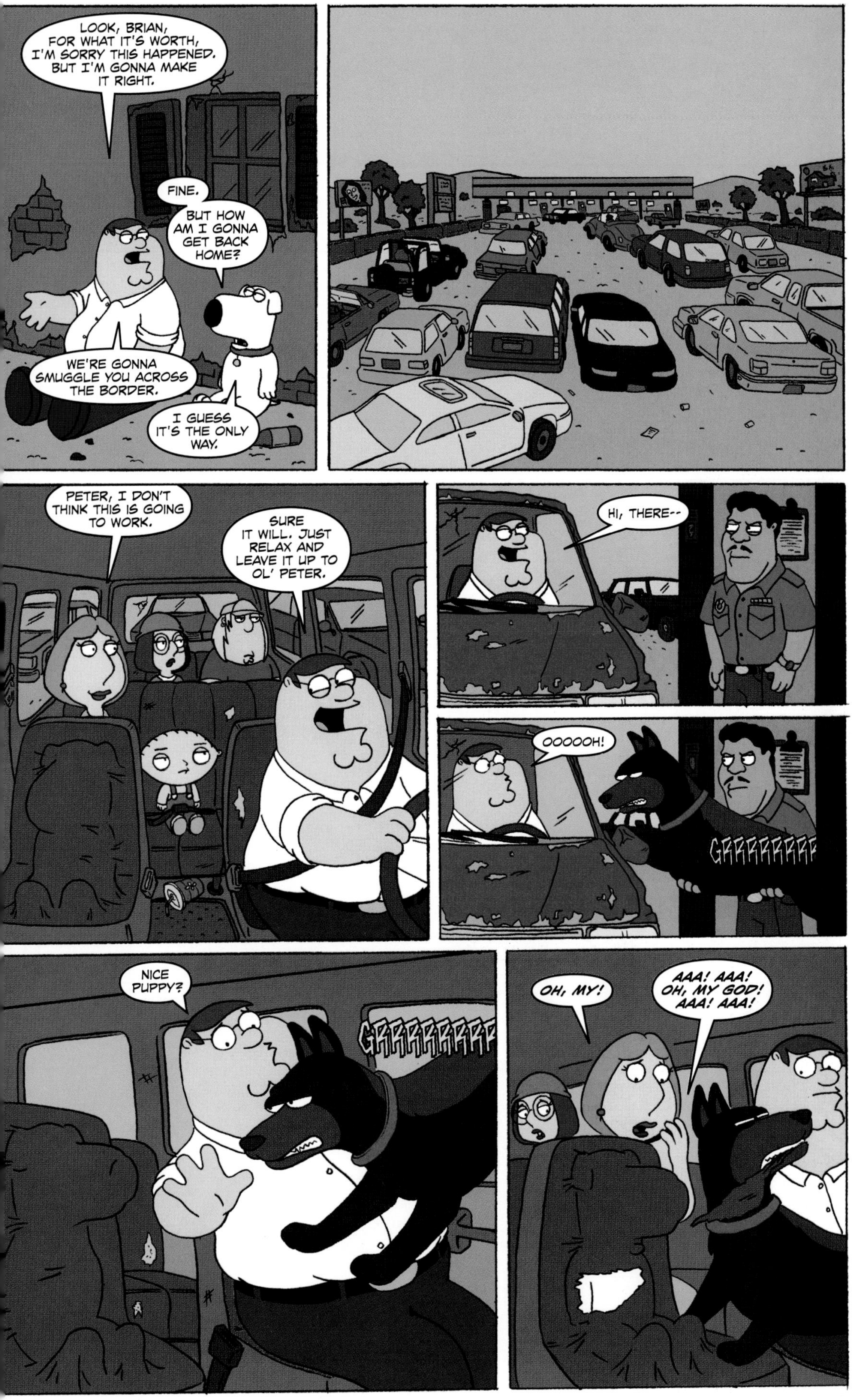
LOOK, BRIAN, FOR WHAT IT'S WORTH, I'M SORRY THIS HAPPENED. BUT I'M GONNA MAKE IT RIGHT.
FINE.
BUT HOW AM I GONNA GET BACK HOME?
WE'RE GONNA SMUGGLE YOU ACROSS THE BORDER.
I GUESS IT'S THE ONLY WAY.
PETER, I DON'T THINK THIS IS GOING TO WORK.
SURE IT WILL. JUST RELAX AND LEAVE IT UP TO OL' PETER.
HI, THERE--
OOOOOH!
GRRRRRRRR
NICE PUPPY?
GRRRRRRRR
OH, MY!
AAA! AAA! OH, MY GOD! AAA! AAA!

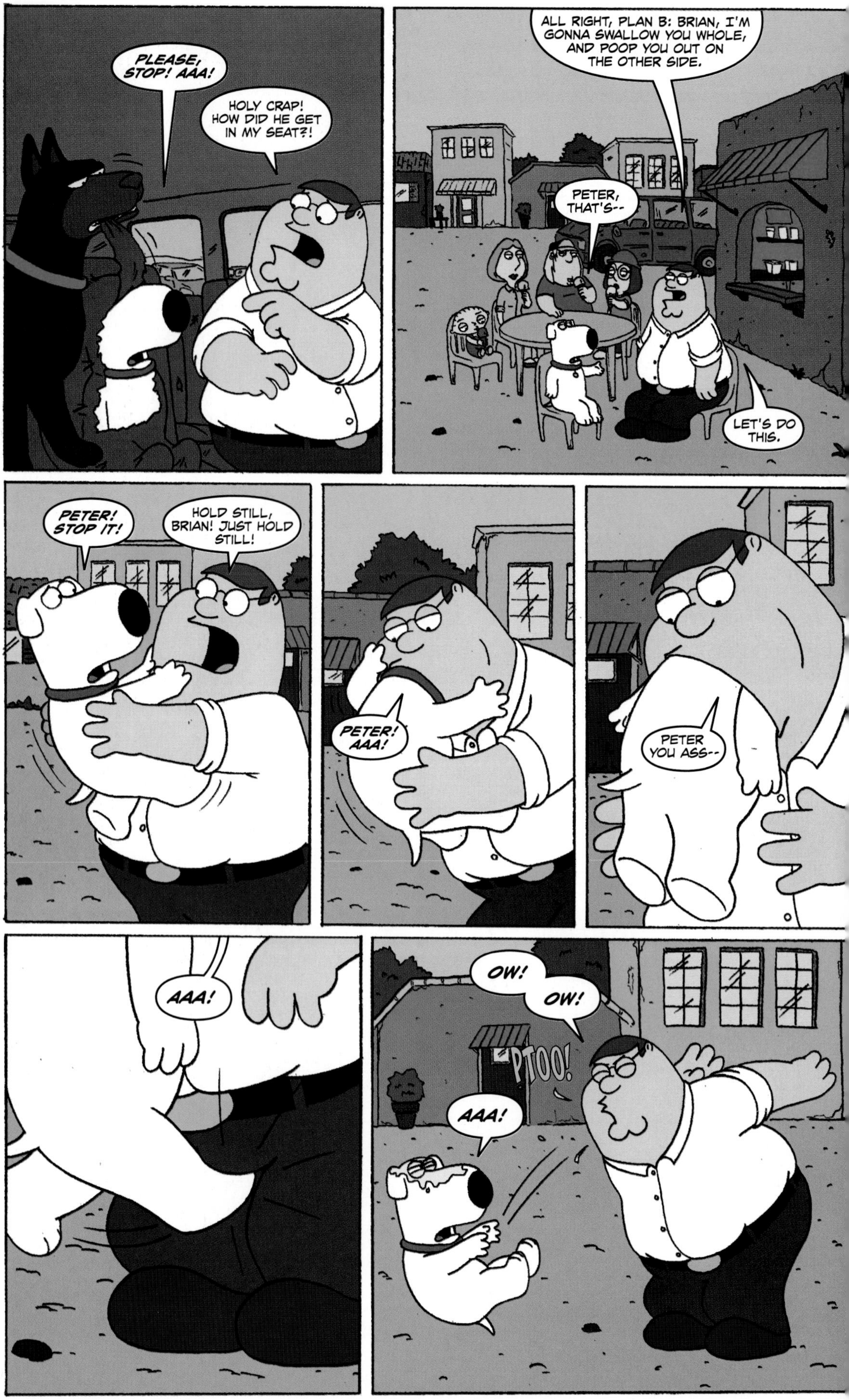
PLEASE, STOP! AAA!
HOLY CRAP! HOW DID HE GET IN MY SEAT?!
ALL RIGHT, PLAN B: BRIAN, I'M GONNA SWALLOW YOU WHOLE, AND POOP YOU OUT ON THE OTHER SIDE.
PETER, THAT'S--
LET'S DO THIS.
PETER! STOP IT!
HOLD STILL, BRIAN! JUST HOLD STILL!
PETER! AAA!
PETER YOU ASS--
AAA!
OW!
OW!
PTOO!
AAA!

Panel 1:
WHAT THE HELL WAS THAT FOR?!

YOU WERE TRYING TO EAT ME!

WELL, YEAH, T-TO SAVE YOU! YOU JERK!

OH, I'M THE JERK?!

Panel 2:
C'MON, CAN'T YOU AT LEAST APPRECIATE WHAT I WAS TRYING TO DO?!

NO, I CAN'T! YOU COULD'VE KILLED ME!

I WAS TRYIN' TO HELP!

Panel 3:
YOU STARTED TO DIGEST ONE OF MY EARS! LOOK AT THIS!

OH, YEAH, THAT'S GROSS. LET'S FIND ANOTHER WAY.

YOU THINK?!

Panel 4:
HEY THERE, FELLOW PATRIOTS.

WHO THE HELL ARE YOU?

Panel 5:
PETER GRIFFIN. I'M A MINUTEMAN FROM THE QUAHOG CHAPTER.

OH, WELL, THEN I RETRACT MY PREVIOUS OVERLY-ANGRY GREETING.

Panel 6:
I KNOW HOW HARD IT IS OUT HERE, DEFENDING AMERICA IN YOUR TANK-TOP TEE SHIRTS AND RED BANDANAS.

WHO WANTS BEER?

HELL, YEAH!

WOO!

AMERICA ROCKS!

Panel 7:
LATER...

HURRY UP! THE COAST IS CLEAR!

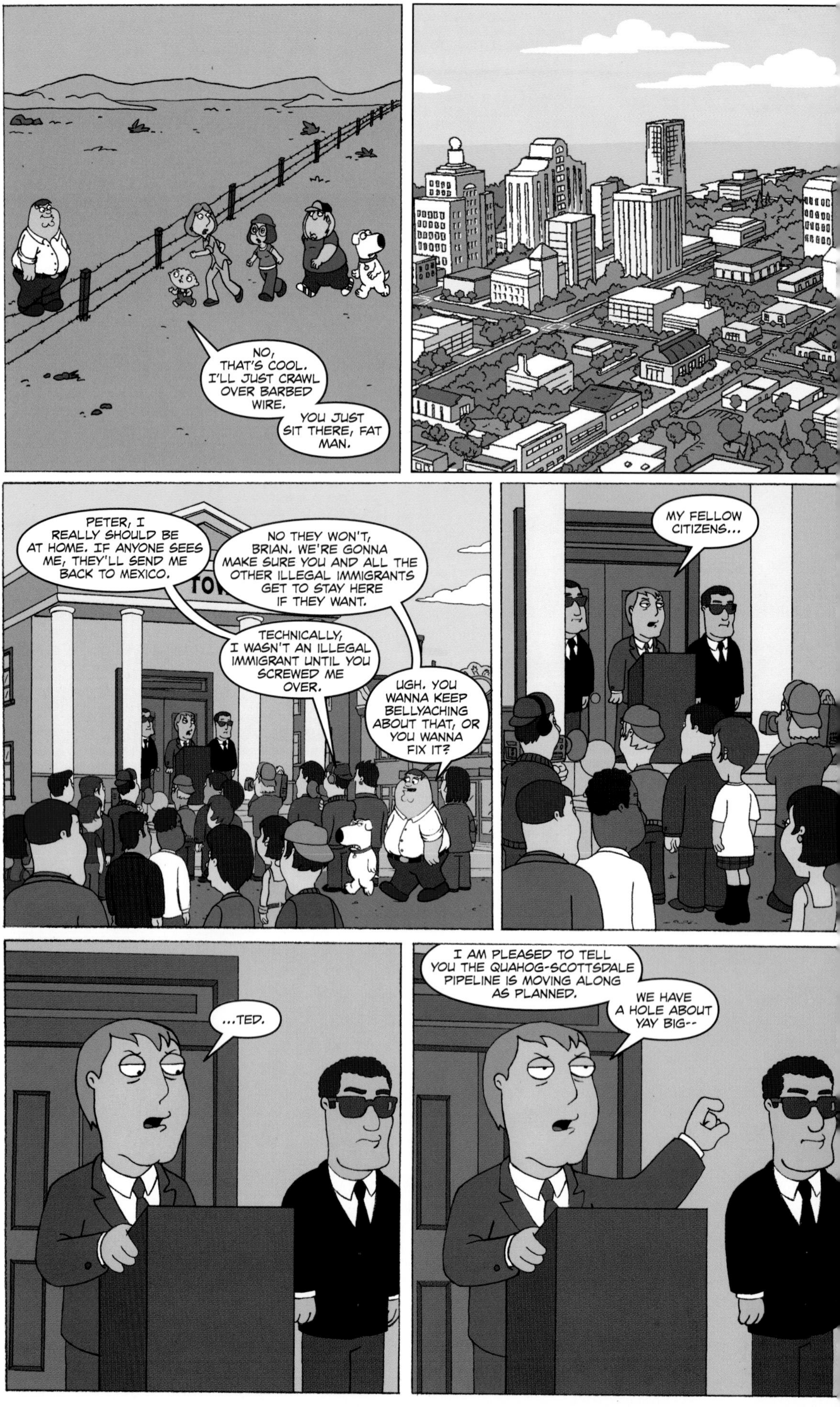
NO, THAT'S COOL. I'LL JUST CRAWL OVER BARBED WIRE.
YOU JUST SIT THERE, FAT MAN.
PETER, I REALLY SHOULD BE AT HOME. IF ANYONE SEES ME, THEY'LL SEND ME BACK TO MEXICO.
NO THEY WON'T, BRIAN. WE'RE GONNA MAKE SURE YOU AND ALL THE OTHER ILLEGAL IMMIGRANTS GET TO STAY HERE IF THEY WANT.
TECHNICALLY, I WASN'T AN ILLEGAL IMMIGRANT UNTIL YOU SCREWED ME OVER.
UGH. YOU WANNA KEEP BELLYACHING ABOUT THAT, OR YOU WANNA FIX IT?
MY FELLOW CITIZENS...
...TED.
I AM PLEASED TO TELL YOU THE QUAHOG-SCOTTSDALE PIPELINE IS MOVING ALONG AS PLANNED.
WE HAVE A HOLE ABOUT YAY BIG--

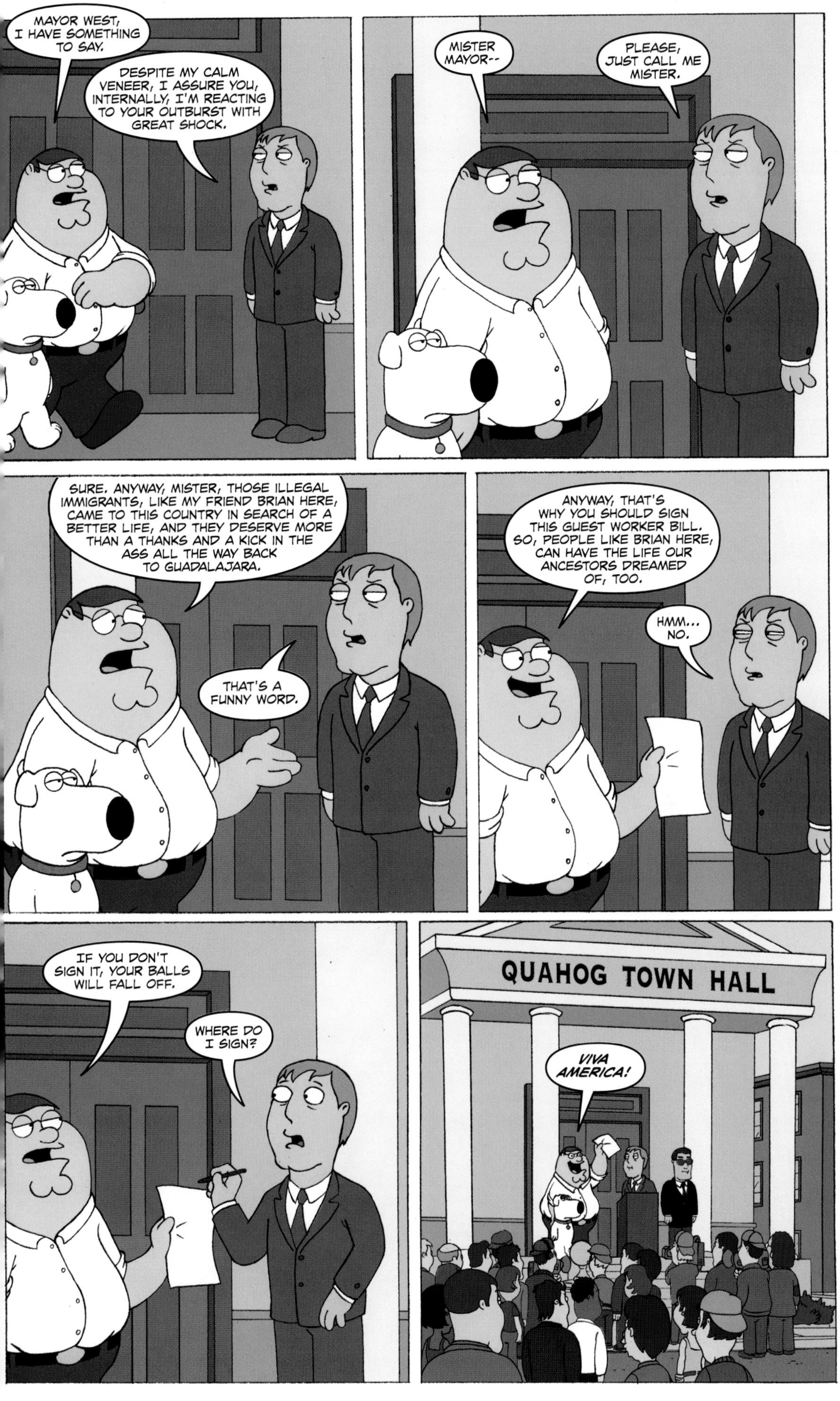

MAYOR WEST, I HAVE SOMETHING TO SAY.
DESPITE MY CALM VENEER, I ASSURE YOU, INTERNALLY, I'M REACTING TO YOUR OUTBURST WITH GREAT SHOCK.
MISTER MAYOR--
PLEASE, JUST CALL ME MISTER.
SURE. ANYWAY, MISTER, THOSE ILLEGAL IMMIGRANTS, LIKE MY FRIEND BRIAN HERE, CAME TO THIS COUNTRY IN SEARCH OF A BETTER LIFE, AND THEY DESERVE MORE THAN A THANKS AND A KICK IN THE ASS ALL THE WAY BACK TO GUADALAJARA.
THAT'S A FUNNY WORD.
ANYWAY, THAT'S WHY YOU SHOULD SIGN THIS GUEST WORKER BILL. SO, PEOPLE LIKE BRIAN HERE, CAN HAVE THE LIFE OUR ANCESTORS DREAMED OF, TOO.
HMM... NO.
IF YOU DON'T SIGN IT, YOUR BALLS WILL FALL OFF.
WHERE DO I SIGN?
QUAHOG TOWN HALL
VIVA AMERICA!

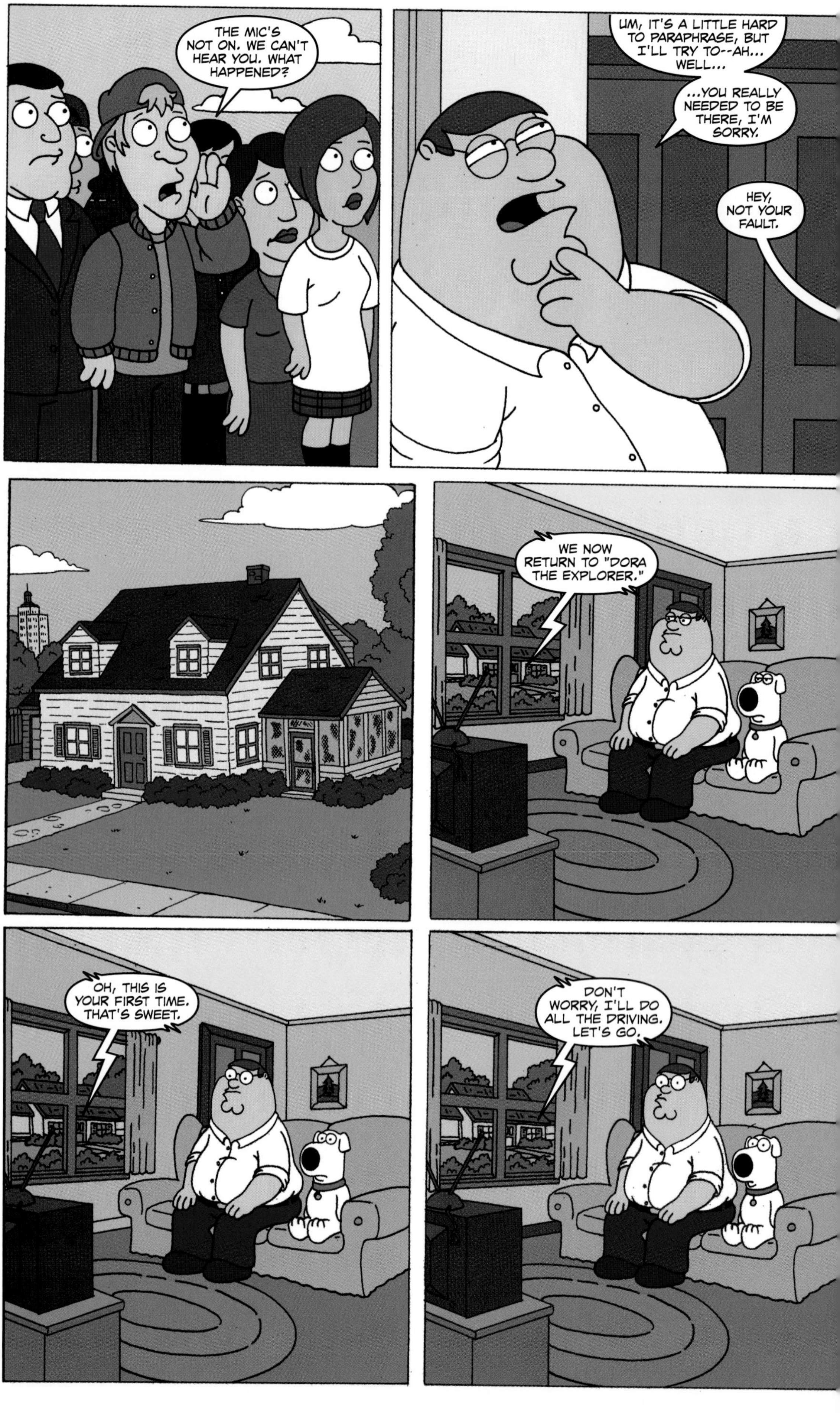
THE MIC'S NOT ON. WE CAN'T HEAR YOU. WHAT HAPPENED?
UM, IT'S A LITTLE HARD TO PARAPHRASE, BUT I'LL TRY TO--AH... WELL...
...YOU REALLY NEEDED TO BE THERE, I'M SORRY.
HEY, NOT YOUR FAULT.
WE NOW RETURN TO "DORA THE EXPLORER."
OH, THIS IS YOUR FIRST TIME. THAT'S SWEET.
DON'T WORRY, I'LL DO ALL THE DRIVING. LET'S GO.

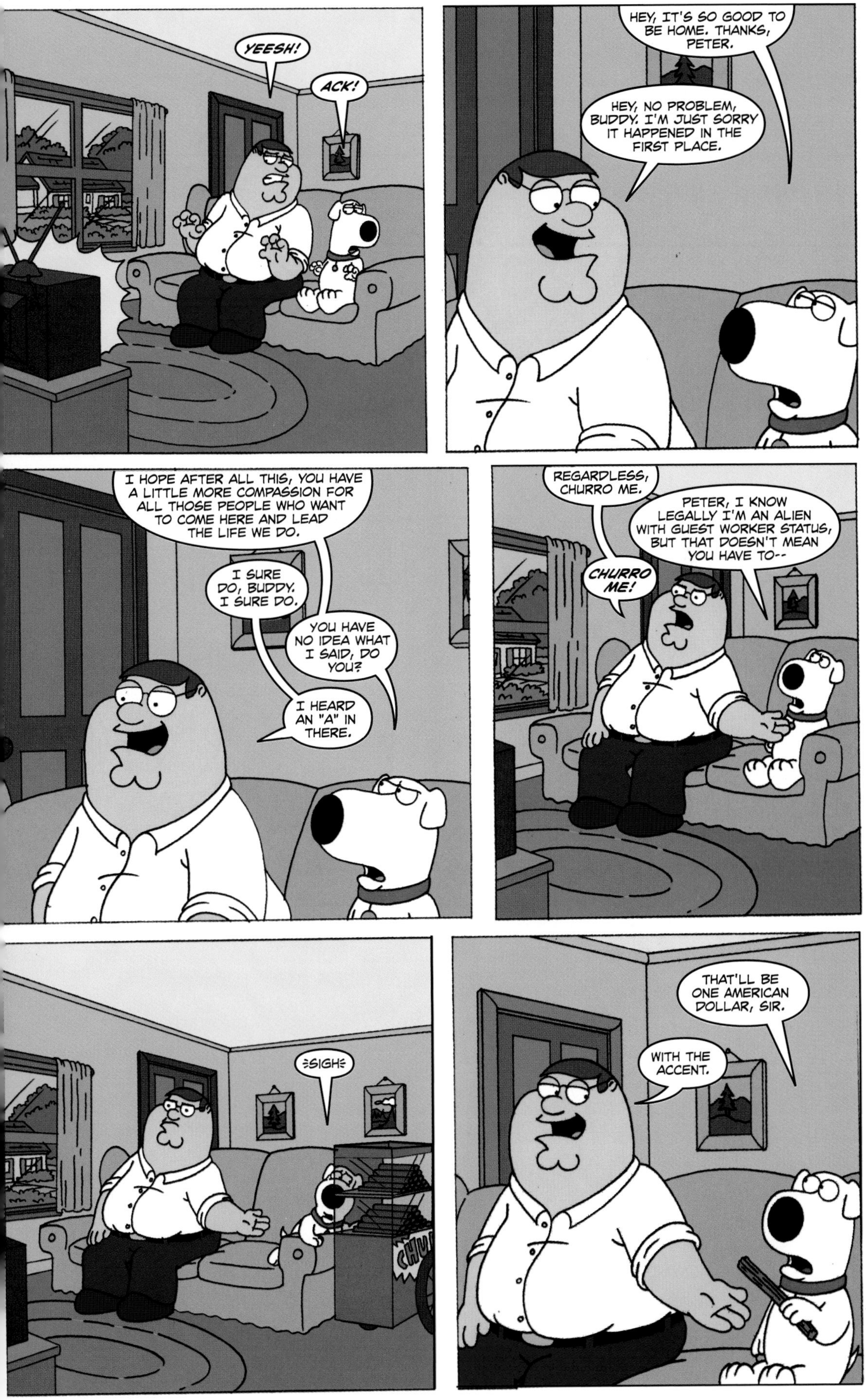
YEESH!
ACK!
HEY, IT'S SO GOOD TO BE HOME. THANKS, PETER.
HEY, NO PROBLEM, BUDDY. I'M JUST SORRY IT HAPPENED IN THE FIRST PLACE.
I HOPE AFTER ALL THIS, YOU HAVE A LITTLE MORE COMPASSION FOR ALL THOSE PEOPLE WHO WANT TO COME HERE AND LEAD THE LIFE WE DO.
I SURE DO, BUDDY. I SURE DO.
YOU HAVE NO IDEA WHAT I SAID, DO YOU?
I HEARD AN "A" IN THERE.
REGARDLESS, CHURRO ME.
PETER, I KNOW LEGALLY I'M AN ALIEN WITH GUEST WORKER STATUS, BUT THAT DOESN'T MEAN YOU HAVE TO--
CHURRO ME!
SIGH
THAT'LL BE ONE AMERICAN DOLLAR, SIR.
WITH THE ACCENT.

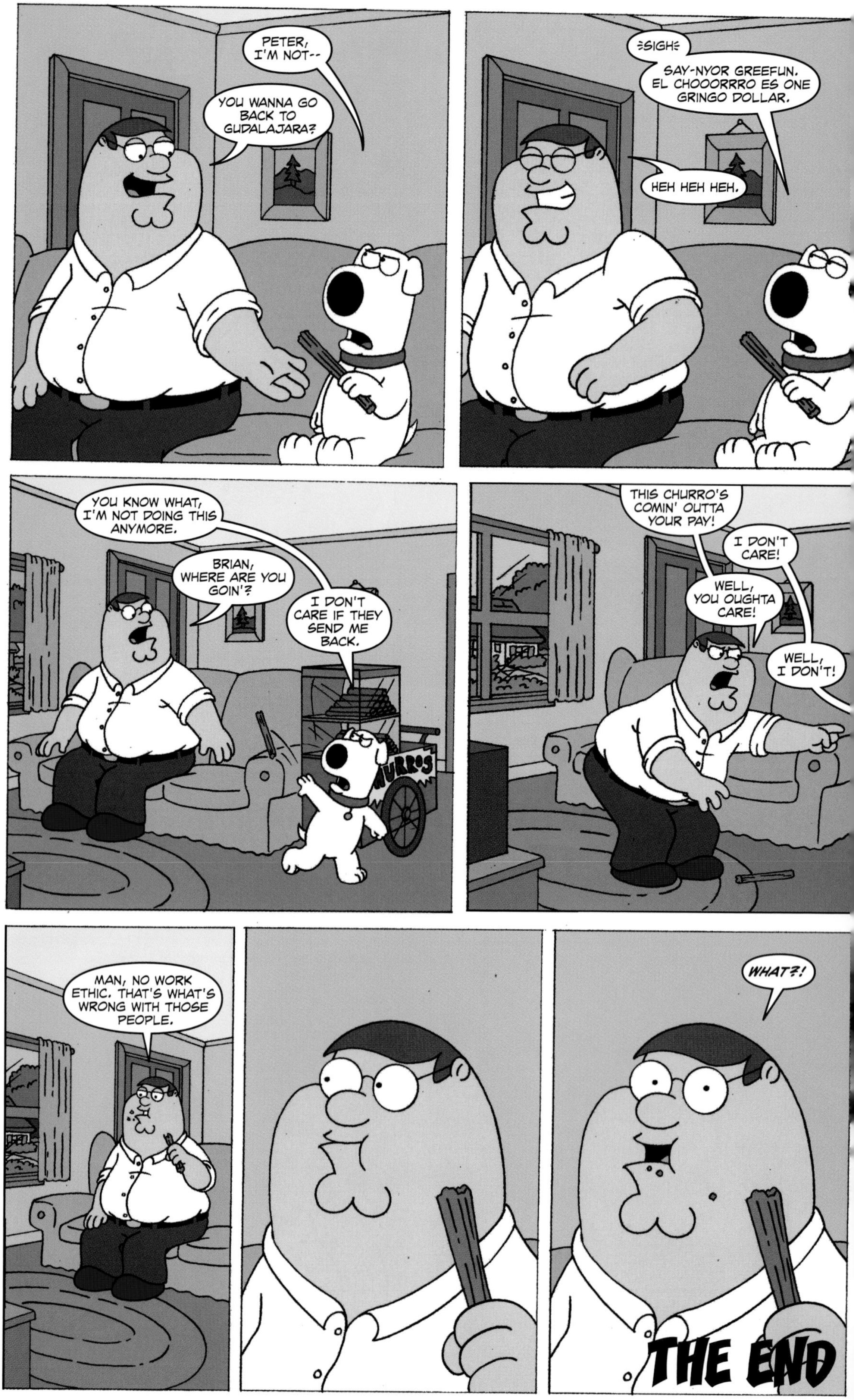
PETER, I'M NOT--
YOU WANNA GO BACK TO GUDALAJARA?
SIGH
SAY-NYOR GREEFUN. EL CHOOORRRO ES ONE GRINGO DOLLAR.
HEH HEH HEH.
YOU KNOW WHAT, I'M NOT DOING THIS ANYMORE.
BRIAN, WHERE ARE YOU GOIN'?
I DON'T CARE IF THEY SEND ME BACK.
CHURROS
THIS CHURRO'S COMIN' OUTTA YOUR PAY!
I DON'T CARE!
WELL, YOU OUGHTA CARE!
WELL, I DON'T!
MAN, NO WORK ETHIC. THAT'S WHAT'S WRONG WITH THOSE PEOPLE.
WHAT?!
THE END

AND NOW, BACK TO "FAMILY COMES FIRST... RIGHT AFTER T.V.!"

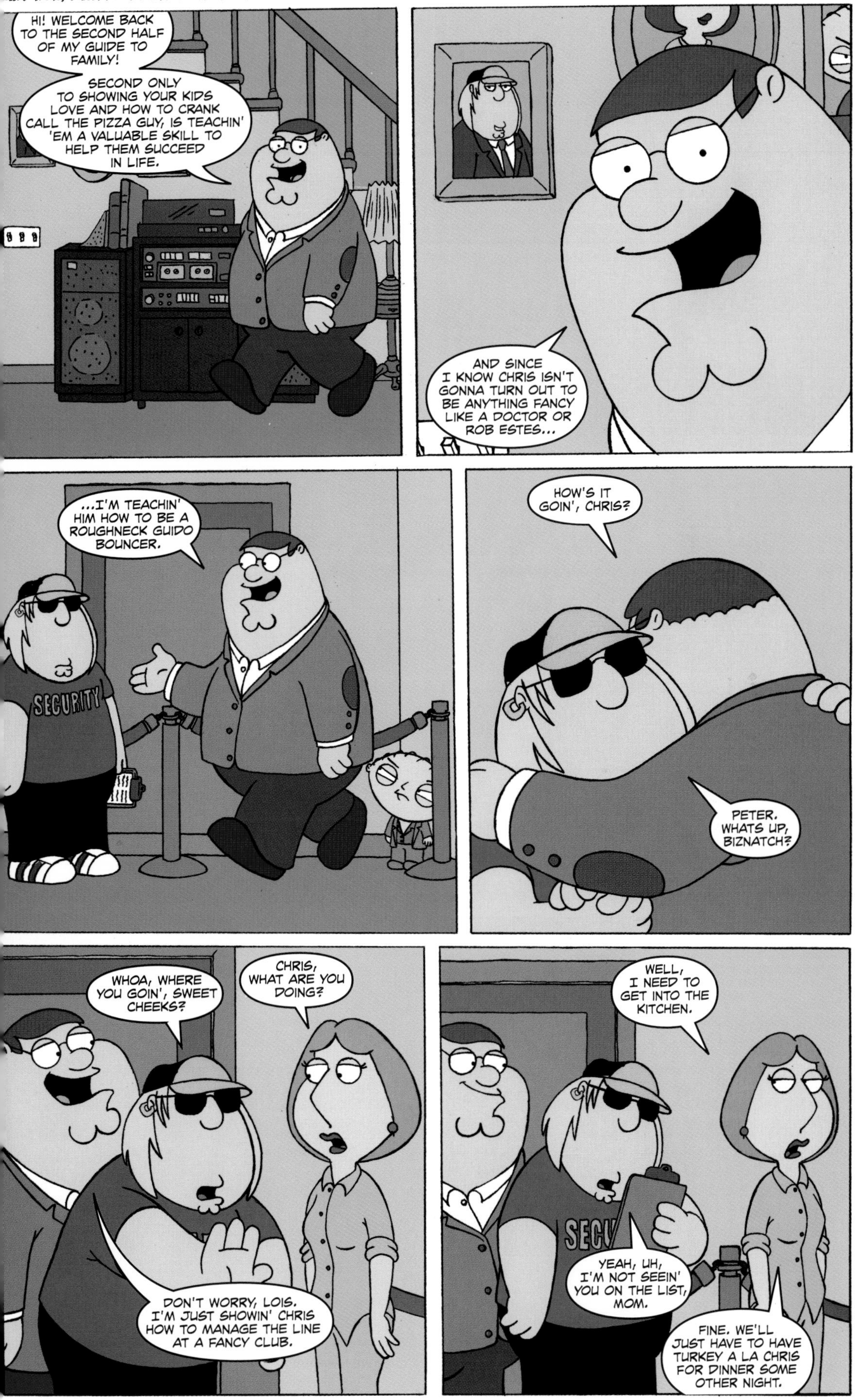
HI! WELCOME BACK TO THE SECOND HALF OF MY GUIDE TO FAMILY!
SECOND ONLY TO SHOWING YOUR KIDS LOVE AND HOW TO CRANK CALL THE PIZZA GUY, IS TEACHIN' 'EM A VALUABLE SKILL TO HELP THEM SUCCEED IN LIFE.
AND SINCE I KNOW CHRIS ISN'T GONNA TURN OUT TO BE ANYTHING FANCY LIKE A DOCTOR OR ROB ESTES...
...I'M TEACHIN' HIM HOW TO BE A ROUGHNECK GUIDO BOUNCER.
SECURITY
HOW'S IT GOIN', CHRIS?
PETER. WHATS UP, BIZNATCH?
WHOA, WHERE YOU GOIN', SWEET CHEEKS?
CHRIS, WHAT ARE YOU DOING?
DON'T WORRY, LOIS. I'M JUST SHOWIN' CHRIS HOW TO MANAGE THE LINE AT A FANCY CLUB.
WELL, I NEED TO GET INTO THE KITCHEN.
YEAH, UH, I'M NOT SEEIN' YOU ON THE LIST, MOM.
FINE. WE'LL JUST HAVE TO HAVE TURKEY A LA CHRIS FOR DINNER SOME OTHER NIGHT.

ALL RIGHT. HEAD ON IN.

I'LL DEAL WITH YOU LATER, PETER.

SHE GETS IN?!

OH, COME ON! WHO'S SHE SLEEPING WITH?!

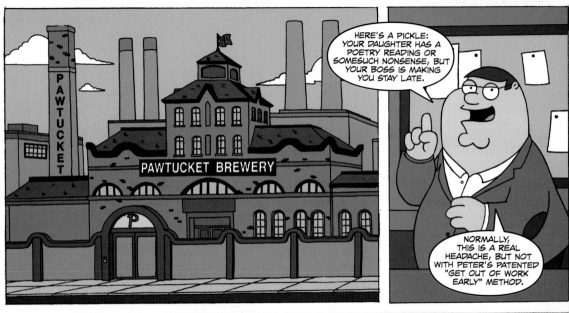

HERE'S A PICKLE: YOUR DAUGHTER HAS A POETRY READING OR SOMESUCH NONSENSE, BUT YOUR BOSS IS MAKING YOU STAY LATE.

PAWTUCKET BREWERY

NORMALLY, THIS IS A REAL HEADACHE, BUT NOT WITH PETER'S PATENTED "GET OUT OF WORK EARLY" METHOD.

JUST FIND A FAT MEXICAN GUY WHO LOOKS LIKE YOU. THIS WAY, YOU GET TO SNEAK OUT, AND YOUR BOSS THINKS YOU'RE STILL BURNING THE MIDNIGHT OIL.

ALL RIGHT, GRIFFIN, NOW HERE ARE THE ORDERS FOR--

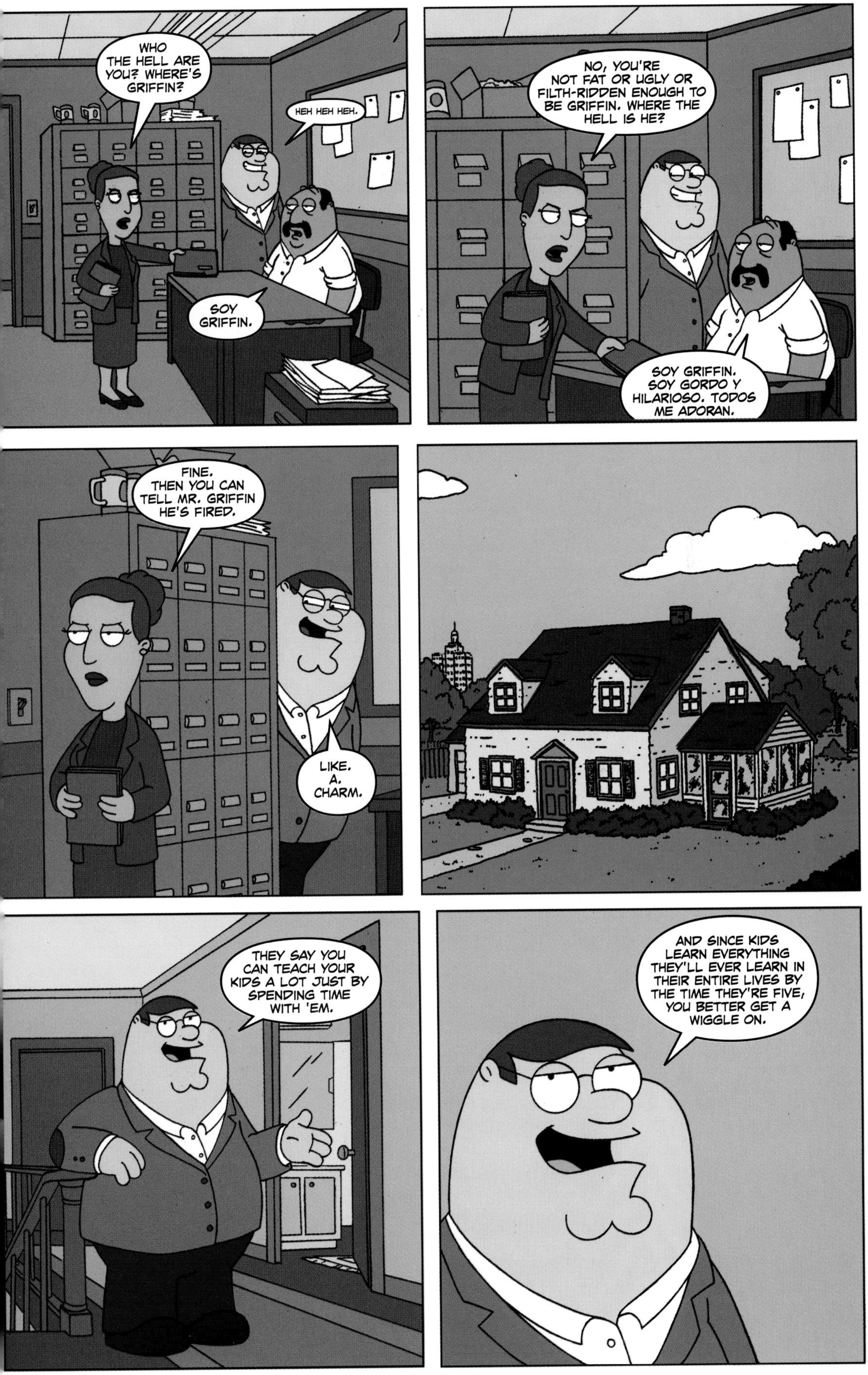
WHO THE HELL ARE YOU? WHERE'S GRIFFIN?
HEH HEH HEH.
SOY GRIFFIN.
NO, YOU'RE NOT FAT OR UGLY OR FILTH-RIDDEN ENOUGH TO BE GRIFFIN. WHERE THE HELL IS HE?
SOY GRIFFIN. SOY GORDO Y HILARIOSO. TODOS ME ADORAN.
FINE. THEN YOU CAN TELL MR. GRIFFIN HE'S FIRED.
LIKE. A. CHARM.
THEY SAY YOU CAN TEACH YOUR KIDS A LOT JUST BY SPENDING TIME WITH 'EM.
AND SINCE KIDS LEARN EVERYTHING THEY'LL EVER LEARN IN THEIR ENTIRE LIVES BY THE TIME THEY'RE FIVE, YOU BETTER GET A WIGGLE ON.

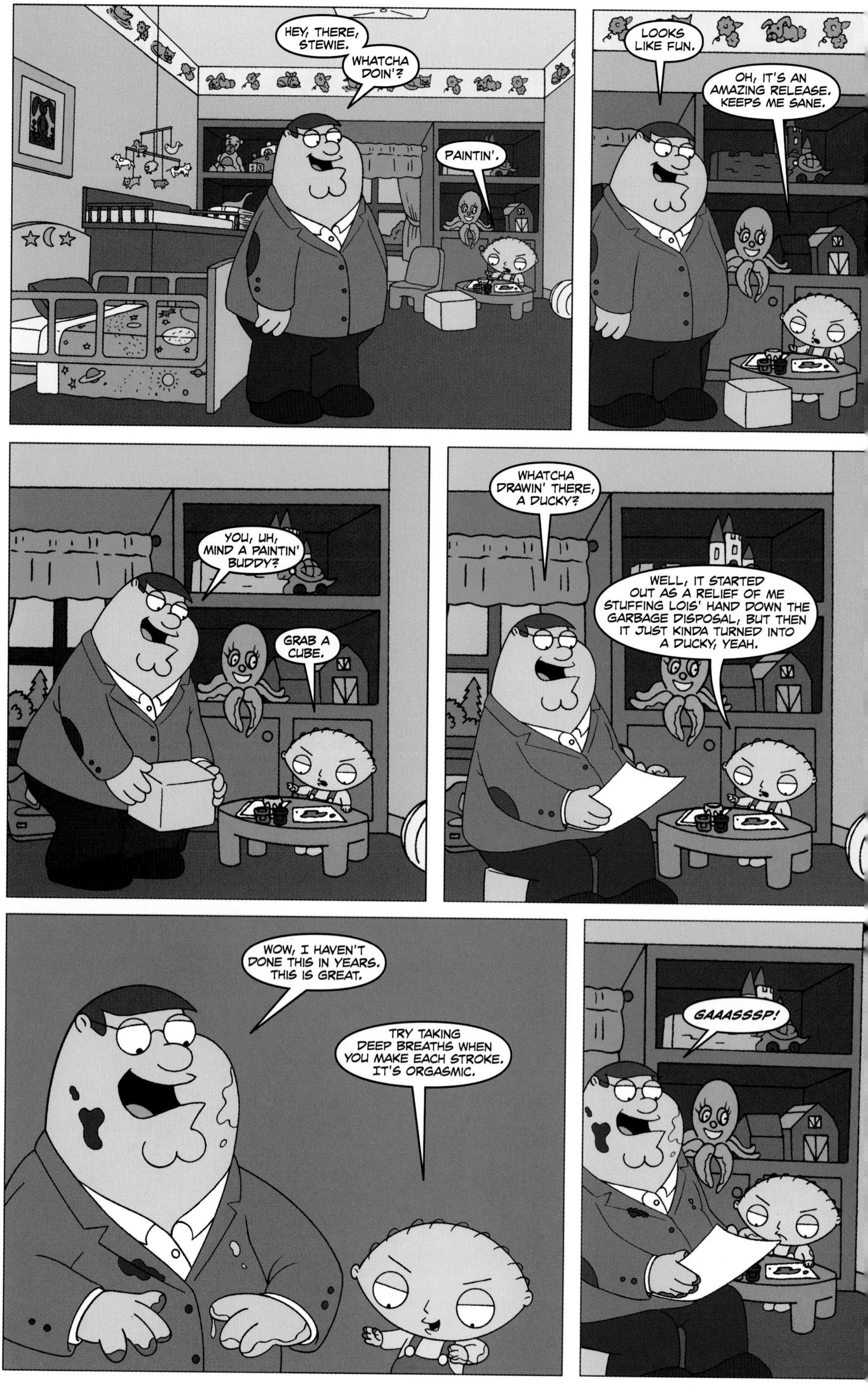
HEY, THERE, STEWIE.
WHATCHA DOIN'?
PAINTIN'.
LOOKS LIKE FUN.
OH, IT'S AN AMAZING RELEASE. KEEPS ME SANE.
YOU, UH, MIND A PAINTIN' BUDDY?
GRAB A CUBE.
WHATCHA DRAWIN' THERE, A DUCKY?
WELL, IT STARTED OUT AS A RELIEF OF ME STUFFING LOIS' HAND DOWN THE GARBAGE DISPOSAL, BUT THEN IT JUST KINDA TURNED INTO A DUCKY, YEAH.
WOW, I HAVEN'T DONE THIS IN YEARS. THIS IS GREAT.
TRY TAKING DEEP BREATHS WHEN YOU MAKE EACH STROKE. IT'S ORGASMIC.
GAAASSSP!

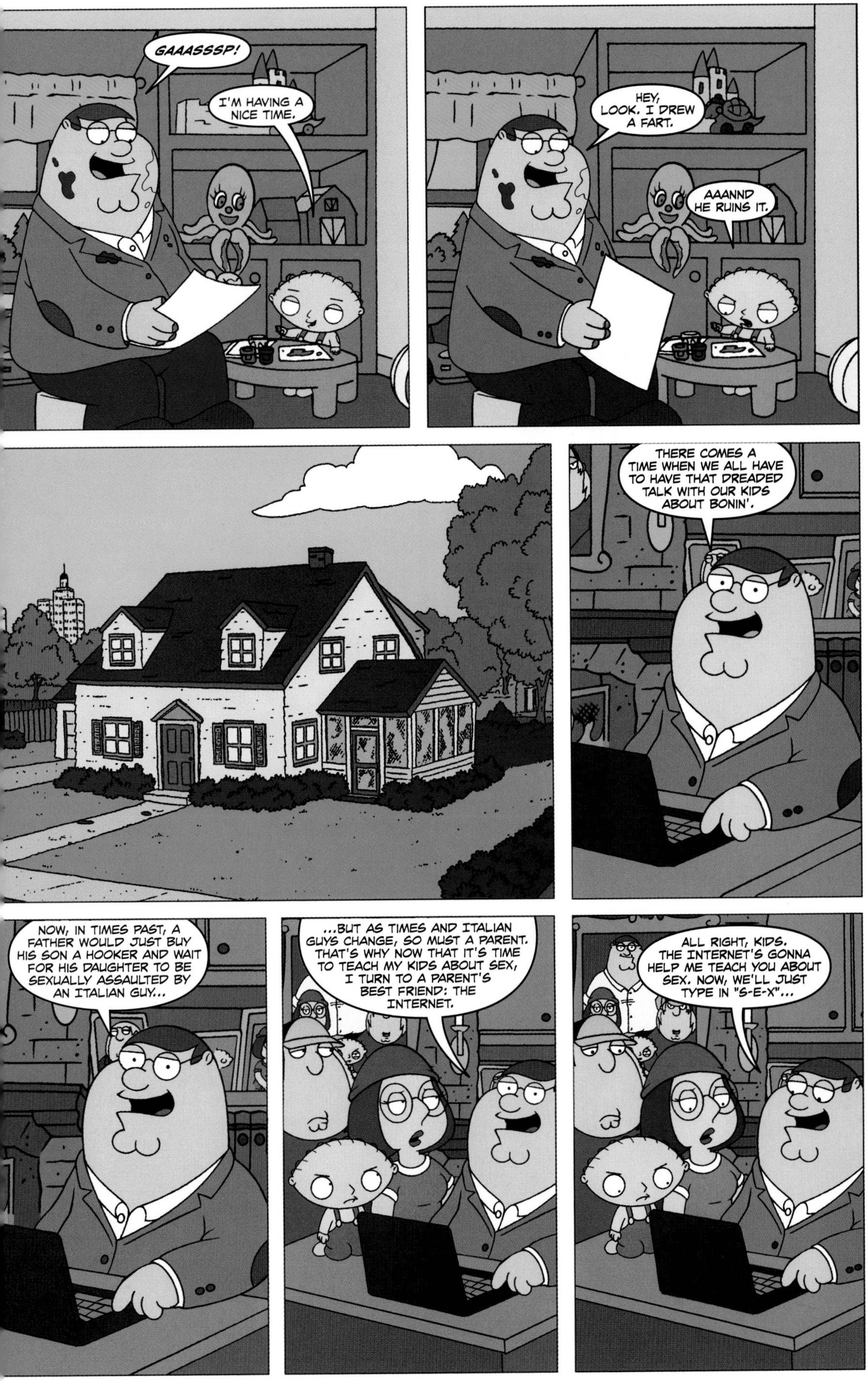
GAAASSSP!
I'M HAVING A NICE TIME.
HEY, LOOK. I DREW A FART.
AAANND HE RUINS IT.
THERE COMES A TIME WHEN WE ALL HAVE TO HAVE THAT DREADED TALK WITH OUR KIDS ABOUT BONIN'.
NOW, IN TIMES PAST, A FATHER WOULD JUST BUY HIS SON A HOOKER AND WAIT FOR HIS DAUGHTER TO BE SEXUALLY ASSAULTED BY AN ITALIAN GUY...
...BUT AS TIMES AND ITALIAN GUYS CHANGE, SO MUST A PARENT. THAT'S WHY NOW THAT IT'S TIME TO TEACH MY KIDS ABOUT SEX, I TURN TO A PARENT'S BEST FRIEND: THE INTERNET.
ALL RIGHT, KIDS. THE INTERNET'S GONNA HELP ME TEACH YOU ABOUT SEX. NOW, WE'LL JUST TYPE IN "S-E-X"...

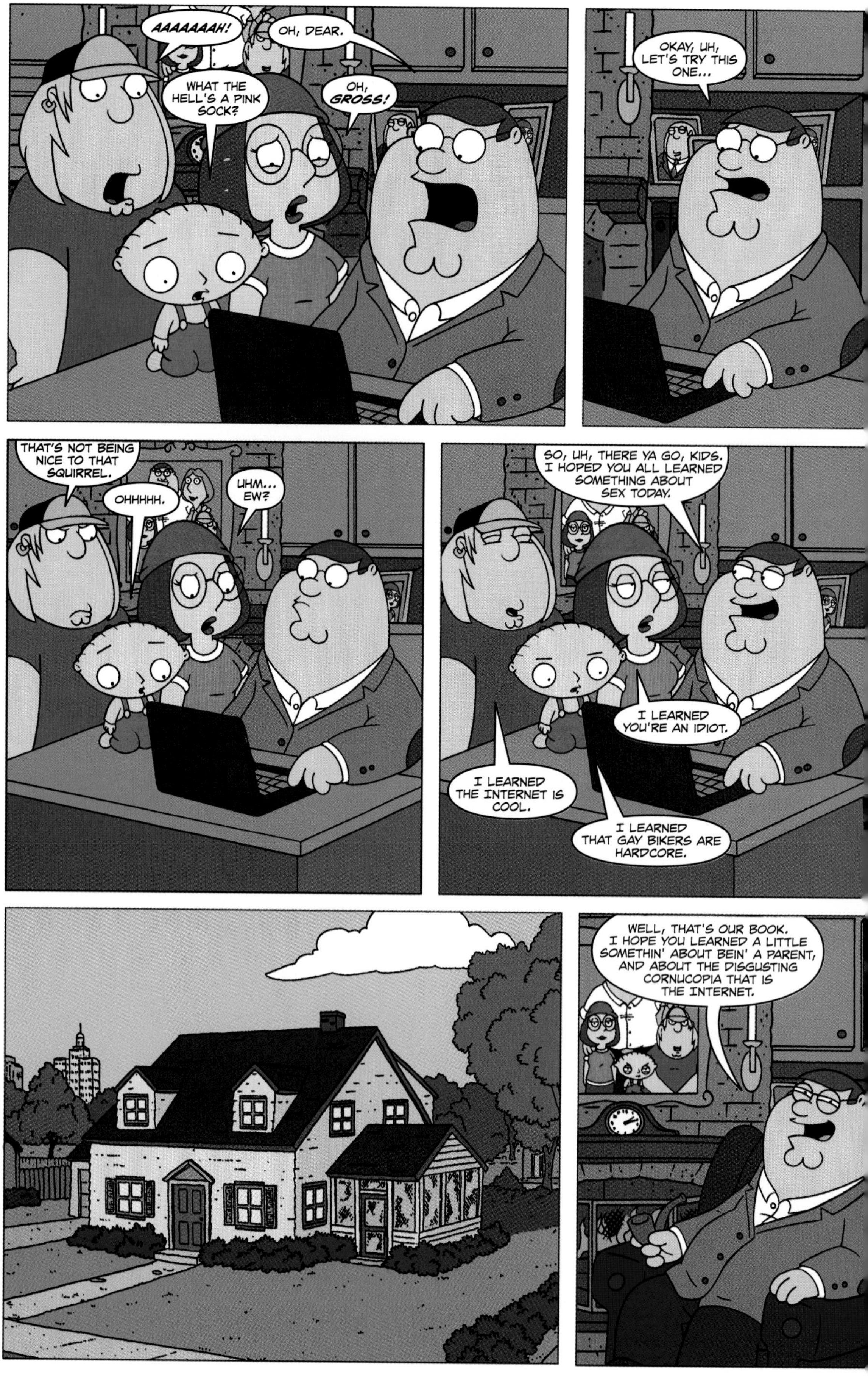
AAAAAAAH!
OH, DEAR.
WHAT THE HELL'S A PINK SOCK?
OH, GROSS!
OKAY, UH, LET'S TRY THIS ONE...
THAT'S NOT BEING NICE TO THAT SQUIRREL.
OHHHHHH.
UHM... EW?
SO, UH, THERE YA GO, KIDS. I HOPED YOU ALL LEARNED SOMETHING ABOUT SEX TODAY.
I LEARNED YOU'RE AN IDIOT.
I LEARNED THE INTERNET IS COOL.
I LEARNED THAT GAY BIKERS ARE HARDCORE.
WELL, THAT'S OUR BOOK. I HOPE YOU LEARNED A LITTLE SOMETHIN' ABOUT BEIN' A PARENT, AND ABOUT THE DISGUSTING CORNUCOPIA THAT IS THE INTERNET.

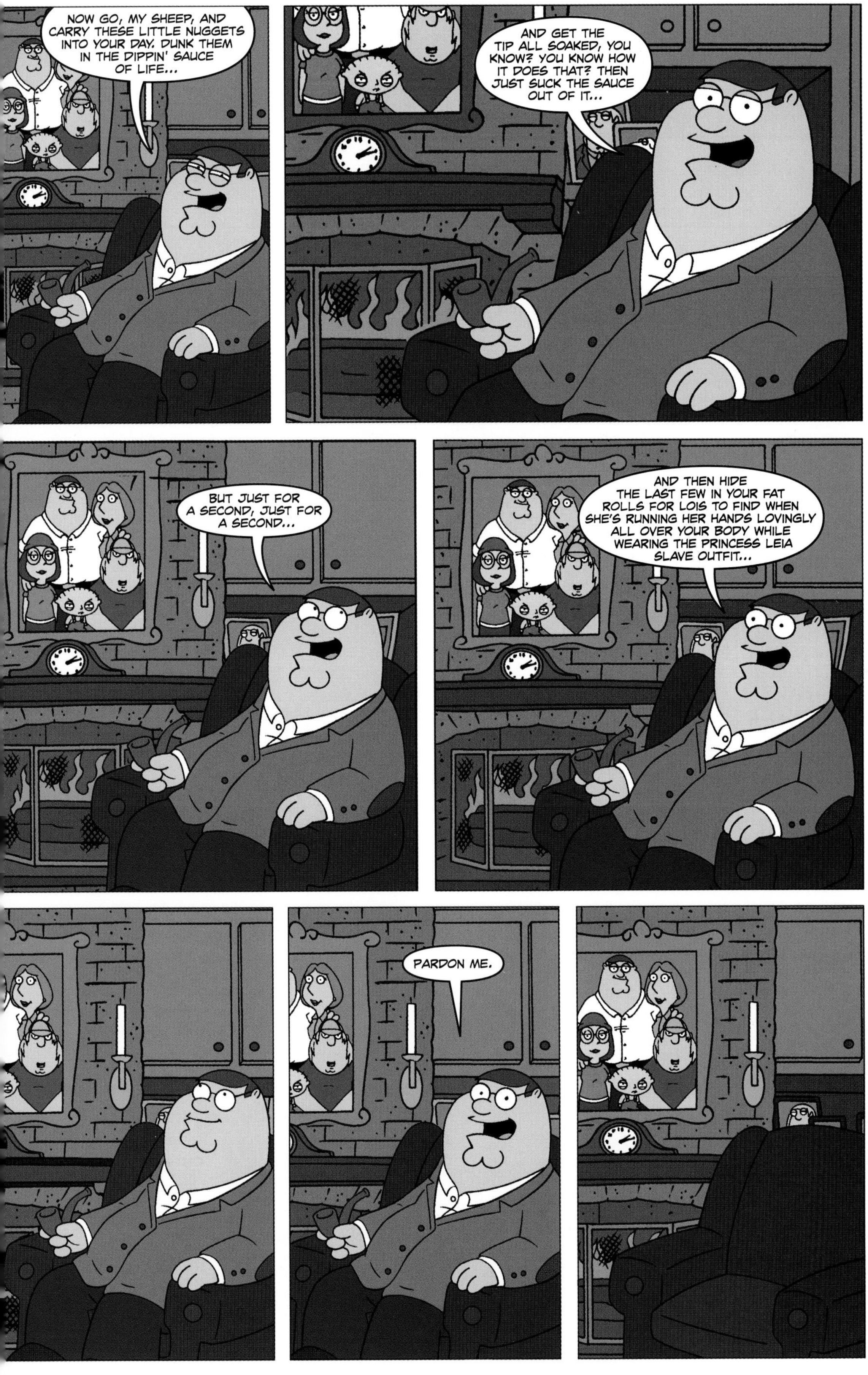
NOW GO, MY SHEEP, AND CARRY THESE LITTLE NUGGETS INTO YOUR DAY. DUNK THEM IN THE DIPPIN' SAUCE OF LIFE...
AND GET THE TIP ALL SOAKED, YOU KNOW? YOU KNOW HOW IT DOES THAT? THEN JUST SUCK THE SAUCE OUT OF IT...
BUT JUST FOR A SECOND, JUST FOR A SECOND...
AND THEN HIDE THE LAST FEW IN YOUR FAT ROLLS FOR LOIS TO FIND WHEN SHE'S RUNNING HER HANDS LOVINGLY ALL OVER YOUR BODY WHILE WEARING THE PRINCESS LEIA SLAVE OUTFIT...
PARDON ME.

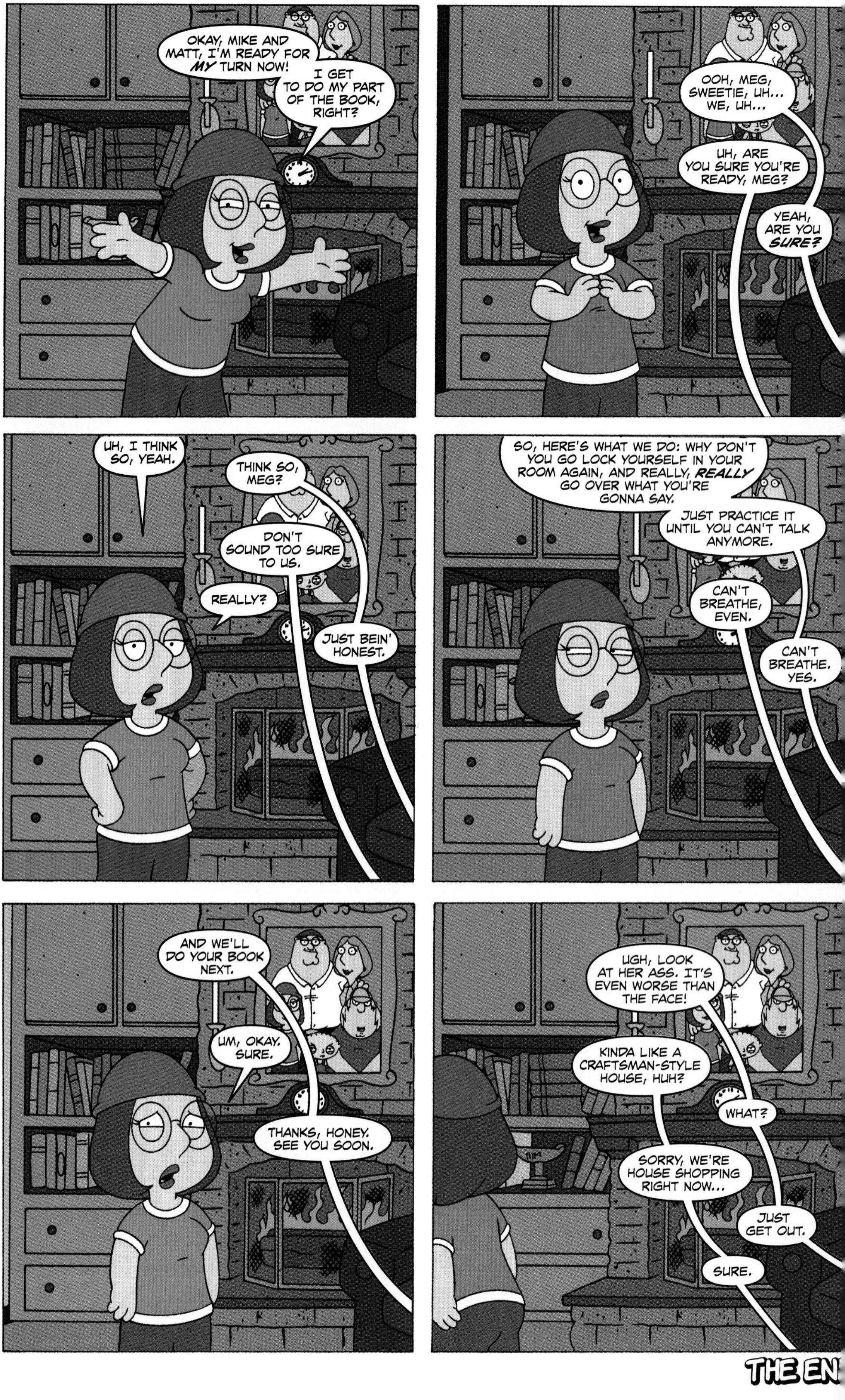
OKAY, MIKE AND MATT, I'M READY FOR *MY* TURN NOW!
I GET TO DO MY PART OF THE BOOK, RIGHT?
OOH, MEG, SWEETIE, UH... WE, UH...
UH, ARE YOU SURE YOU'RE READY, MEG?
YEAH, ARE YOU *SURE?*
UH, I THINK SO, YEAH.
THINK SO, MEG?
DON'T SOUND TOO SURE TO US.
REALLY?
JUST BEIN' HONEST.
SO, HERE'S WHAT WE DO: WHY DON'T YOU GO LOCK YOURSELF IN YOUR ROOM AGAIN, AND REALLY, *REALLY* GO OVER WHAT YOU'RE GONNA SAY.
JUST PRACTICE IT UNTIL YOU CAN'T TALK ANYMORE.
CAN'T BREATHE, EVEN.
CAN'T BREATHE. YES.
AND WE'LL DO YOUR BOOK NEXT.
UM, OKAY. SURE.
THANKS, HONEY. SEE YOU SOON.
UGH, LOOK AT HER ASS. IT'S EVEN WORSE THAN THE FACE!
KINDA LIKE A CRAFTSMAN-STYLE HOUSE, HUH?
WHAT?
SORRY, WE'RE HOUSE SHOPPING RIGHT NOW...
JUST GET OUT.
SURE.
THE EN

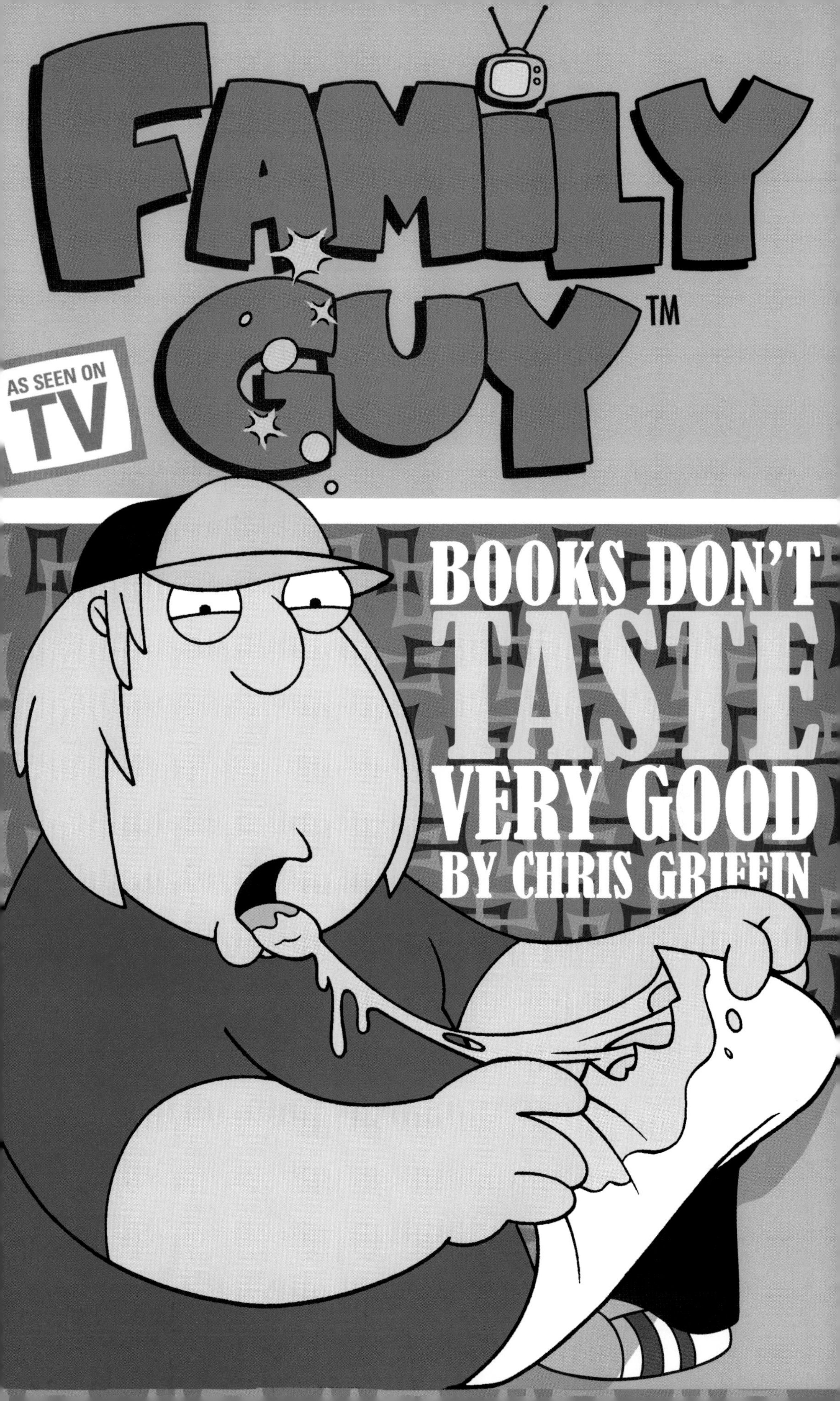
FAMILY GUY™
AS SEEN ON TV
BOOKS DON'T
TASTE
VERY GOOD
BY CHRIS GRIFFIN

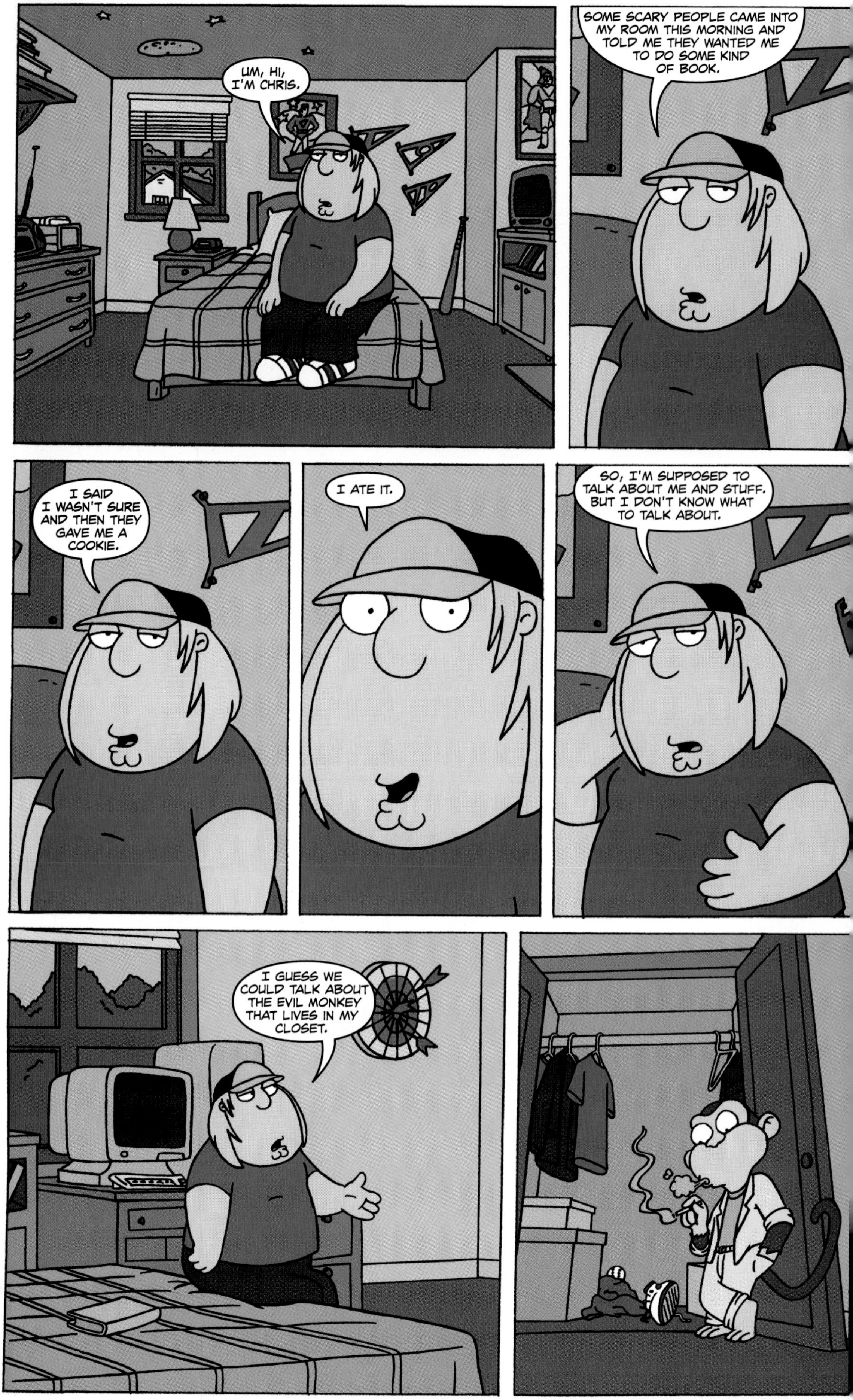

UM, HI, I'M CHRIS.
SOME SCARY PEOPLE CAME INTO MY ROOM THIS MORNING AND TOLD ME THEY WANTED ME TO DO SOME KIND OF BOOK.
I SAID I WASN'T SURE AND THEN THEY GAVE ME A COOKIE.
I ATE IT.
SO, I'M SUPPOSED TO TALK ABOUT ME AND STUFF. BUT I DON'T KNOW WHAT TO TALK ABOUT.
I GUESS WE COULD TALK ABOUT THE EVIL MONKEY THAT LIVES IN MY CLOSET.

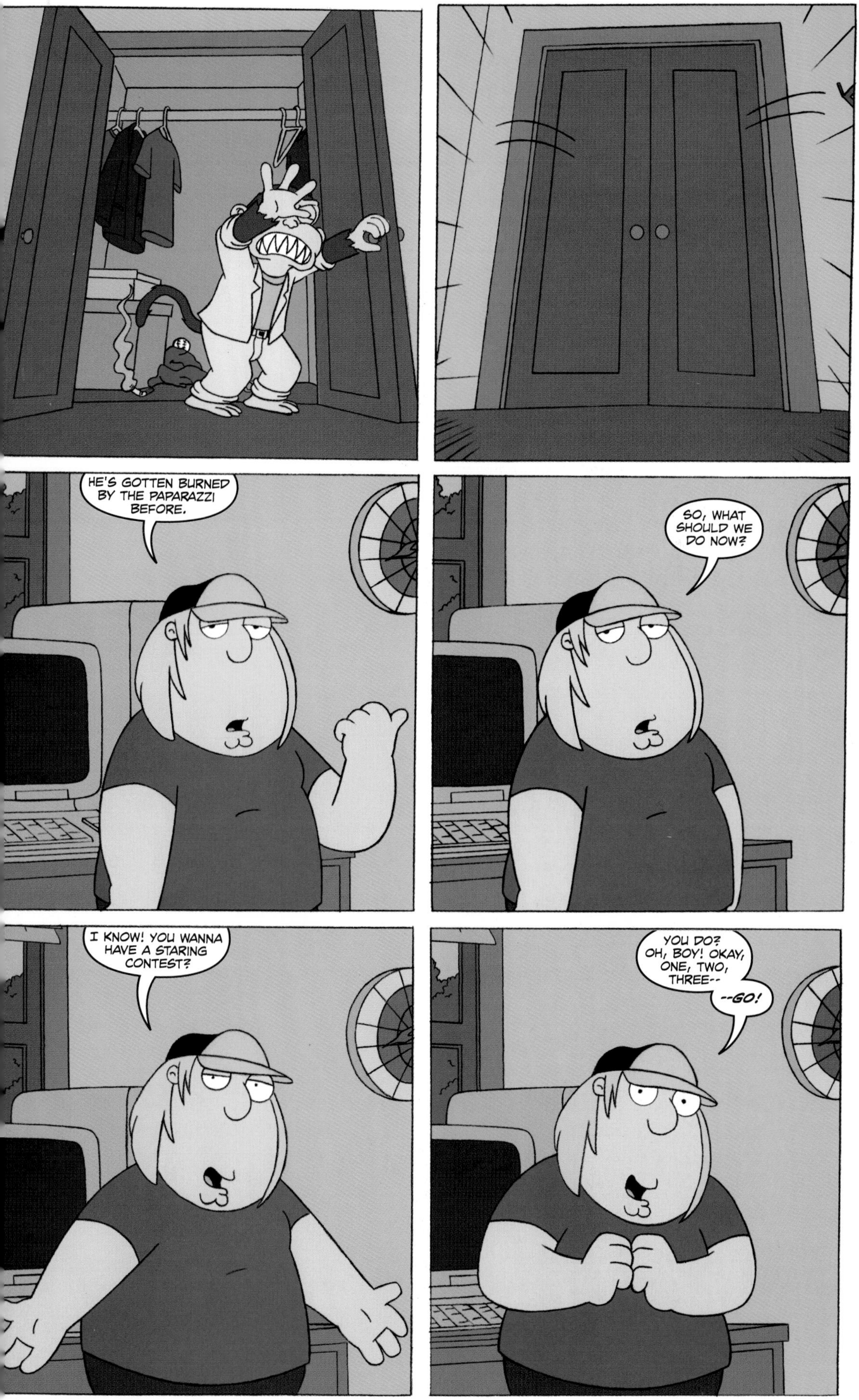
HE'S GOTTEN BURNED BY THE PAPARAZZI BEFORE.
SO, WHAT SHOULD WE DO NOW?
I KNOW! YOU WANNA HAVE A STARING CONTEST?
YOU DO? OH, BOY! OKAY, ONE, TWO, THREE--
--GO!

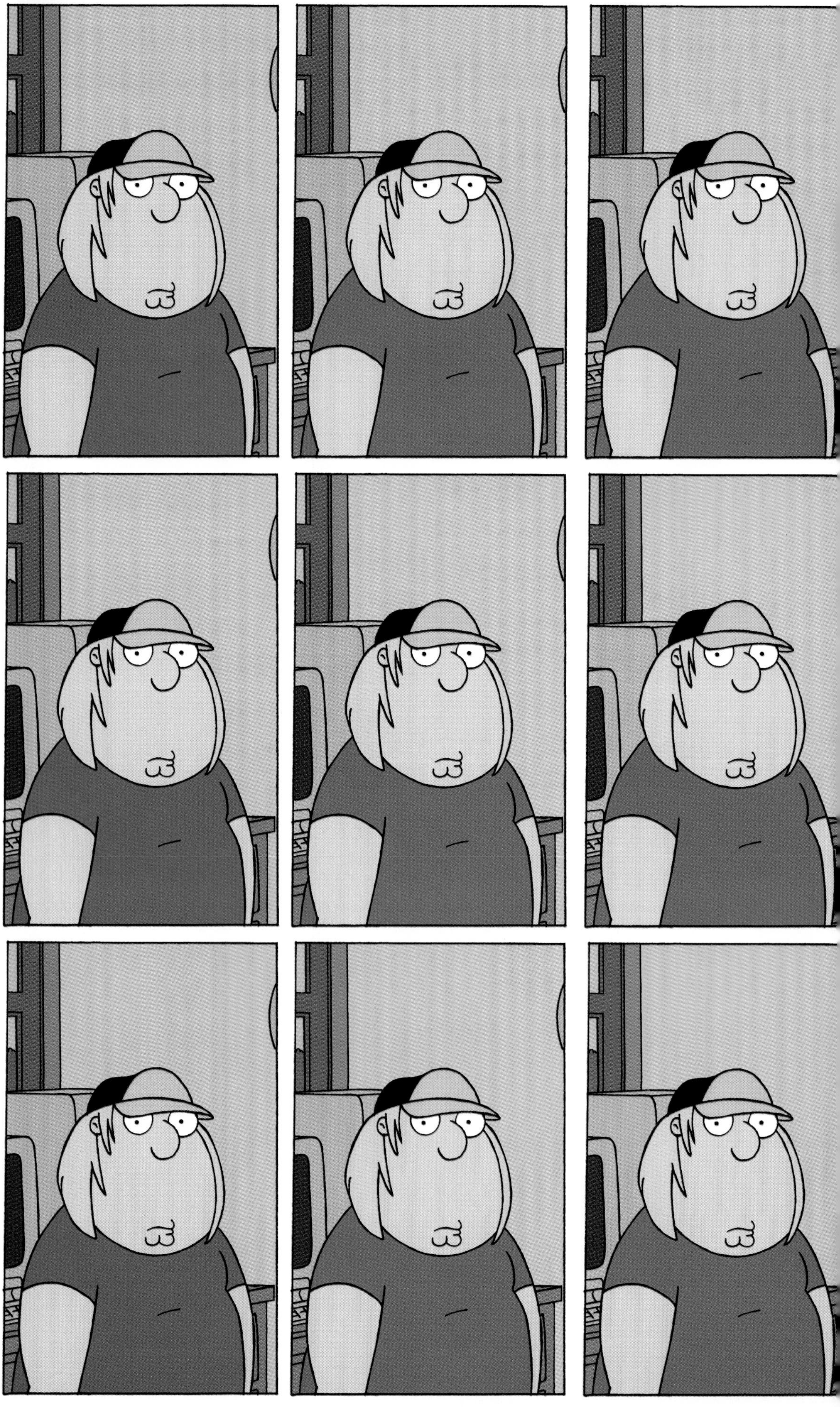

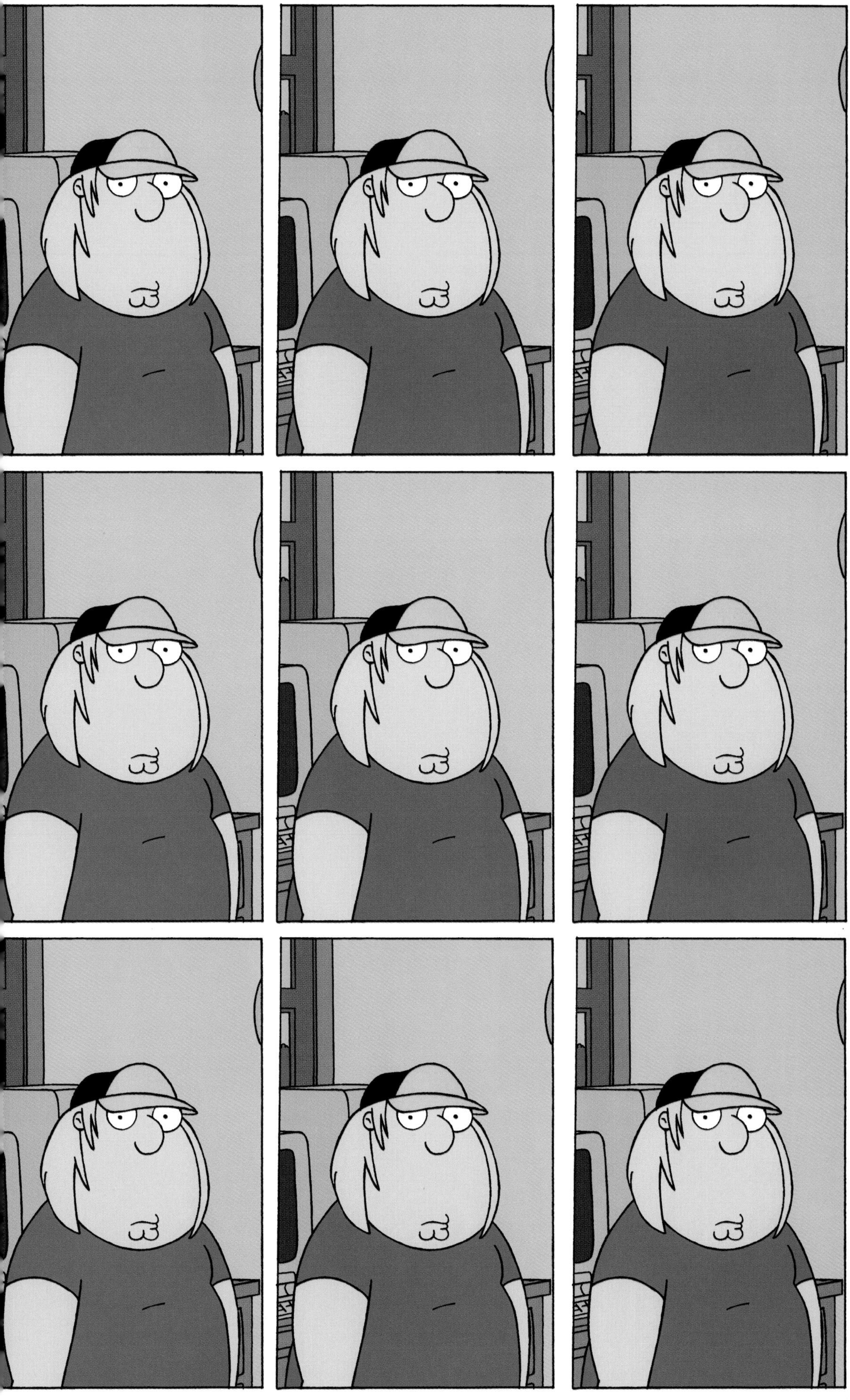

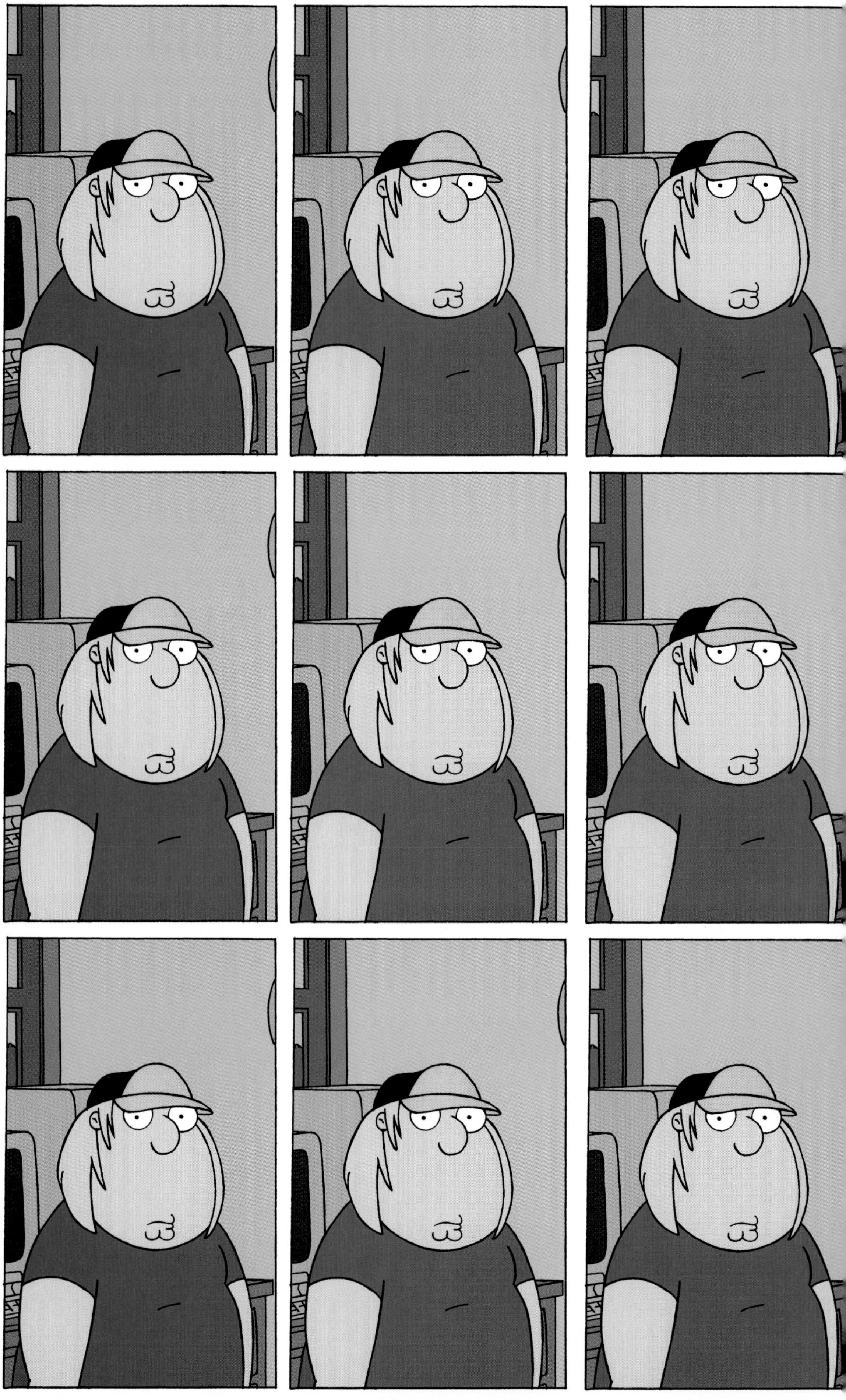

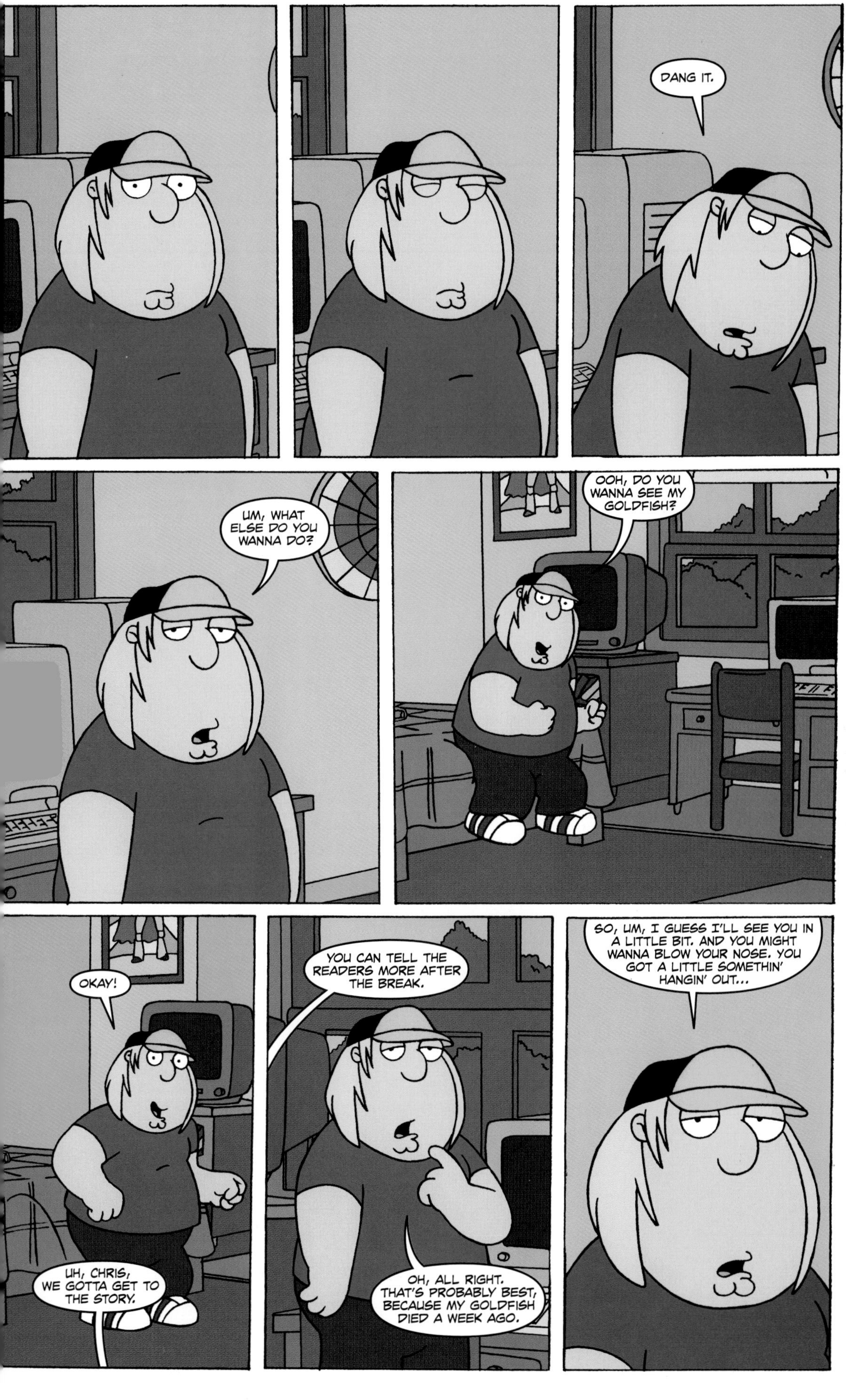
DANG IT.
UM, WHAT ELSE DO YOU WANNA DO?
OOH, DO YOU WANNA SEE MY GOLDFISH?
OKAY!
UH, CHRIS, WE GOTTA GET TO THE STORY.
YOU CAN TELL THE READERS MORE AFTER THE BREAK.
OH, ALL RIGHT. THAT'S PROBABLY BEST, BECAUSE MY GOLDFISH DIED A WEEK AGO.
SO, UM, I GUESS I'LL SEE YOU IN A LITTLE BIT. AND YOU MIGHT WANNA BLOW YOUR NOSE. YOU GOT A LITTLE SOMETHIN' HANGIN' OUT...

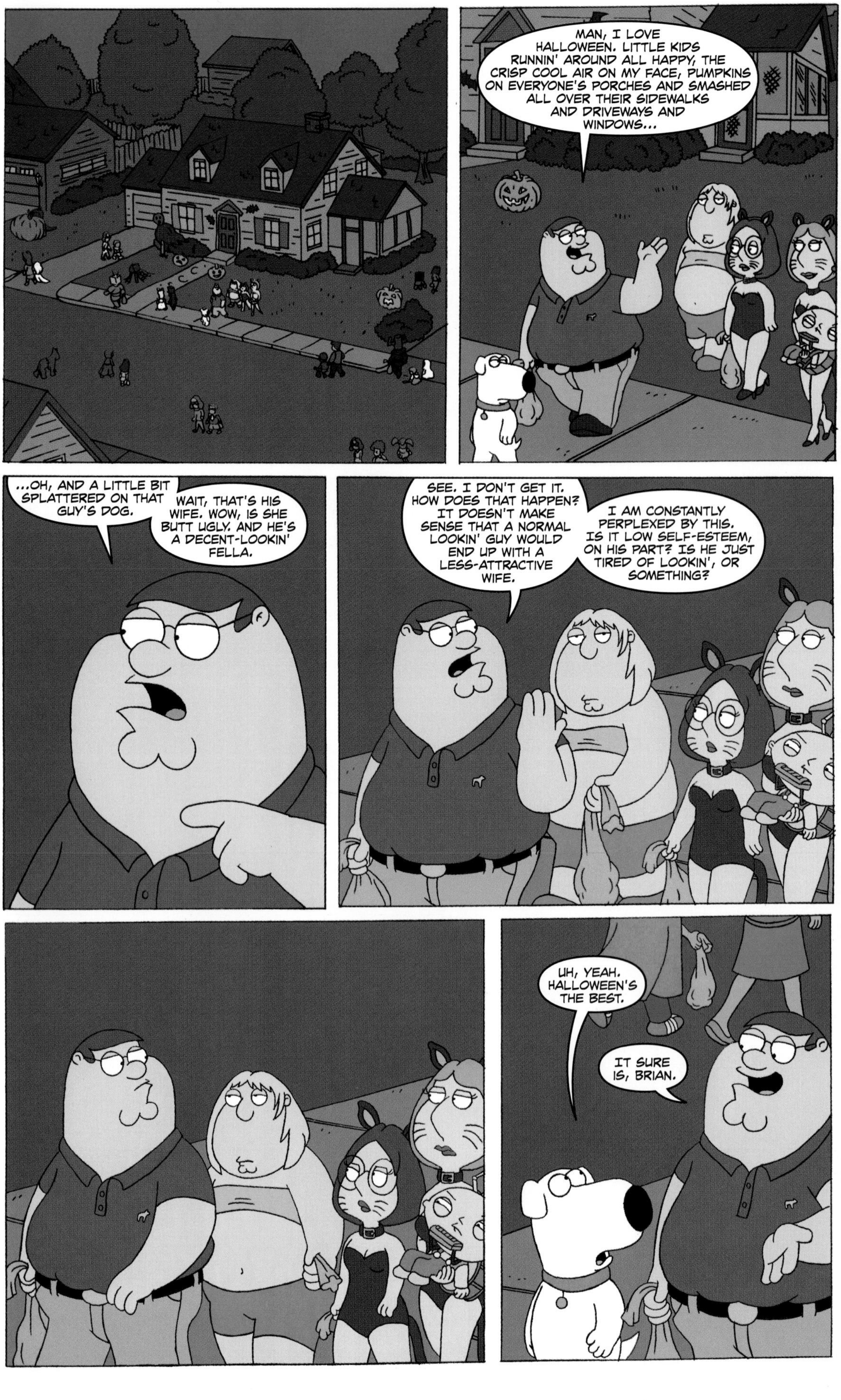
MAN, I LOVE HALLOWEEN. LITTLE KIDS RUNNIN' AROUND ALL HAPPY, THE CRISP COOL AIR ON MY FACE, PUMPKINS ON EVERYONE'S PORCHES AND SMASHED ALL OVER THEIR SIDEWALKS AND DRIVEWAYS AND WINDOWS...
...OH, AND A LITTLE BIT SPLATTERED ON THAT GUY'S DOG.
WAIT, THAT'S HIS WIFE. WOW, IS SHE BUTT UGLY. AND HE'S A DECENT-LOOKIN' FELLA.
SEE. I DON'T GET IT. HOW DOES THAT HAPPEN? IT DOESN'T MAKE SENSE THAT A NORMAL LOOKIN' GUY WOULD END UP WITH A LESS-ATTRACTIVE WIFE.
I AM CONSTANTLY PERPLEXED BY THIS. IS IT LOW SELF-ESTEEM, ON HIS PART? IS HE JUST TIRED OF LOOKIN', OR SOMETHING?
UH, YEAH. HALLOWEEN'S THE BEST.
IT SURE IS, BRIAN.

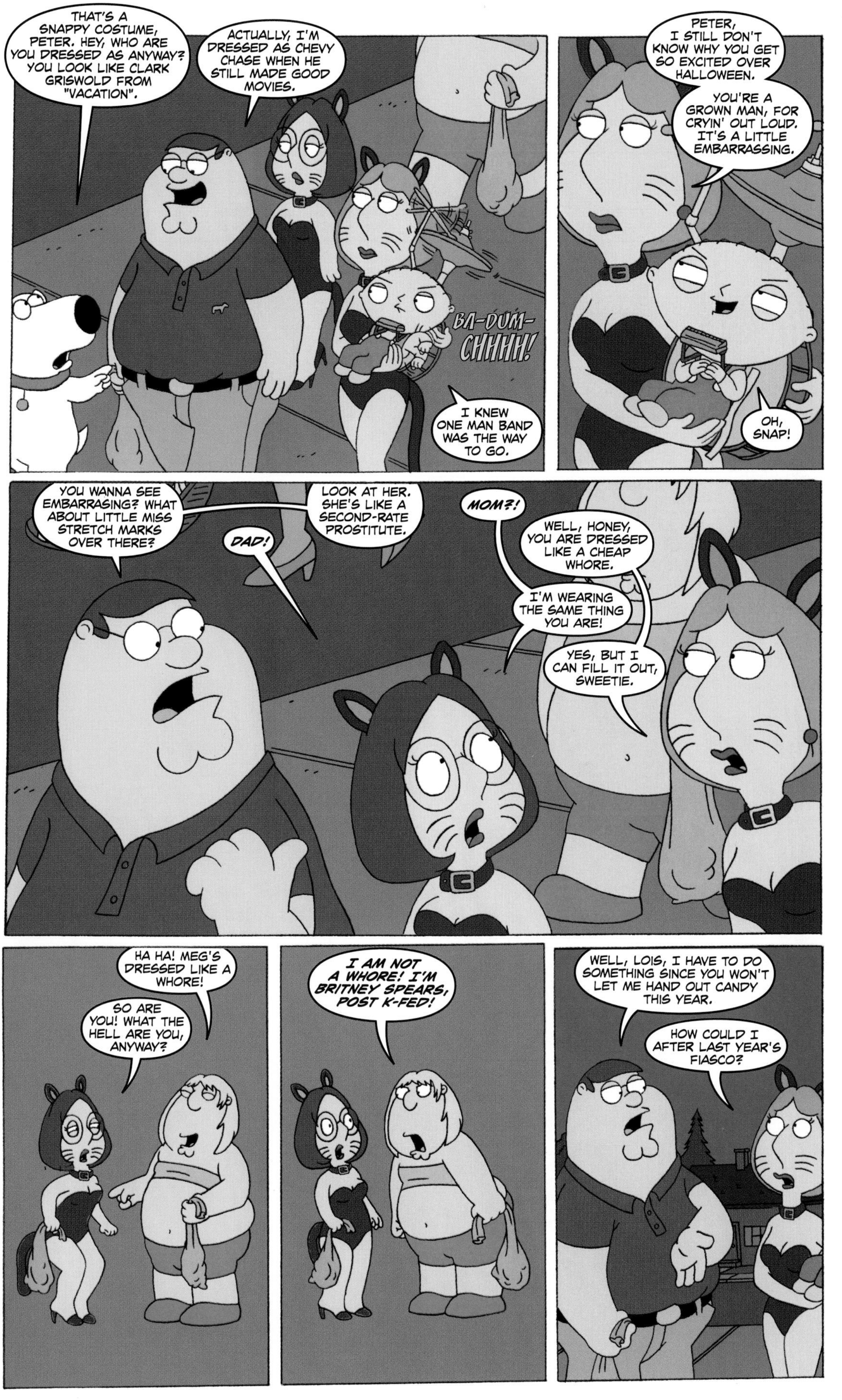

THAT'S A SNAPPY COSTUME, PETER. HEY, WHO ARE YOU DRESSED AS ANYWAY? YOU LOOK LIKE CLARK GRISWOLD FROM "VACATION".
ACTUALLY, I'M DRESSED AS CHEVY CHASE WHEN HE STILL MADE GOOD MOVIES.
BA-DUM-CHHHH!
I KNEW ONE MAN BAND WAS THE WAY TO GO.
PETER, I STILL DON'T KNOW WHY YOU GET SO EXCITED OVER HALLOWEEN.
YOU'RE A GROWN MAN, FOR CRYIN' OUT LOUD. IT'S A LITTLE EMBARRASSING.
OH, SNAP!
YOU WANNA SEE EMBARRASING? WHAT ABOUT LITTLE MISS STRETCH MARKS OVER THERE?
LOOK AT HER. SHE'S LIKE A SECOND-RATE PROSTITUTE.
DAD!
MOM?!
WELL, HONEY, YOU ARE DRESSED LIKE A CHEAP WHORE.
I'M WEARING THE SAME THING YOU ARE!
YES, BUT I CAN FILL IT OUT, SWEETIE.
HA HA! MEG'S DRESSED LIKE A WHORE!
SO ARE YOU! WHAT THE HELL ARE YOU, ANYWAY?
I AM NOT A WHORE! I'M BRITNEY SPEARS, POST K-FED!
WELL, LOIS, I HAVE TO DO SOMETHING SINCE YOU WON'T LET ME HAND OUT CANDY THIS YEAR.
HOW COULD I AFTER LAST YEAR'S FIASCO?

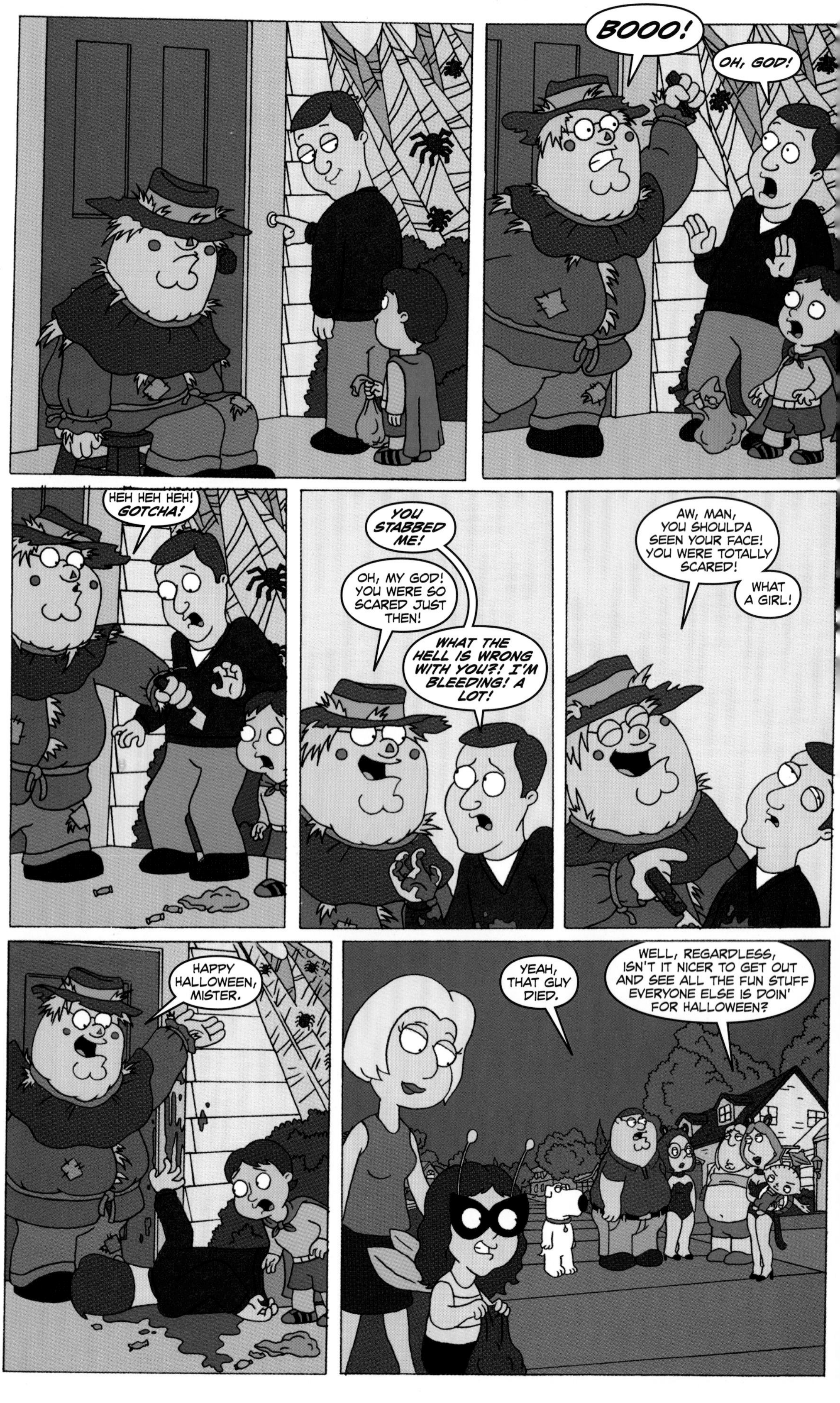
BOOO!
OH, GOD!
HEH HEH HEH! GOTCHA!
YOU STABBED ME!
OH, MY GOD! YOU WERE SO SCARED JUST THEN!
WHAT THE HELL IS WRONG WITH YOU?! I'M BLEEDING! A LOT!
AW, MAN, YOU SHOULDA SEEN YOUR FACE! YOU WERE TOTALLY SCARED!
WHAT A GIRL!
HAPPY HALLOWEEN, MISTER.
YEAH, THAT GUY DIED.
WELL, REGARDLESS, ISN'T IT NICER TO GET OUT AND SEE ALL THE FUN STUFF EVERYONE ELSE IS DOIN' FOR HALLOWEEN?

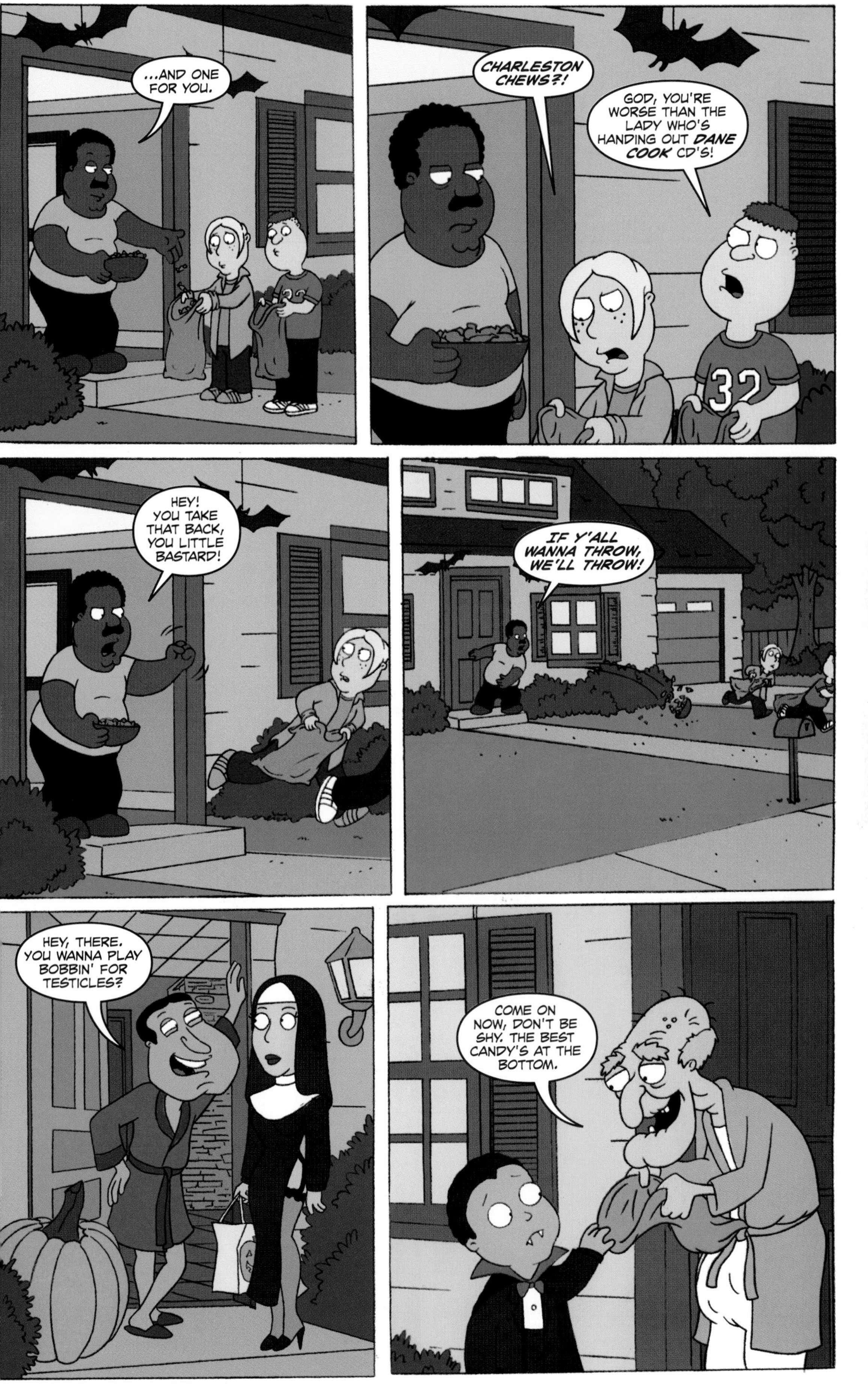
...AND ONE FOR YOU.
CHARLESTON CHEWS?!
GOD, YOU'RE WORSE THAN THE LADY WHO'S HANDING OUT DANE COOK CD'S!
HEY! YOU TAKE THAT BACK, YOU LITTLE BASTARD!
IF Y'ALL WANNA THROW, WE'LL THROW!
HEY, THERE. YOU WANNA PLAY BOBBIN' FOR TESTICLES?
COME ON NOW, DON'T BE SHY. THE BEST CANDY'S AT THE BOTTOM.

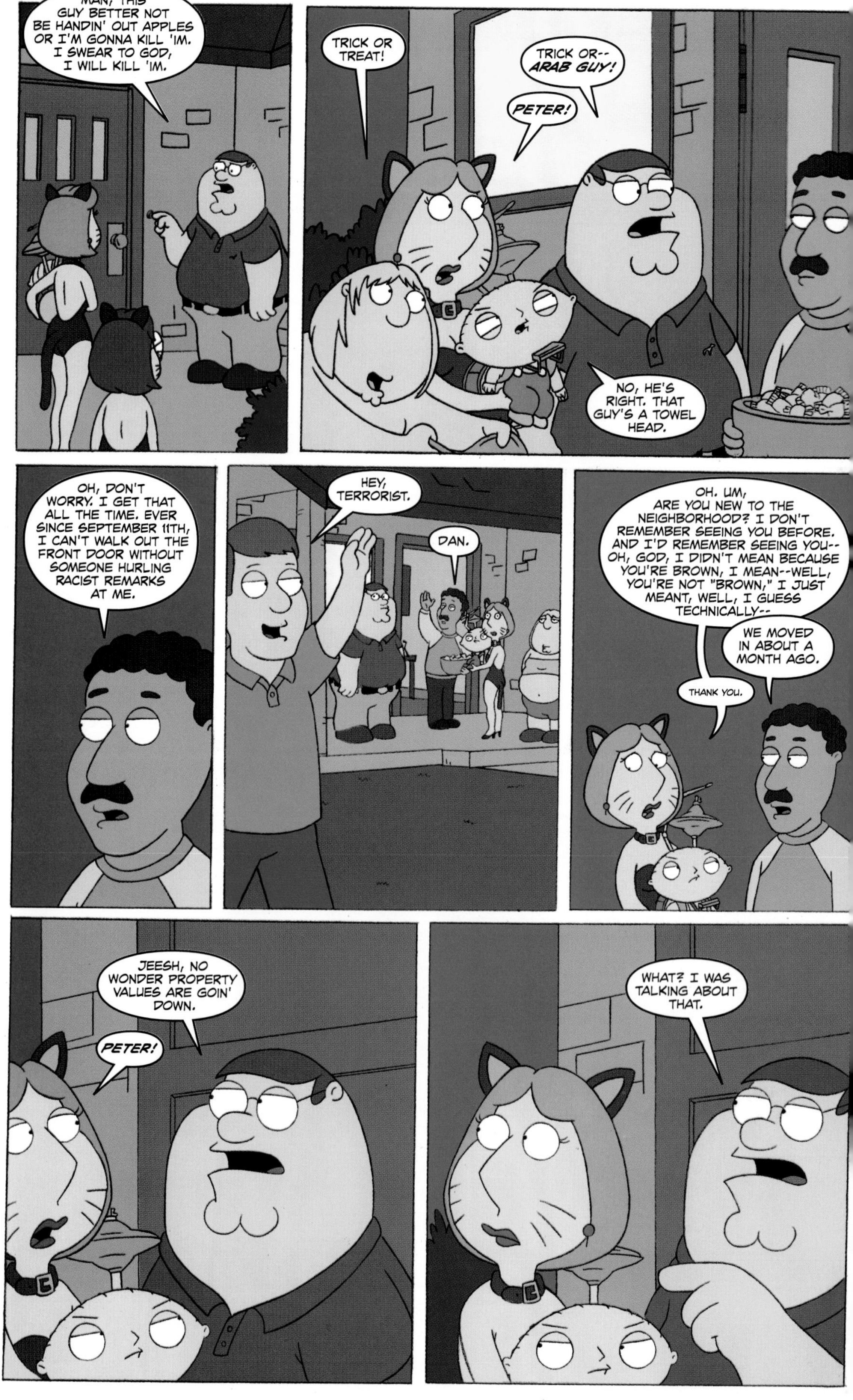
MAN, THIS GUY BETTER NOT BE HANDIN' OUT APPLES OR I'M GONNA KILL 'IM. I SWEAR TO GOD, I WILL KILL 'IM.
TRICK OR TREAT!
TRICK OR-- ARAB GUY!
PETER!
NO, HE'S RIGHT. THAT GUY'S A TOWEL HEAD.
OH, DON'T WORRY. I GET THAT ALL THE TIME. EVER SINCE SEPTEMBER 11TH, I CAN'T WALK OUT THE FRONT DOOR WITHOUT SOMEONE HURLING RACIST REMARKS AT ME.
HEY, TERRORIST.
DAN.
OH. UM, ARE YOU NEW TO THE NEIGHBORHOOD? I DON'T REMEMBER SEEING YOU BEFORE. AND I'D REMEMBER SEEING YOU-- OH, GOD, I DIDN'T MEAN BECAUSE YOU'RE BROWN, I MEAN--WELL, YOU'RE NOT "BROWN," I JUST MEANT, WELL, I GUESS TECHNICALLY--
WE MOVED IN ABOUT A MONTH AGO.
THANK YOU.
JEESH, NO WONDER PROPERTY VALUES ARE GOIN' DOWN.
PETER!
WHAT? I WAS TALKING ABOUT THAT.

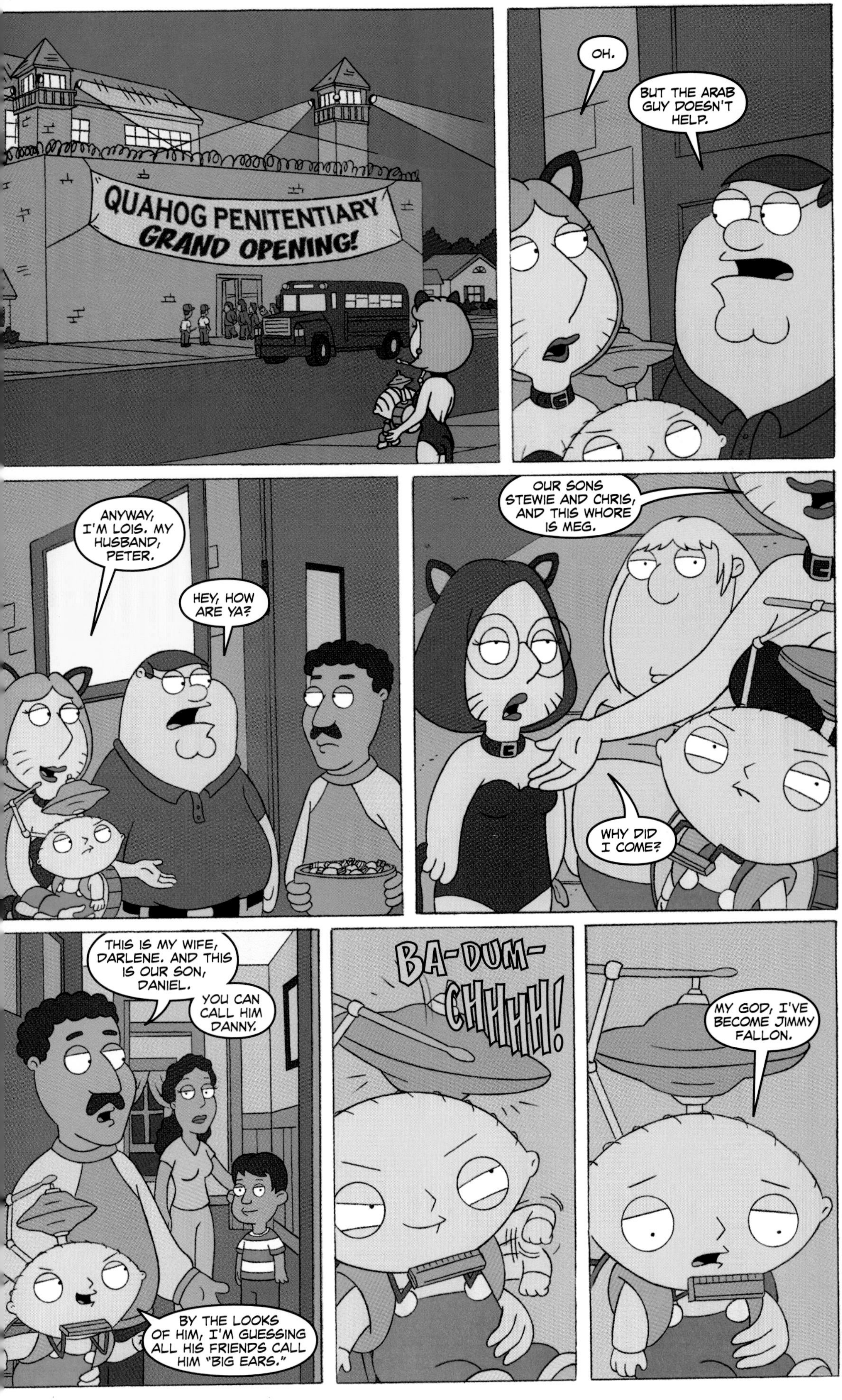
QUAHOG PENITENTIARY
GRAND OPENING!
OH.
BUT THE ARAB GUY DOESN'T HELP.
ANYWAY, I'M LOIS. MY HUSBAND, PETER.
HEY, HOW ARE YA?
OUR SONS STEWIE AND CHRIS, AND THIS WHORE IS MEG.
WHY DID I COME?
THIS IS MY WIFE, DARLENE. AND THIS IS OUR SON, DANIEL.
YOU CAN CALL HIM DANNY.
BY THE LOOKS OF HIM, I'M GUESSING ALL HIS FRIENDS CALL HIM "BIG EARS."
BA-DUM-CHHHH!
MY GOD, I'VE BECOME JIMMY FALLON.

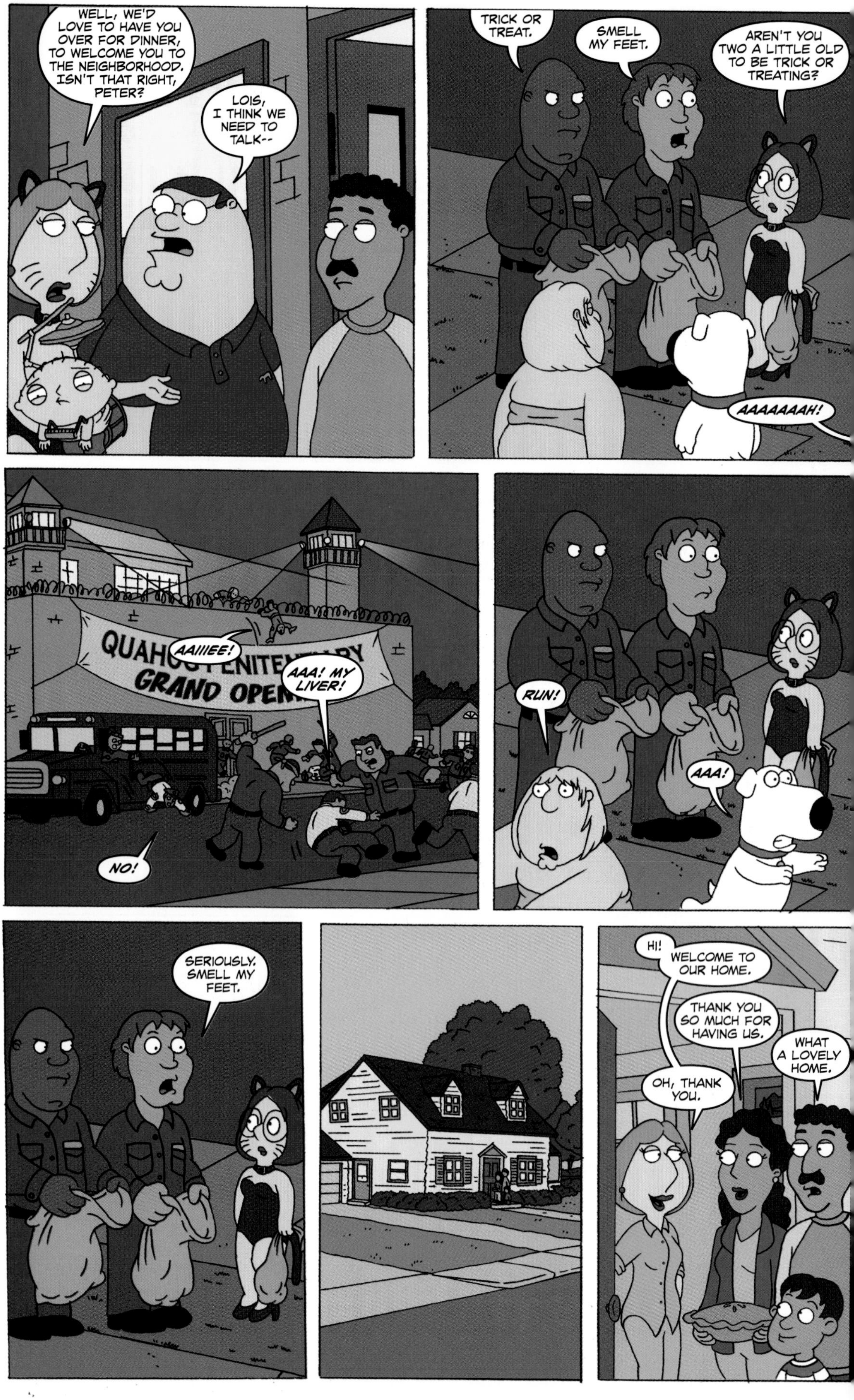

WELL, WE'D LOVE TO HAVE YOU OVER FOR DINNER, TO WELCOME YOU TO THE NEIGHBORHOOD. ISN'T THAT RIGHT, PETER?
LOIS, I THINK WE NEED TO TALK--
TRICK OR TREAT.
SMELL MY FEET.
AREN'T YOU TWO A LITTLE OLD TO BE TRICK OR TREATING?
AAAAAAAH!
QUAHOG PENITENTIARY GRAND OPEN
AAIIIEE!
AAA! MY LIVER!
NO!
RUN!
AAA!
SERIOUSLY. SMELL MY FEET.
HI!
WELCOME TO OUR HOME.
THANK YOU SO MUCH FOR HAVING US.
WHAT A LOVELY HOME.
OH, THANK YOU.

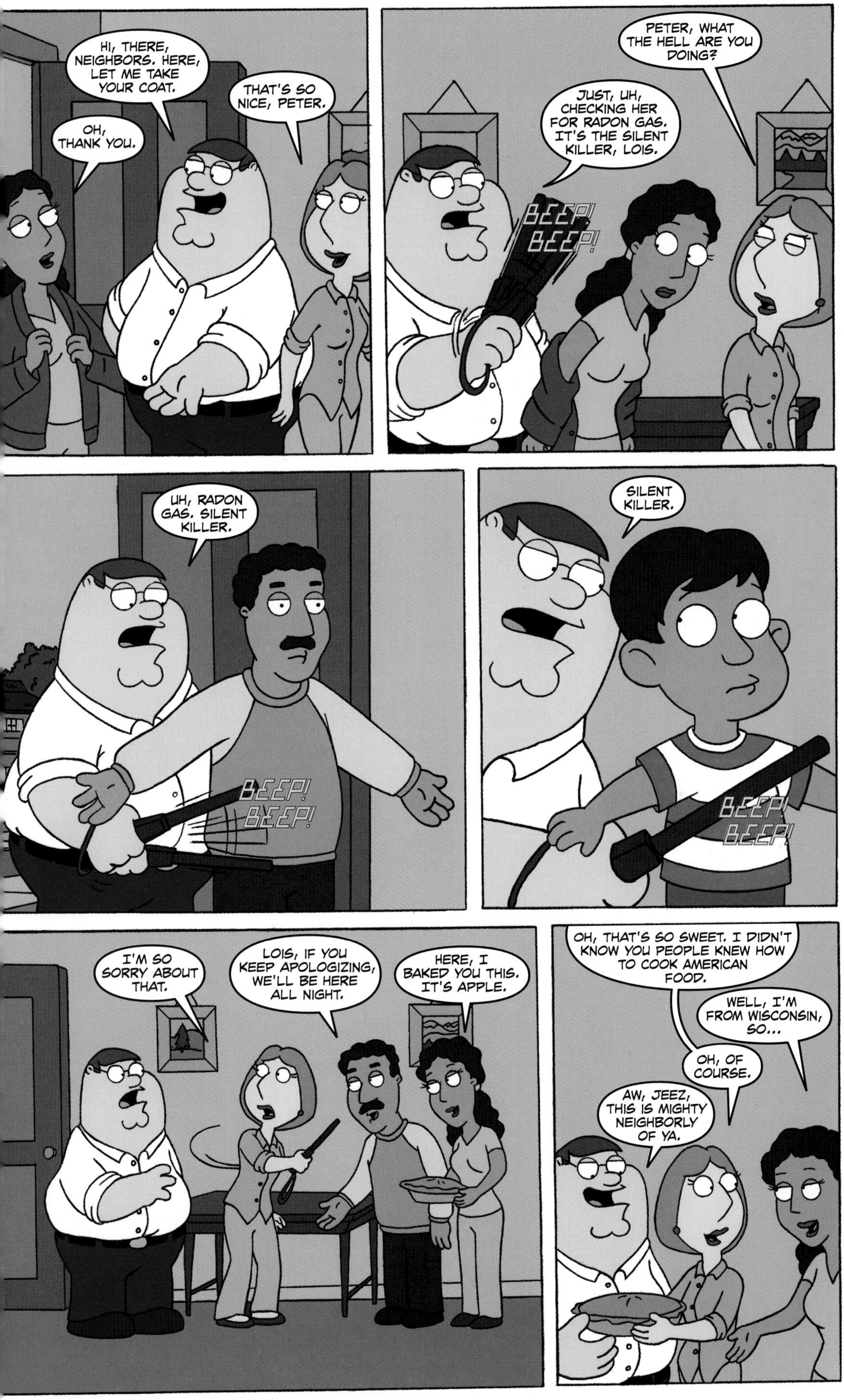

HI, THERE, NEIGHBORS. HERE, LET ME TAKE YOUR COAT.
OH, THANK YOU.
THAT'S SO NICE, PETER.
PETER, WHAT THE HELL ARE YOU DOING?
JUST, UH, CHECKING HER FOR RADON GAS. IT'S THE SILENT KILLER, LOIS.
BEEP! BEEP!
UH, RADON GAS. SILENT KILLER.
BEEP! BEEP!
SILENT KILLER.
BEEP! BEEP!
I'M SO SORRY ABOUT THAT.
LOIS, IF YOU KEEP APOLOGIZING, WE'LL BE HERE ALL NIGHT.
HERE, I BAKED YOU THIS. IT'S APPLE.
OH, THAT'S SO SWEET. I DIDN'T KNOW YOU PEOPLE KNEW HOW TO COOK AMERICAN FOOD.
WELL, I'M FROM WISCONSIN, SO...
OH, OF COURSE.
AW, JEEZ, THIS IS MIGHTY NEIGHBORLY OF YA.

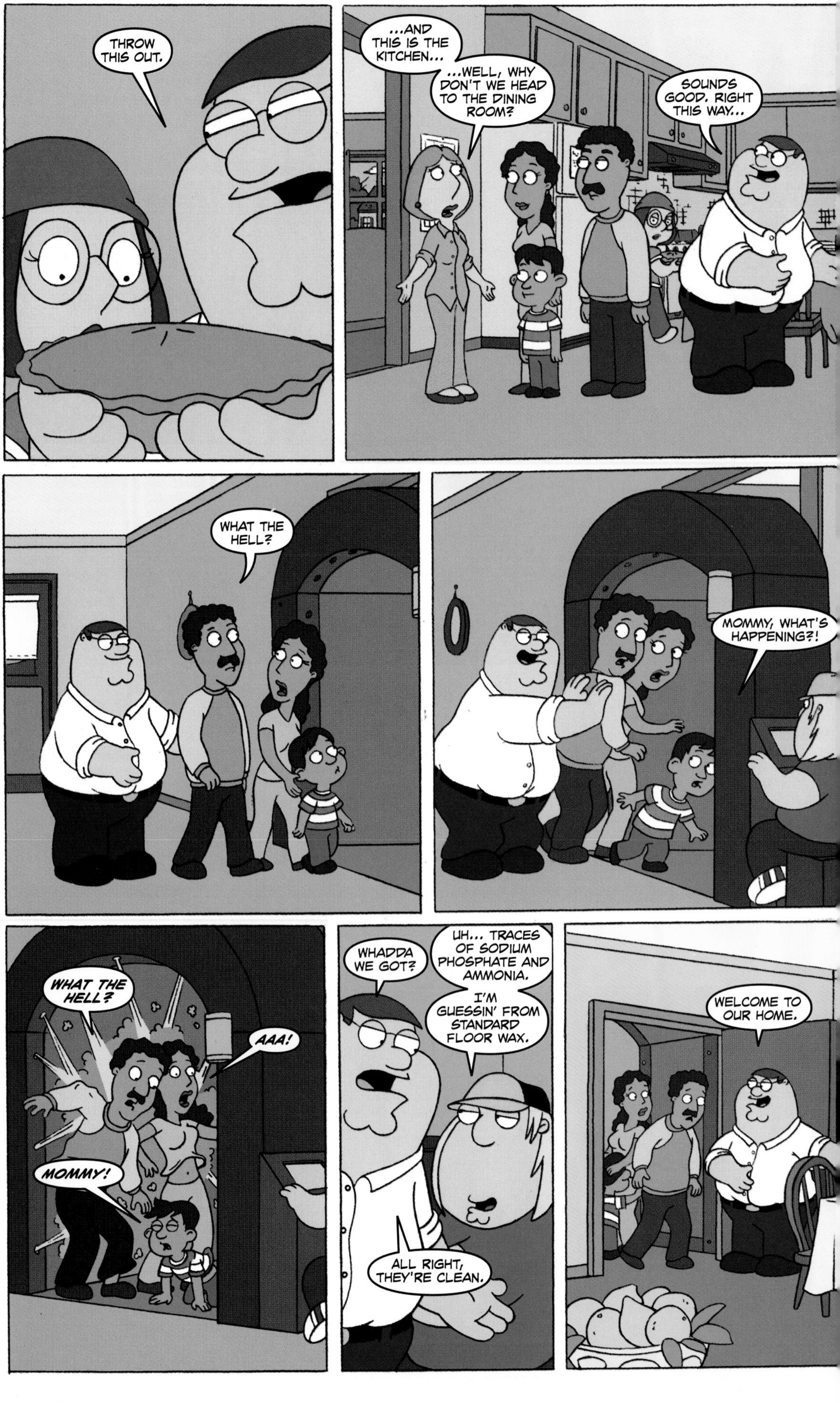
THROW THIS OUT.
...AND THIS IS THE KITCHEN...
...WELL, WHY DON'T WE HEAD TO THE DINING ROOM?
SOUNDS GOOD. RIGHT THIS WAY...
WHAT THE HELL?
MOMMY, WHAT'S HAPPENING?!
WHAT THE HELL?
AAA!
MOMMY!
WHADDA WE GOT?
UH... TRACES OF SODIUM PHOSPHATE AND AMMONIA.
I'M GUESSIN' FROM STANDARD FLOOR WAX.
ALL RIGHT, THEY'RE CLEAN.
WELCOME TO OUR HOME.

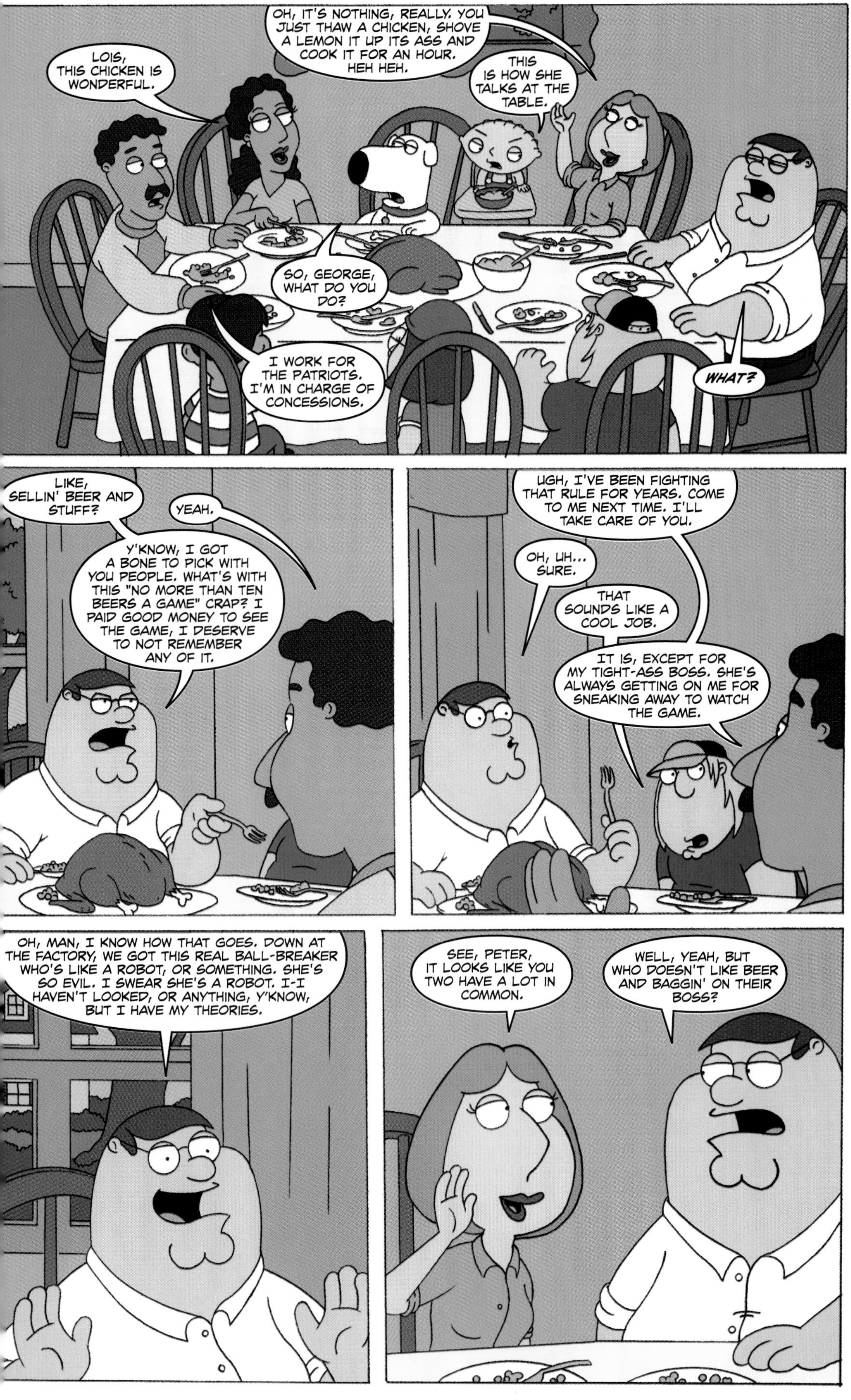

LOIS, THIS CHICKEN IS WONDERFUL.
OH, IT'S NOTHING, REALLY. YOU JUST THAW A CHICKEN, SHOVE A LEMON IT UP ITS ASS AND COOK IT FOR AN HOUR. HEH HEH.
THIS IS HOW SHE TALKS AT THE TABLE.
SO, GEORGE, WHAT DO YOU DO?
I WORK FOR THE PATRIOTS. I'M IN CHARGE OF CONCESSIONS.
WHAT?
LIKE, SELLIN' BEER AND STUFF?
YEAH.
Y'KNOW, I GOT A BONE TO PICK WITH YOU PEOPLE. WHAT'S WITH THIS "NO MORE THAN TEN BEERS A GAME" CRAP? I PAID GOOD MONEY TO SEE THE GAME, I DESERVE TO NOT REMEMBER ANY OF IT.
UGH, I'VE BEEN FIGHTING THAT RULE FOR YEARS. COME TO ME NEXT TIME. I'LL TAKE CARE OF YOU.
OH, UH... SURE.
THAT SOUNDS LIKE A COOL JOB.
IT IS, EXCEPT FOR MY TIGHT-ASS BOSS. SHE'S ALWAYS GETTING ON ME FOR SNEAKING AWAY TO WATCH THE GAME.
OH, MAN, I KNOW HOW THAT GOES. DOWN AT THE FACTORY, WE GOT THIS REAL BALL-BREAKER WHO'S LIKE A ROBOT, OR SOMETHING. SHE'S SO EVIL. I SWEAR SHE'S A ROBOT. I-I HAVEN'T LOOKED, OR ANYTHING, Y'KNOW, BUT I HAVE MY THEORIES.
SEE, PETER, IT LOOKS LIKE YOU TWO HAVE A LOT IN COMMON.
WELL, YEAH, BUT WHO DOESN'T LIKE BEER AND BAGGIN' ON THEIR BOSS?

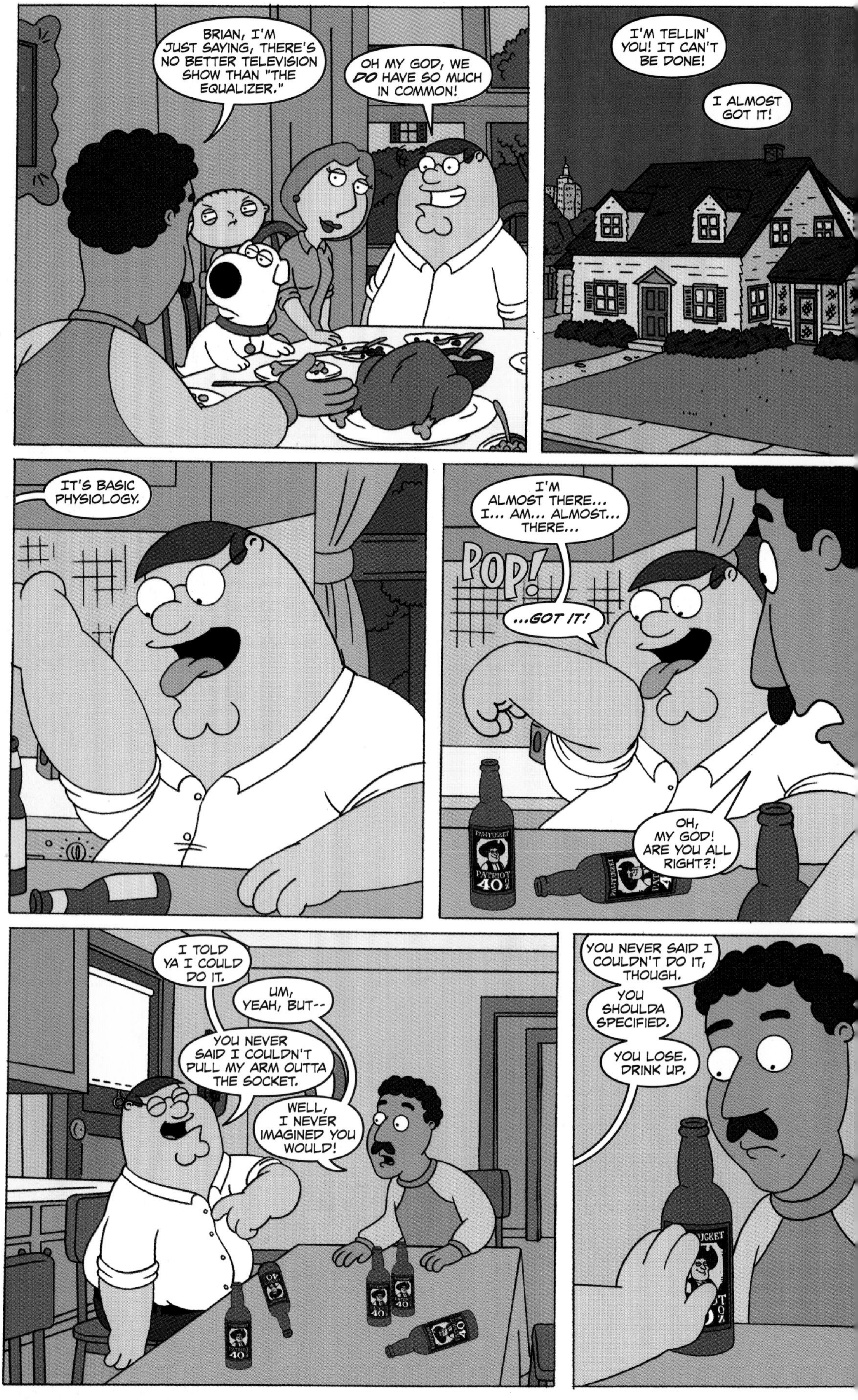
BRIAN, I'M JUST SAYING, THERE'S NO BETTER TELEVISION SHOW THAN "THE EQUALIZER."
OH MY GOD, WE *DO* HAVE SO MUCH IN COMMON!
I'M TELLIN' YOU! IT CAN'T BE DONE!
I ALMOST GOT IT!
IT'S BASIC PHYSIOLOGY.
I'M ALMOST THERE... I... AM... ALMOST... THERE...
POP!
...GOT IT!
OH, MY GOD! ARE YOU ALL RIGHT?!
PAWTUCKET PATRIOT 40 OZ
I TOLD YA I COULD DO IT.
UM, YEAH, BUT--
YOU NEVER SAID I COULDN'T PULL MY ARM OUTTA THE SOCKET.
WELL, I NEVER IMAGINED YOU WOULD!
YOU NEVER SAID I COULDN'T DO IT, THOUGH.
YOU SHOULDA SPECIFIED.
YOU LOSE. DRINK UP.

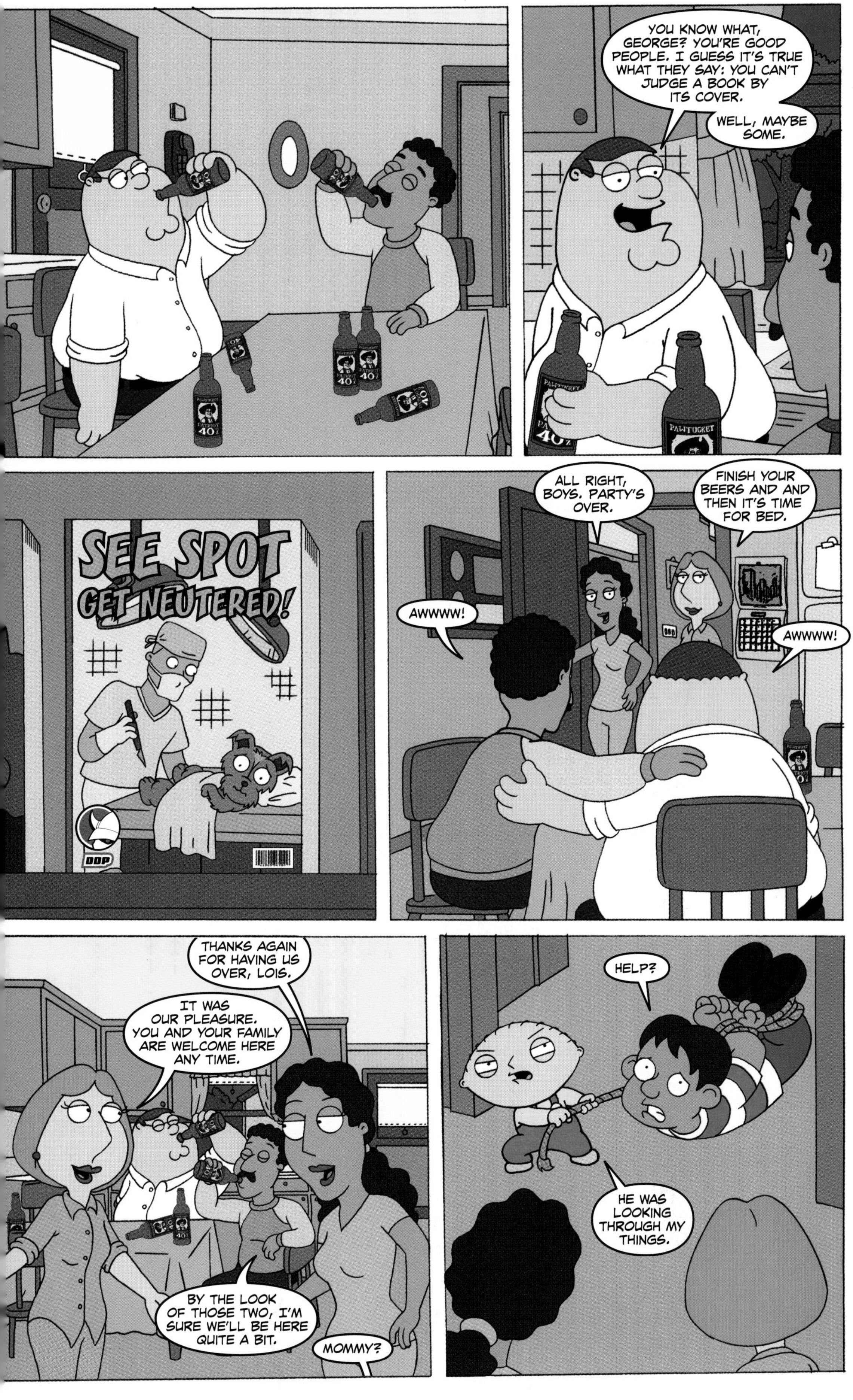
YOU KNOW WHAT, GEORGE? YOU'RE GOOD PEOPLE. I GUESS IT'S TRUE WHAT THEY SAY: YOU CAN'T JUDGE A BOOK BY ITS COVER.
WELL, MAYBE SOME.
PAWTUCKET
SEE SPOT GET NEUTERED!
DDP
ALL RIGHT, BOYS. PARTY'S OVER.
FINISH YOUR BEERS AND AND THEN IT'S TIME FOR BED.
AWWWW!
AWWWW!
THANKS AGAIN FOR HAVING US OVER, LOIS.
IT WAS OUR PLEASURE. YOU AND YOUR FAMILY ARE WELCOME HERE ANY TIME.
BY THE LOOK OF THOSE TWO, I'M SURE WE'LL BE HERE QUITE A BIT.
MOMMY?
HELP?
HE WAS LOOKING THROUGH MY THINGS.

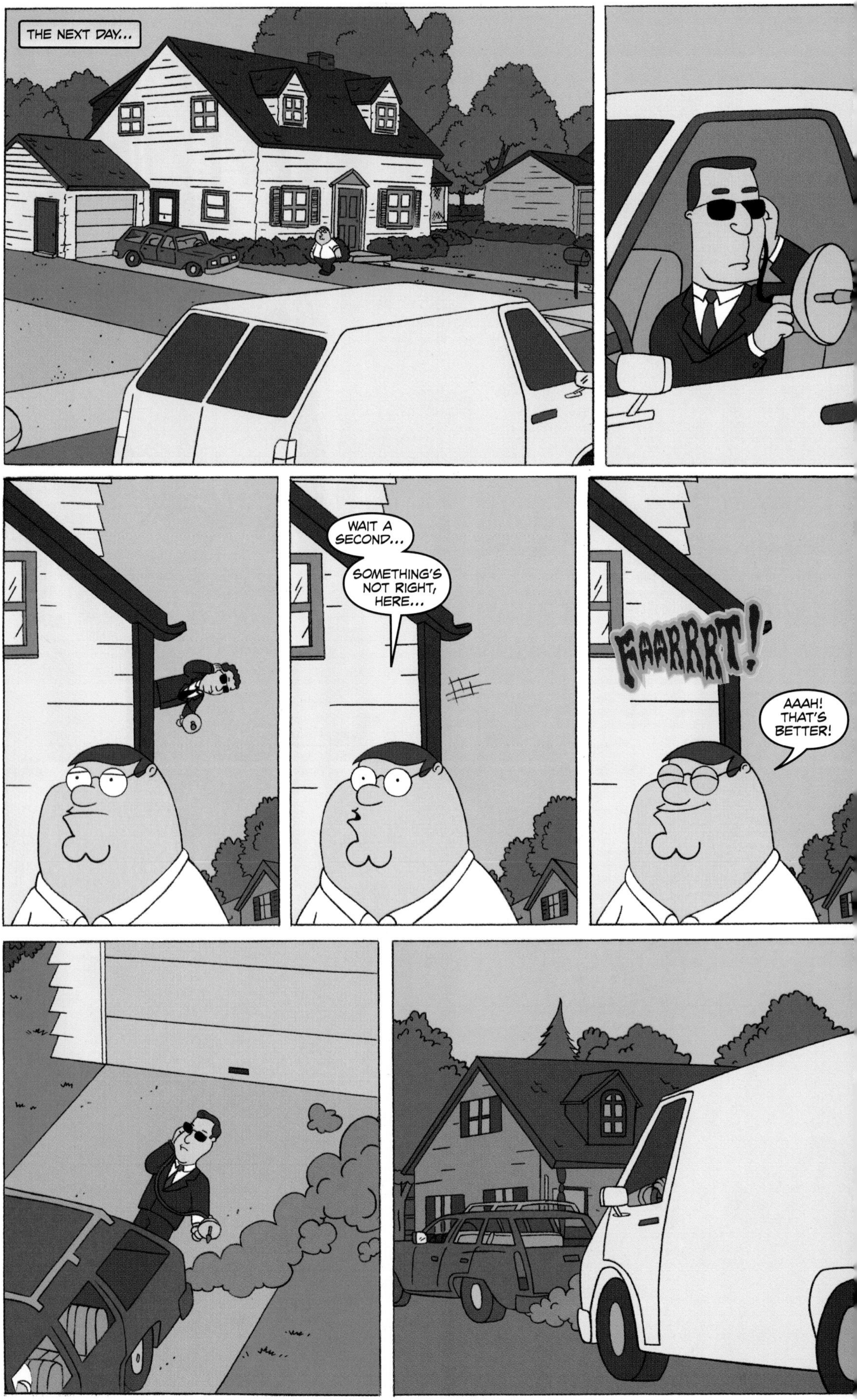
THE NEXT DAY...
WAIT A SECOND...
SOMETHING'S NOT RIGHT, HERE...
FAARRRT!
AAAH! THAT'S BETTER!

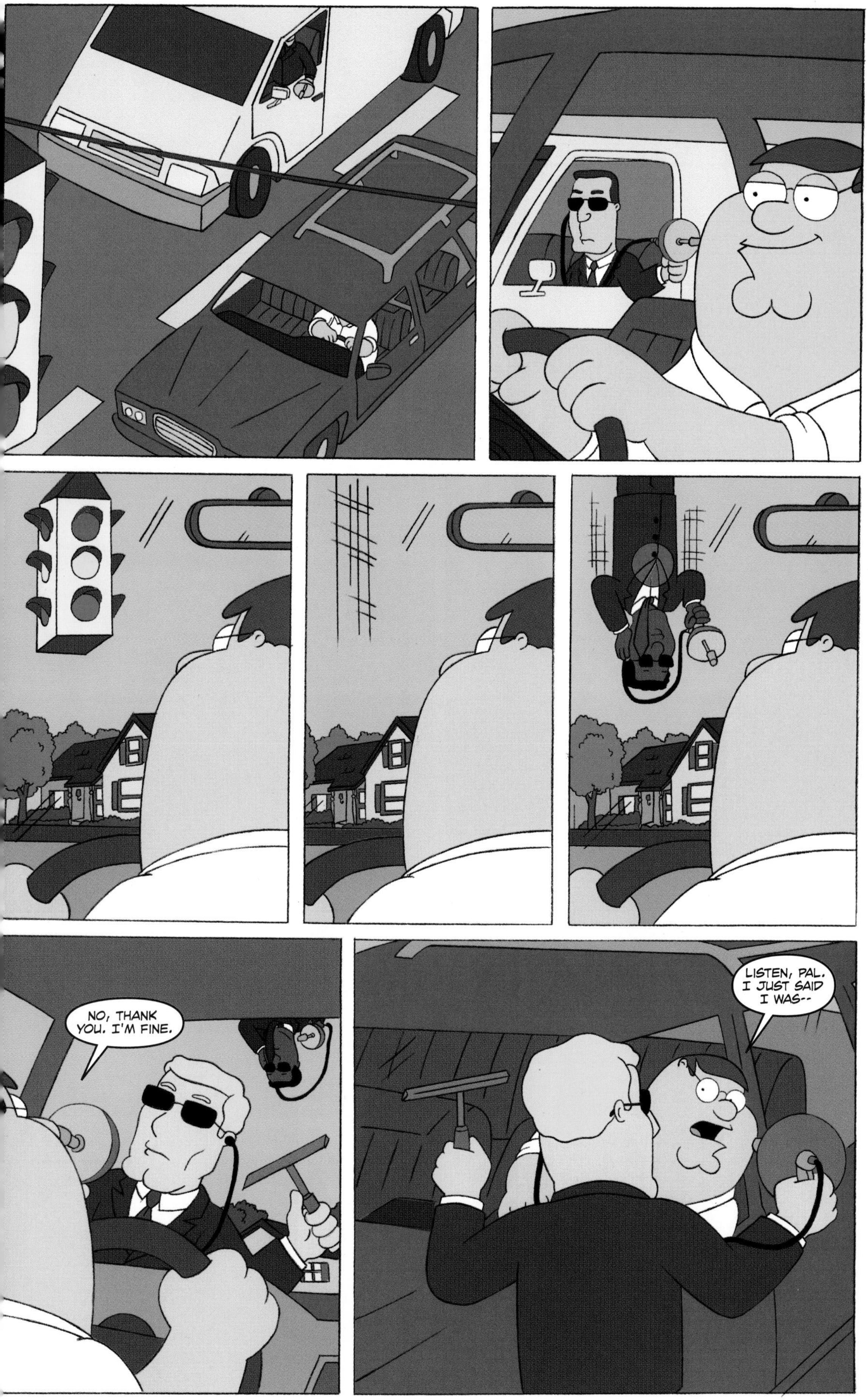
NO, THANK YOU. I'M FINE.
LISTEN, PAL. I JUST SAID I WAS--

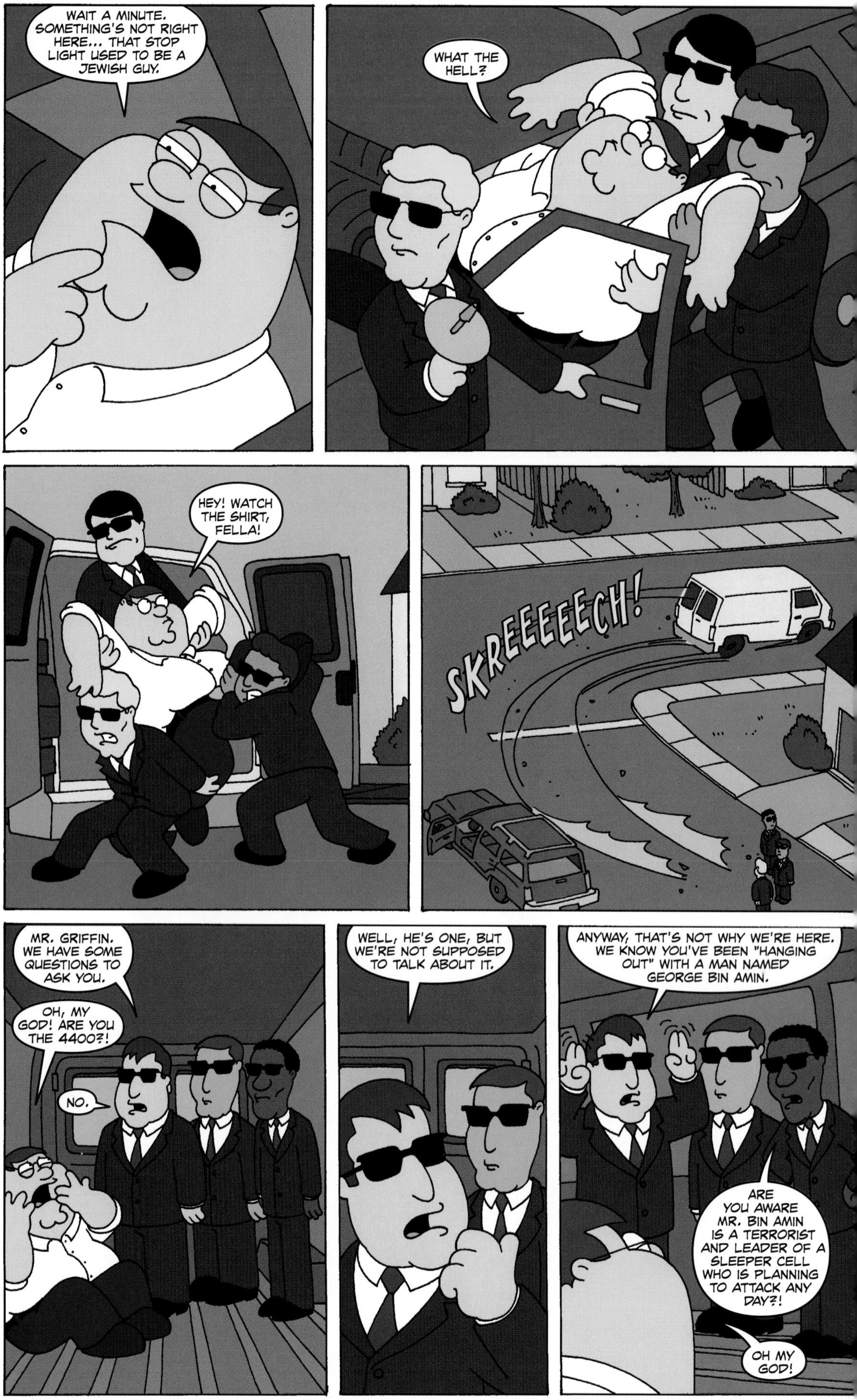
WAIT A MINUTE. SOMETHING'S NOT RIGHT HERE... THAT STOP LIGHT USED TO BE A JEWISH GUY.
WHAT THE HELL?
HEY! WATCH THE SHIRT, FELLA!
SKREEEEEECH!
MR. GRIFFIN. WE HAVE SOME QUESTIONS TO ASK YOU.
OH, MY GOD! ARE YOU THE 4400?!
NO.
WELL, HE'S ONE, BUT WE'RE NOT SUPPOSED TO TALK ABOUT IT.
ANYWAY, THAT'S NOT WHY WE'RE HERE. WE KNOW YOU'VE BEEN "HANGING OUT" WITH A MAN NAMED GEORGE BIN AMIN.
ARE YOU AWARE MR. BIN AMIN IS A TERRORIST AND LEADER OF A SLEEPER CELL WHO IS PLANNING TO ATTACK ANY DAY?!
OH MY GOD!

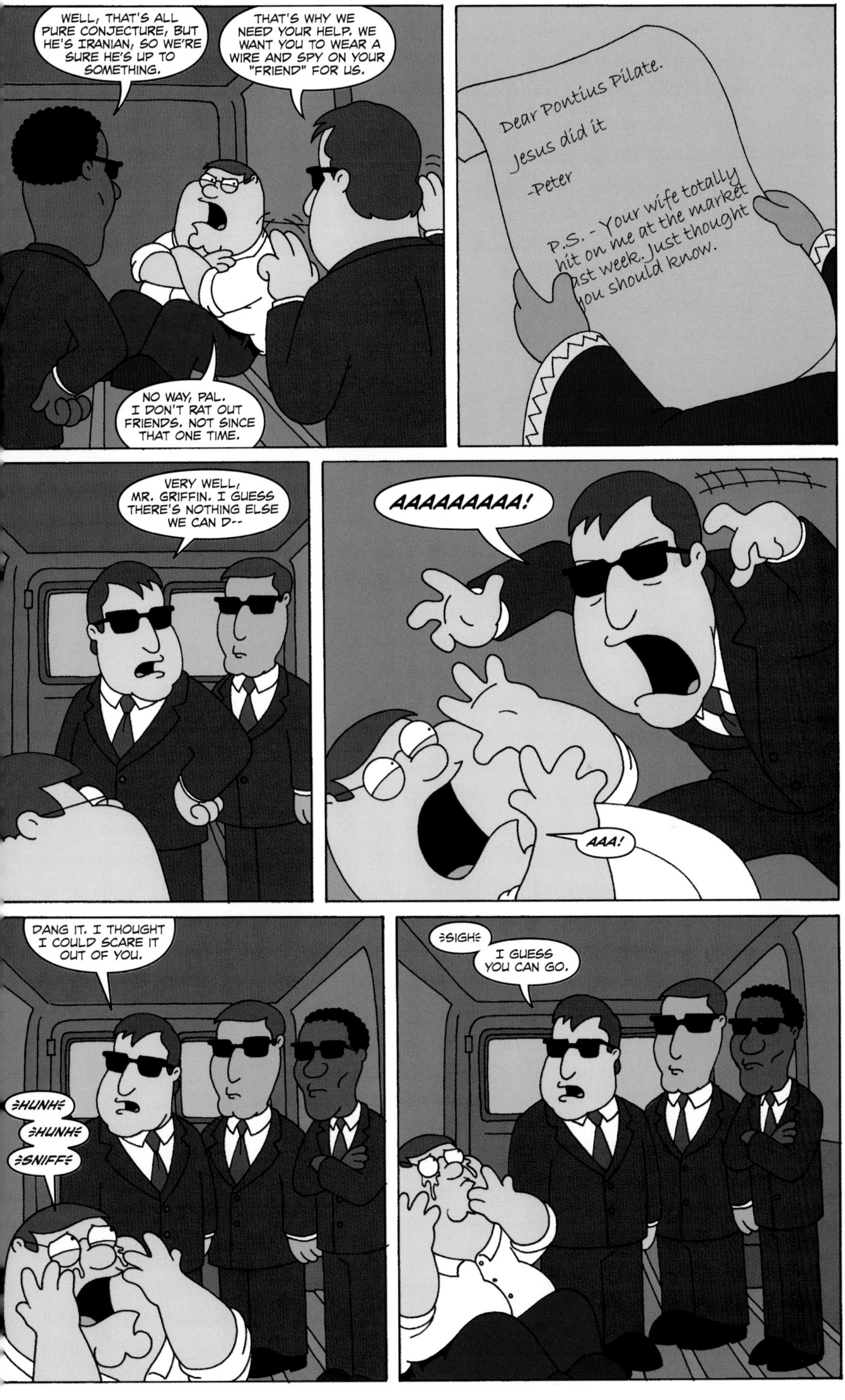
WELL, THAT'S ALL PURE CONJECTURE, BUT HE'S IRANIAN, SO WE'RE SURE HE'S UP TO SOMETHING.
THAT'S WHY WE NEED YOUR HELP. WE WANT YOU TO WEAR A WIRE AND SPY ON YOUR "FRIEND" FOR US.
NO WAY, PAL. I DON'T RAT OUT FRIENDS. NOT SINCE THAT ONE TIME.
Dear Pontius Pilate.
Jesus did it
-Peter
P.S. - Your wife totally hit on me at the market last week. Just thought you should know.
VERY WELL, MR. GRIFFIN. I GUESS THERE'S NOTHING ELSE WE CAN D--
AAAAAAAAA!
AAA!
DANG IT. I THOUGHT I COULD SCARE IT OUT OF YOU.
HUNH
HUNH
SNIFF
SIGH
I GUESS YOU CAN GO.

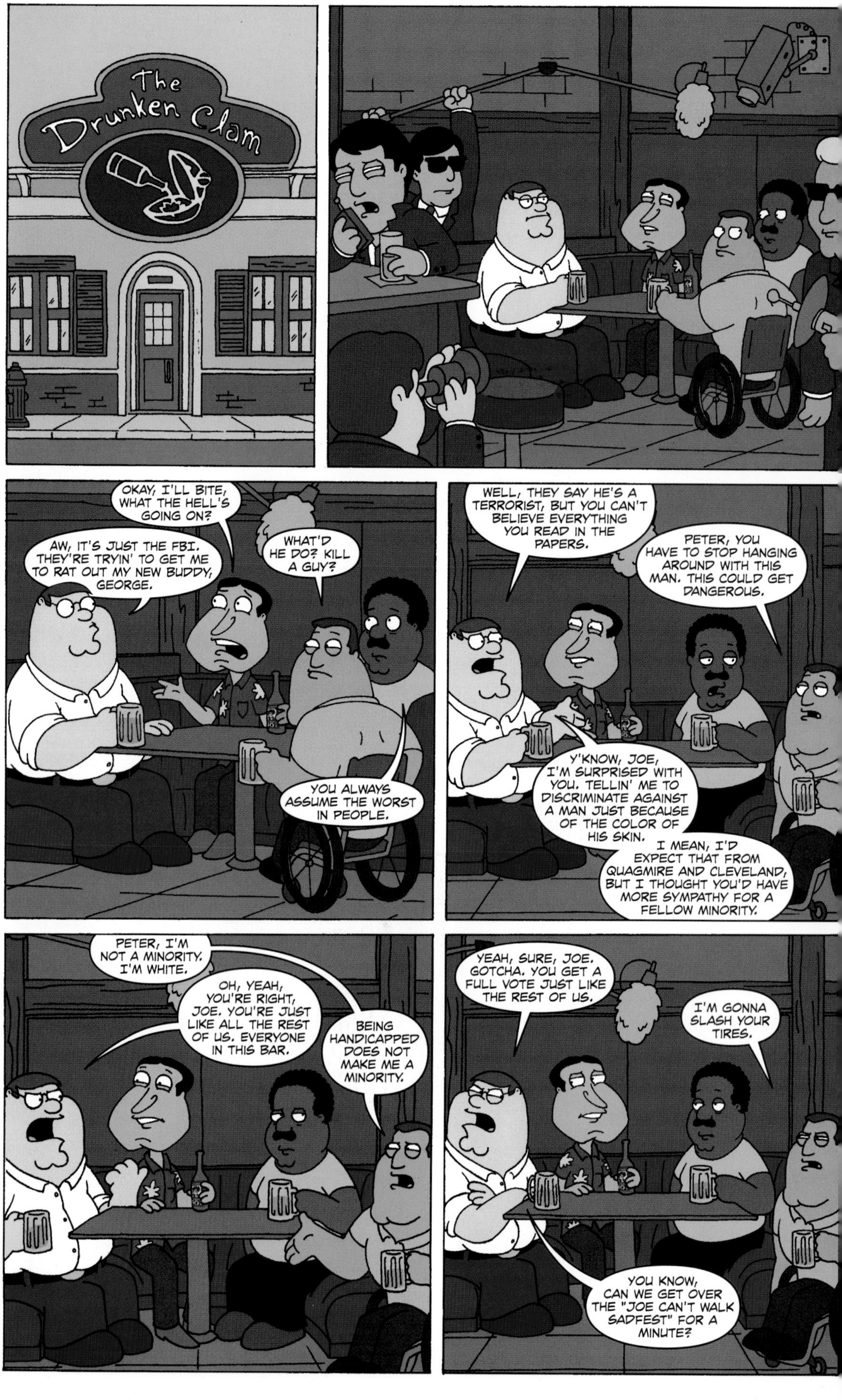
The Drunken Clam
OKAY, I'LL BITE, WHAT THE HELL'S GOING ON?
AW, IT'S JUST THE FBI. THEY'RE TRYIN' TO GET ME TO RAT OUT MY NEW BUDDY, GEORGE.
WHAT'D HE DO? KILL A GUY?
YOU ALWAYS ASSUME THE WORST IN PEOPLE.
WELL, THEY SAY HE'S A TERRORIST, BUT YOU CAN'T BELIEVE EVERYTHING YOU READ IN THE PAPERS.
PETER, YOU HAVE TO STOP HANGING AROUND WITH THIS MAN. THIS COULD GET DANGEROUS.
Y'KNOW, JOE, I'M SURPRISED WITH YOU. TELLIN' ME TO DISCRIMINATE AGAINST A MAN JUST BECAUSE OF THE COLOR OF HIS SKIN.
I MEAN, I'D EXPECT THAT FROM QUAGMIRE AND CLEVELAND, BUT I THOUGHT YOU'D HAVE MORE SYMPATHY FOR A FELLOW MINORITY.
PETER, I'M NOT A MINORITY. I'M WHITE.
OH, YEAH, YOU'RE RIGHT, JOE. YOU'RE JUST LIKE ALL THE REST OF US. EVERYONE IN THIS BAR.
BEING HANDICAPPED DOES NOT MAKE ME A MINORITY.
YEAH, SURE, JOE. GOTCHA. YOU GET A FULL VOTE JUST LIKE THE REST OF US.
I'M GONNA SLASH YOUR TIRES.
YOU KNOW, CAN WE GET OVER THE "JOE CAN'T WALK SADFEST" FOR A MINUTE?

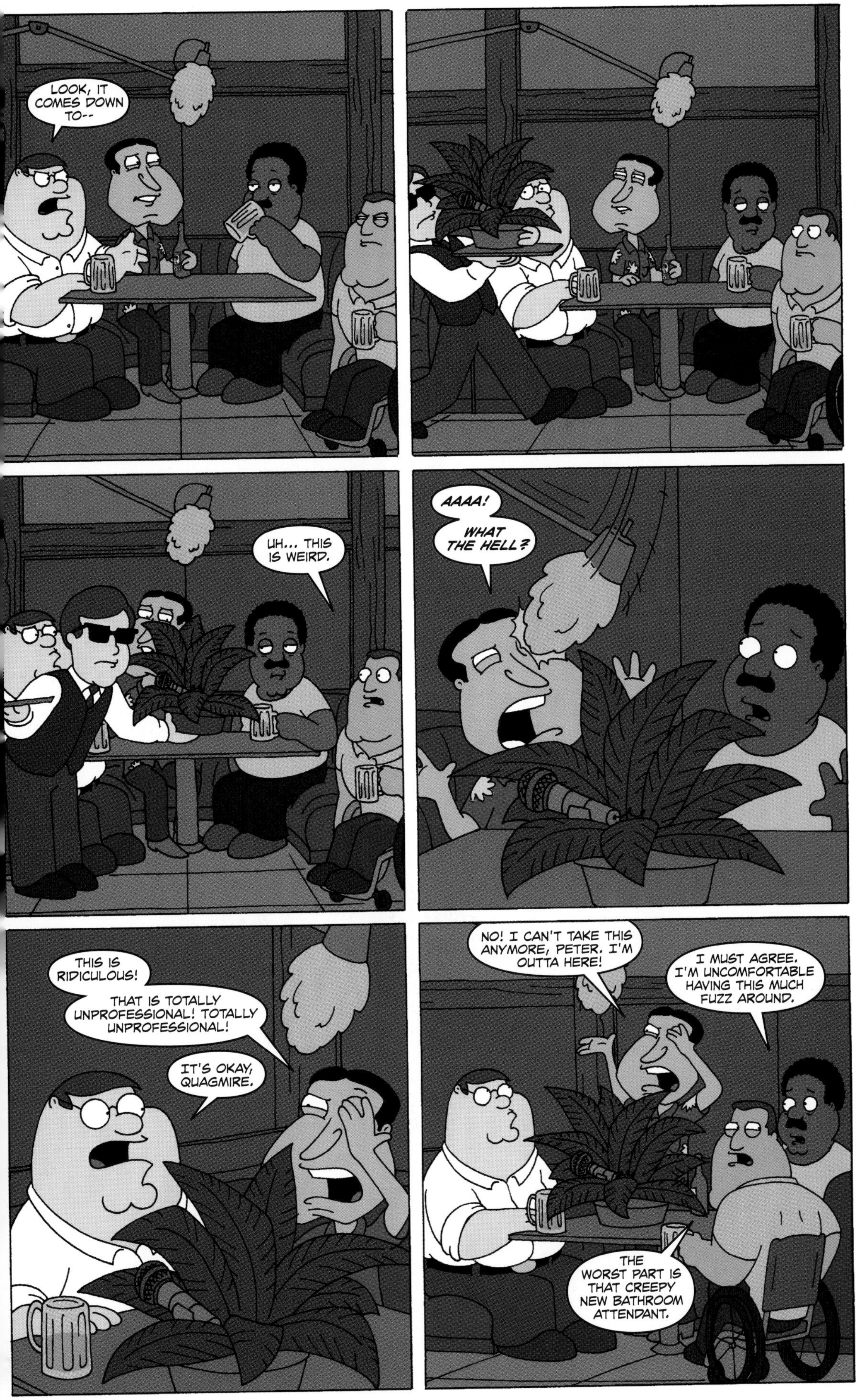
LOOK, IT COMES DOWN TO--
UH... THIS IS WEIRD.
AAAA!
WHAT THE HELL?
THIS IS RIDICULOUS!
THAT IS TOTALLY UNPROFESSIONAL! TOTALLY UNPROFESSIONAL!
IT'S OKAY, QUAGMIRE.
NO! I CAN'T TAKE THIS ANYMORE, PETER. I'M OUTTA HERE!
I MUST AGREE. I'M UNCOMFORTABLE HAVING THIS MUCH FUZZ AROUND.
THE WORST PART IS THAT CREEPY NEW BATHROOM ATTENDANT.

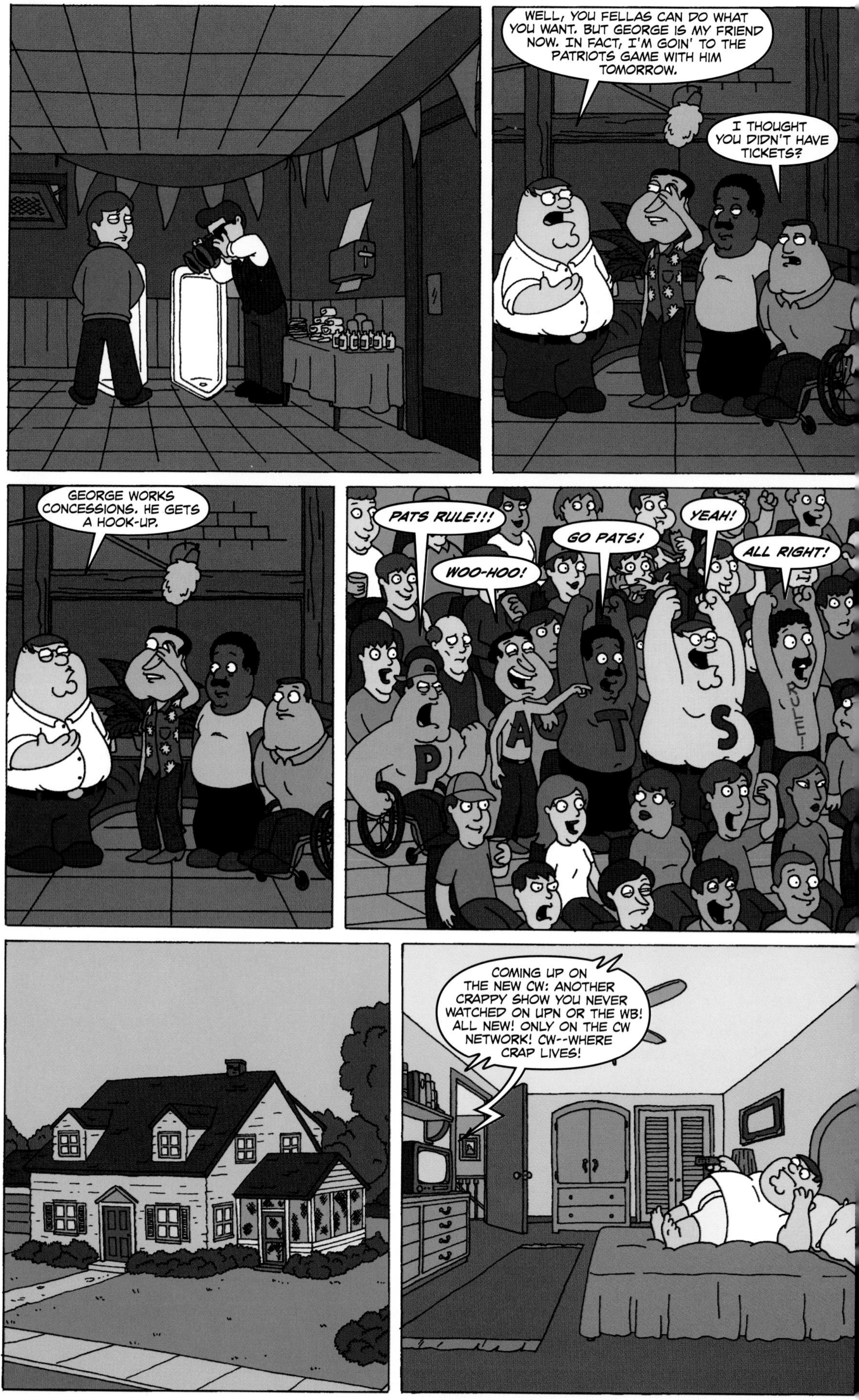
WELL, YOU FELLAS CAN DO WHAT YOU WANT. BUT GEORGE IS MY FRIEND NOW. IN FACT, I'M GOIN' TO THE PATRIOTS GAME WITH HIM TOMORROW.
I THOUGHT YOU DIDN'T HAVE TICKETS?
GEORGE WORKS CONCESSIONS. HE GETS A HOOK-UP.
PATS RULE!!!
WOO-HOO!
GO PATS!
YEAH!
ALL RIGHT!
P
A
T
S
RULE!
COMING UP ON THE NEW CW: ANOTHER CRAPPY SHOW YOU NEVER WATCHED ON UPN OR THE WB! ALL NEW! ONLY ON THE CW NETWORK! CW--WHERE CRAP LIVES!

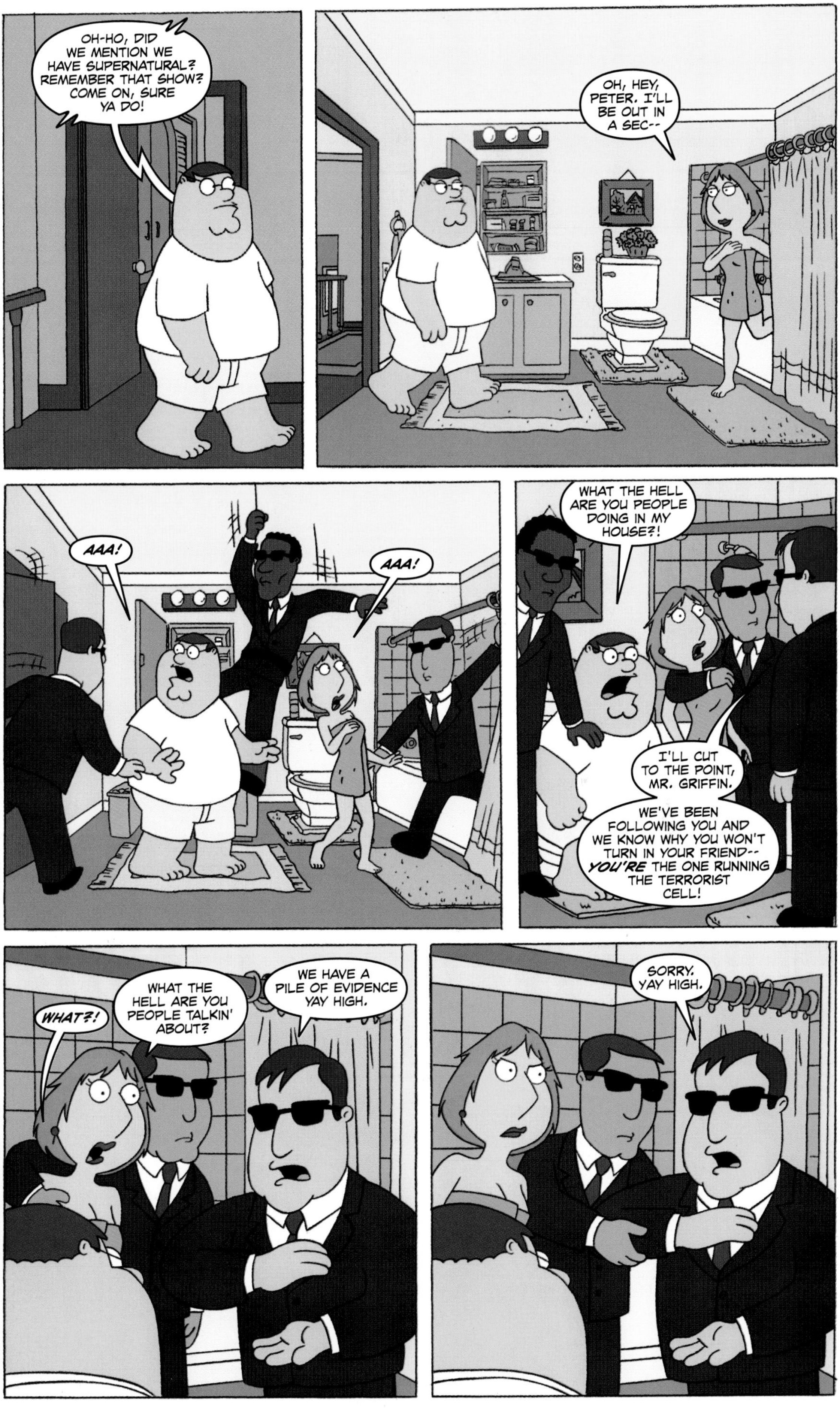
OH-HO, DID WE MENTION WE HAVE SUPERNATURAL? REMEMBER THAT SHOW? COME ON, SURE YA DO!
OH, HEY, PETER. I'LL BE OUT IN A SEC--
AAA!
AAA!
WHAT THE HELL ARE YOU PEOPLE DOING IN MY HOUSE?!
I'LL CUT TO THE POINT, MR. GRIFFIN.
WE'VE BEEN FOLLOWING YOU AND WE KNOW WHY YOU WON'T TURN IN YOUR FRIEND-- YOU'RE THE ONE RUNNING THE TERRORIST CELL!
WHAT?!
WHAT THE HELL ARE YOU PEOPLE TALKIN' ABOUT?
WE HAVE A PILE OF EVIDENCE YAY HIGH.
SORRY. YAY HIGH.

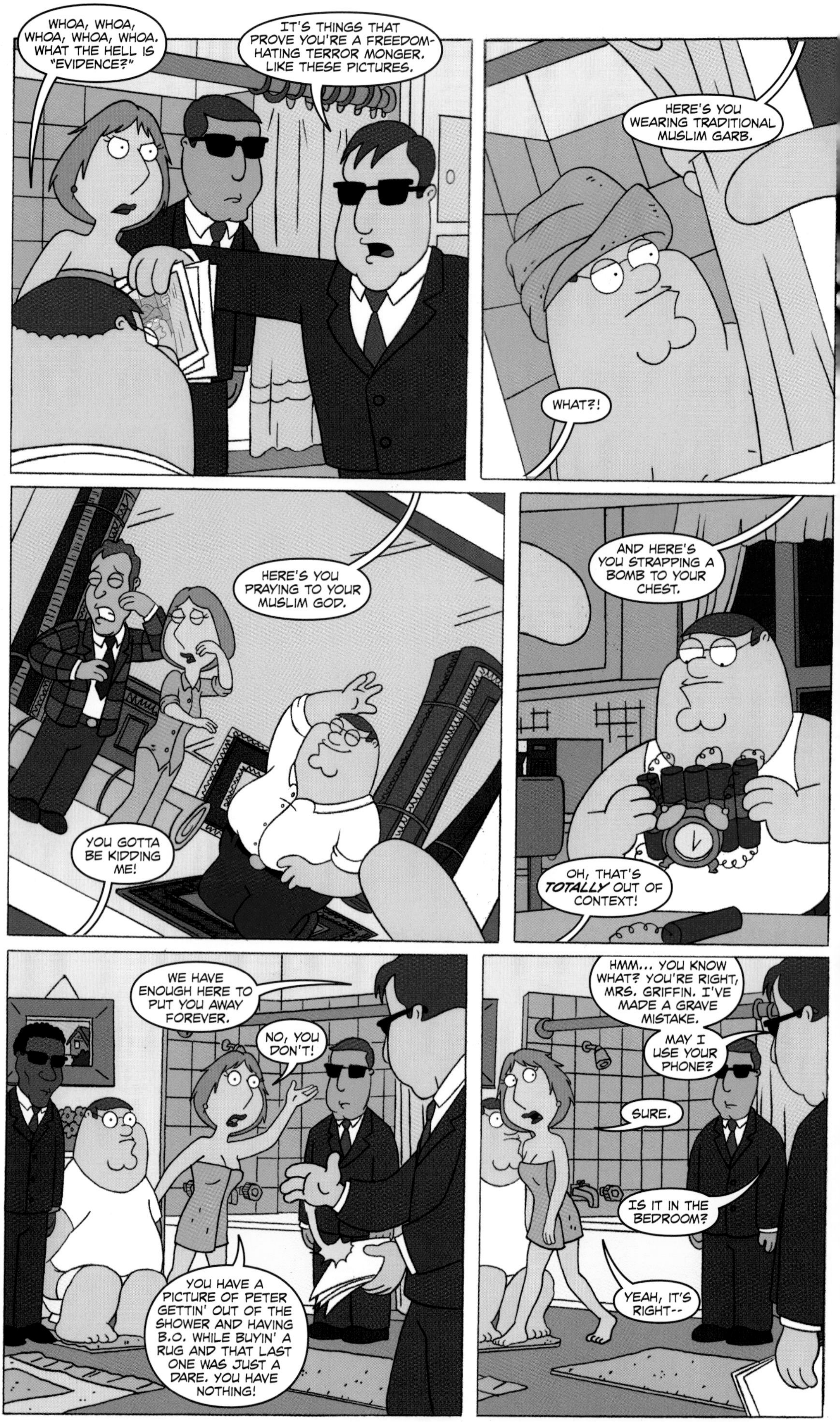
WHOA, WHOA, WHOA, WHOA, WHOA. WHAT THE HELL IS "EVIDENCE?"
IT'S THINGS THAT PROVE YOU'RE A FREEDOM-HATING TERROR MONGER. LIKE THESE PICTURES.
HERE'S YOU WEARING TRADITIONAL MUSLIM GARB.
WHAT?!
HERE'S YOU PRAYING TO YOUR MUSLIM GOD.
YOU GOTTA BE KIDDING ME!
AND HERE'S YOU STRAPPING A BOMB TO YOUR CHEST.
OH, THAT'S *TOTALLY* OUT OF CONTEXT!
WE HAVE ENOUGH HERE TO PUT YOU AWAY FOREVER.
NO, YOU DON'T!
YOU HAVE A PICTURE OF PETER GETTIN' OUT OF THE SHOWER AND HAVING B.O. WHILE BUYIN' A RUG AND THAT LAST ONE WAS JUST A DARE. YOU HAVE NOTHING!
HMM... YOU KNOW WHAT? YOU'RE RIGHT, MRS. GRIFFIN. I'VE MADE A GRAVE MISTAKE.
MAY I USE YOUR PHONE?
SURE.
IS IT IN THE BEDROOM?
YEAH, IT'S RIGHT--

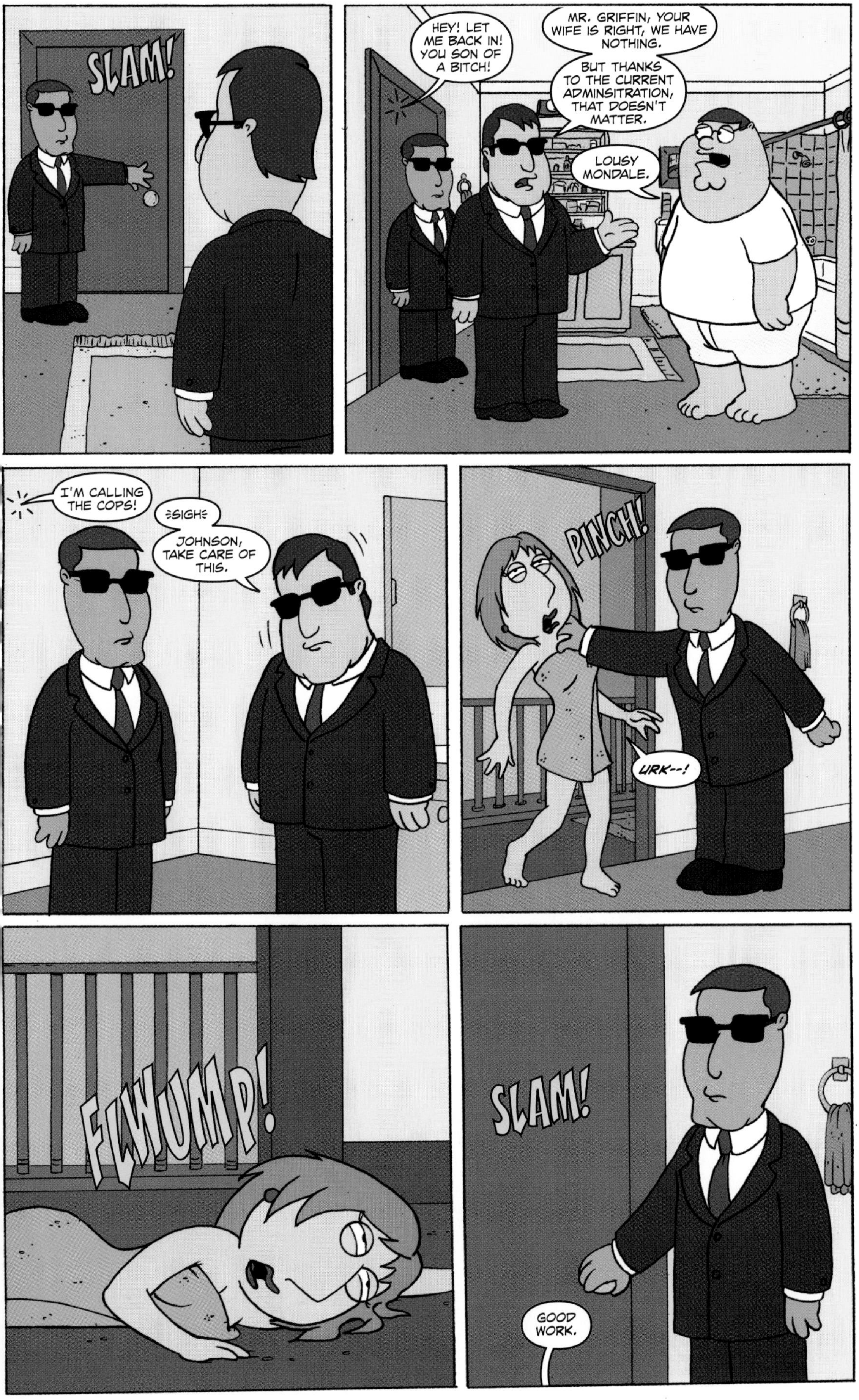
SLAM!
HEY! LET ME BACK IN! YOU SON OF A BITCH!
MR. GRIFFIN, YOUR WIFE IS RIGHT, WE HAVE NOTHING.
BUT THANKS TO THE CURRENT ADMINSITRATION, THAT DOESN'T MATTER.
LOUSY MONDALE.
I'M CALLING THE COPS!
SIGH
JOHNSON, TAKE CARE OF THIS.
PINCH!
URK--!
FLWUMP!
SLAM!
GOOD WORK.

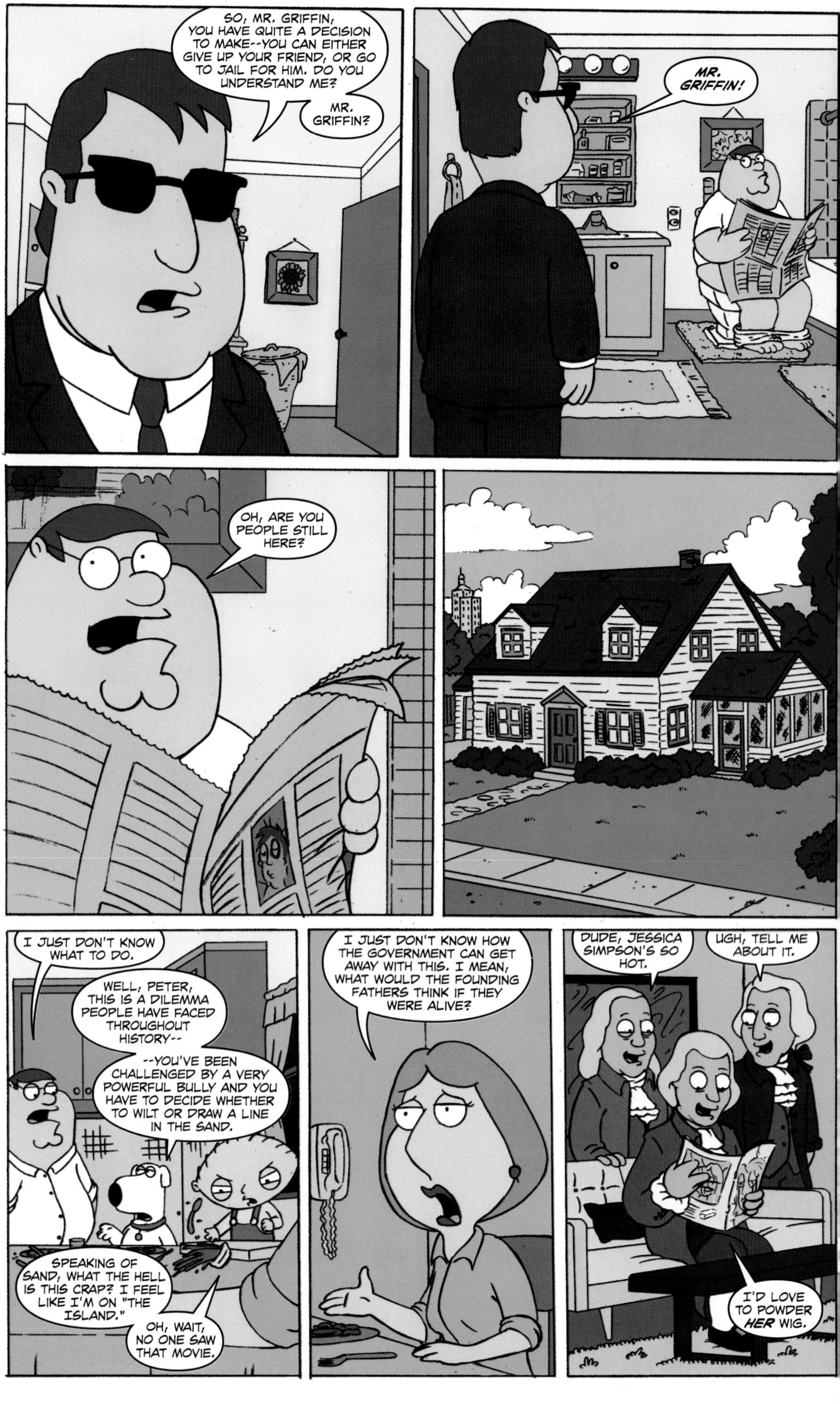
SO, MR. GRIFFIN, YOU HAVE QUITE A DECISION TO MAKE--YOU CAN EITHER GIVE UP YOUR FRIEND, OR GO TO JAIL FOR HIM. DO YOU UNDERSTAND ME?
MR. GRIFFIN?
MR. GRIFFIN!
OH, ARE YOU PEOPLE STILL HERE?
I JUST DON'T KNOW WHAT TO DO.
WELL, PETER, THIS IS A DILEMMA PEOPLE HAVE FACED THROUGHOUT HISTORY--
--YOU'VE BEEN CHALLENGED BY A VERY POWERFUL BULLY AND YOU HAVE TO DECIDE WHETHER TO WILT OR DRAW A LINE IN THE SAND.
SPEAKING OF SAND, WHAT THE HELL IS THIS CRAP? I FEEL LIKE I'M ON "THE ISLAND."
OH, WAIT, NO ONE SAW THAT MOVIE.
I JUST DON'T KNOW HOW THE GOVERNMENT CAN GET AWAY WITH THIS. I MEAN, WHAT WOULD THE FOUNDING FATHERS THINK IF THEY WERE ALIVE?
DUDE, JESSICA SIMPSON'S SO HOT.
UGH, TELL ME ABOUT IT.
I'D LOVE TO POWDER *HER* WIG.

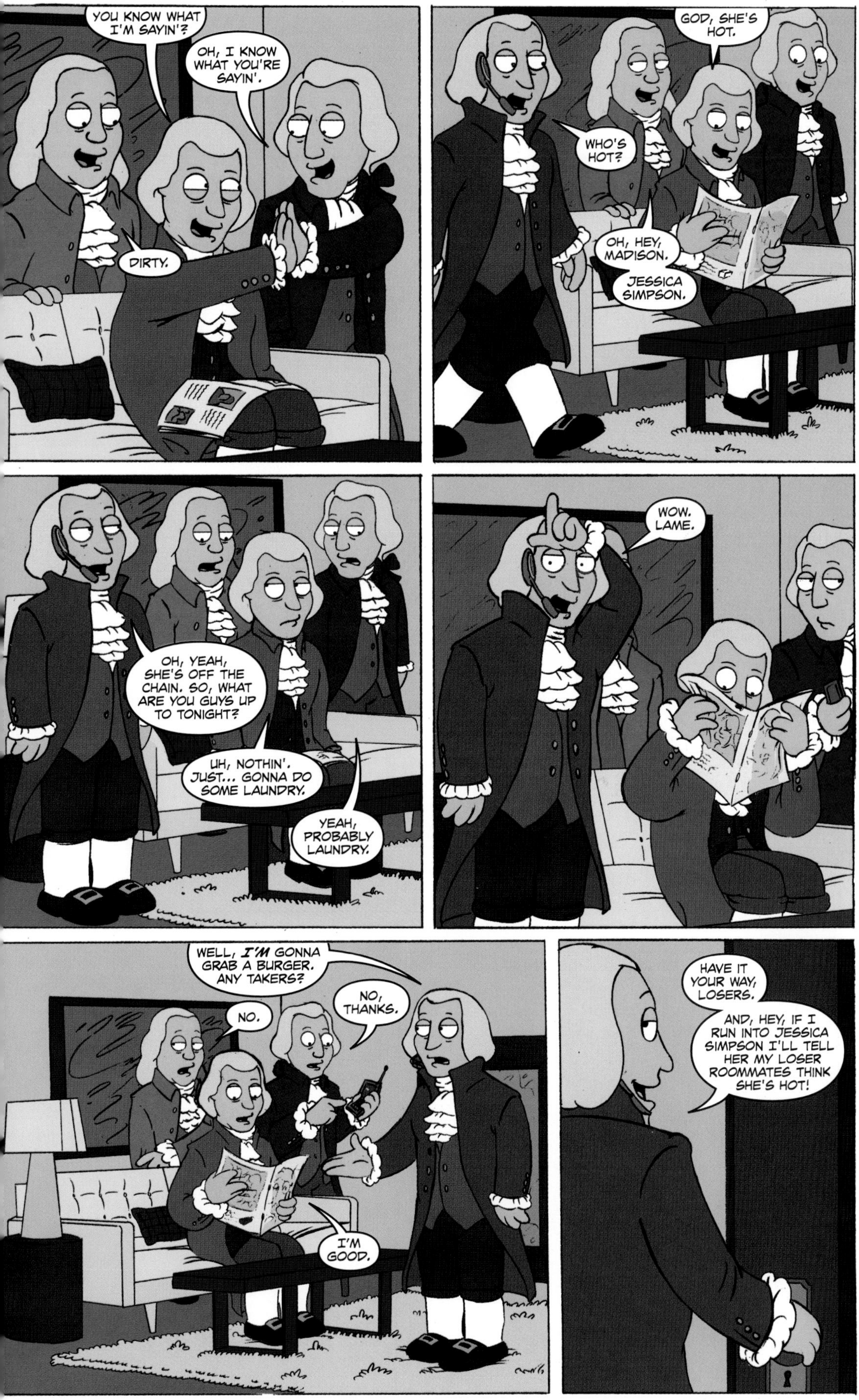
YOU KNOW WHAT I'M SAYIN'?
OH, I KNOW WHAT YOU'RE SAYIN'.
DIRTY.
GOD, SHE'S HOT.
WHO'S HOT?
OH, HEY, MADISON.
JESSICA SIMPSON.
OH, YEAH, SHE'S OFF THE CHAIN. SO, WHAT ARE YOU GUYS UP TO TONIGHT?
UH, NOTHIN'. JUST... GONNA DO SOME LAUNDRY.
YEAH, PROBABLY LAUNDRY.
WOW. LAME.
WELL, I'M GONNA GRAB A BURGER. ANY TAKERS?
NO.
NO, THANKS.
I'M GOOD.
HAVE IT YOUR WAY, LOSERS.
AND, HEY, IF I RUN INTO JESSICA SIMPSON I'LL TELL HER MY LOSER ROOMMATES THINK SHE'S HOT!

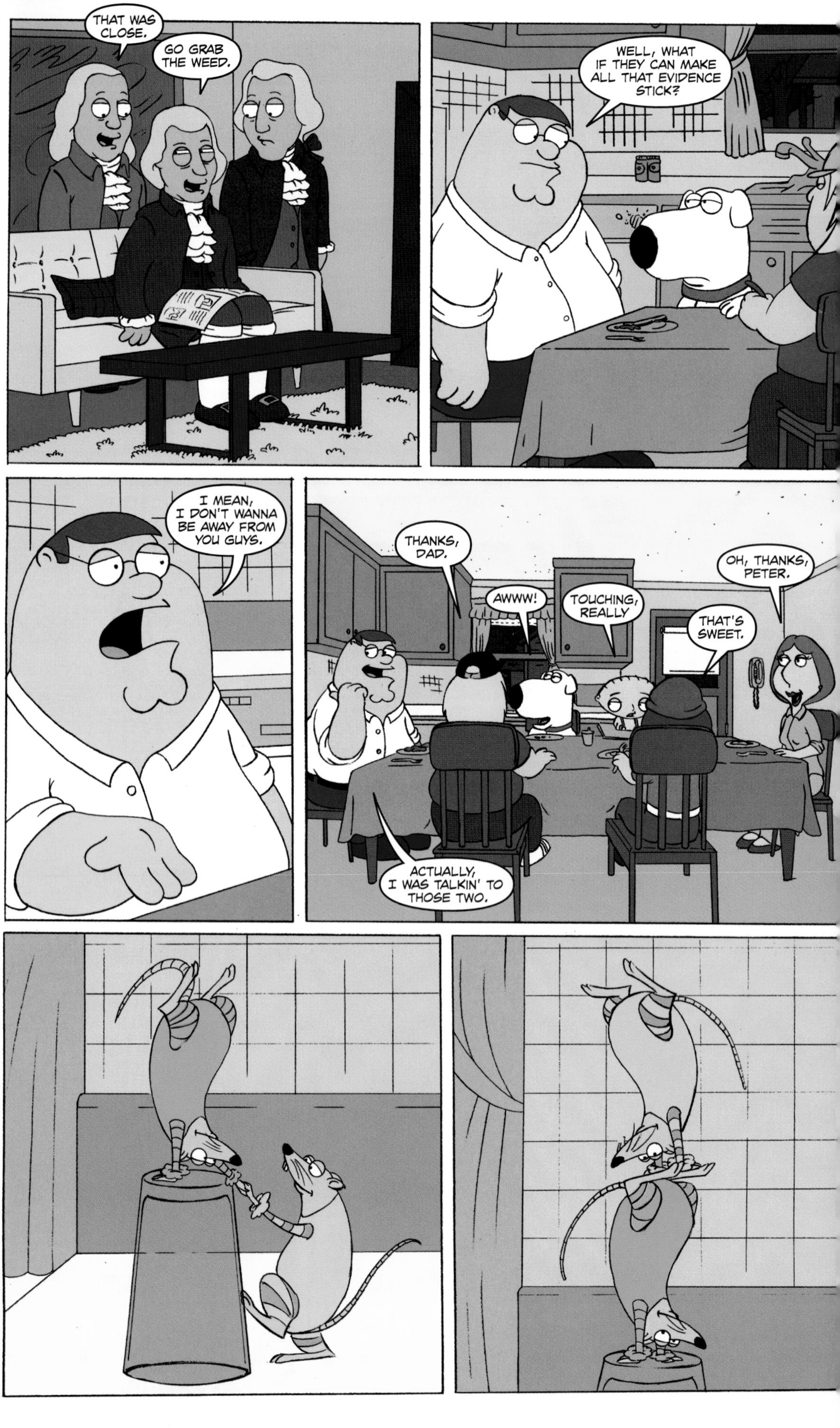
THAT WAS CLOSE.
GO GRAB THE WEED.
WELL, WHAT IF THEY CAN MAKE ALL THAT EVIDENCE STICK?
I MEAN, I DON'T WANNA BE AWAY FROM YOU GUYS.
THANKS, DAD.
AWWW!
TOUCHING, REALLY
OH, THANKS, PETER.
THAT'S SWEET.
ACTUALLY, I WAS TALKIN' TO THOSE TWO.

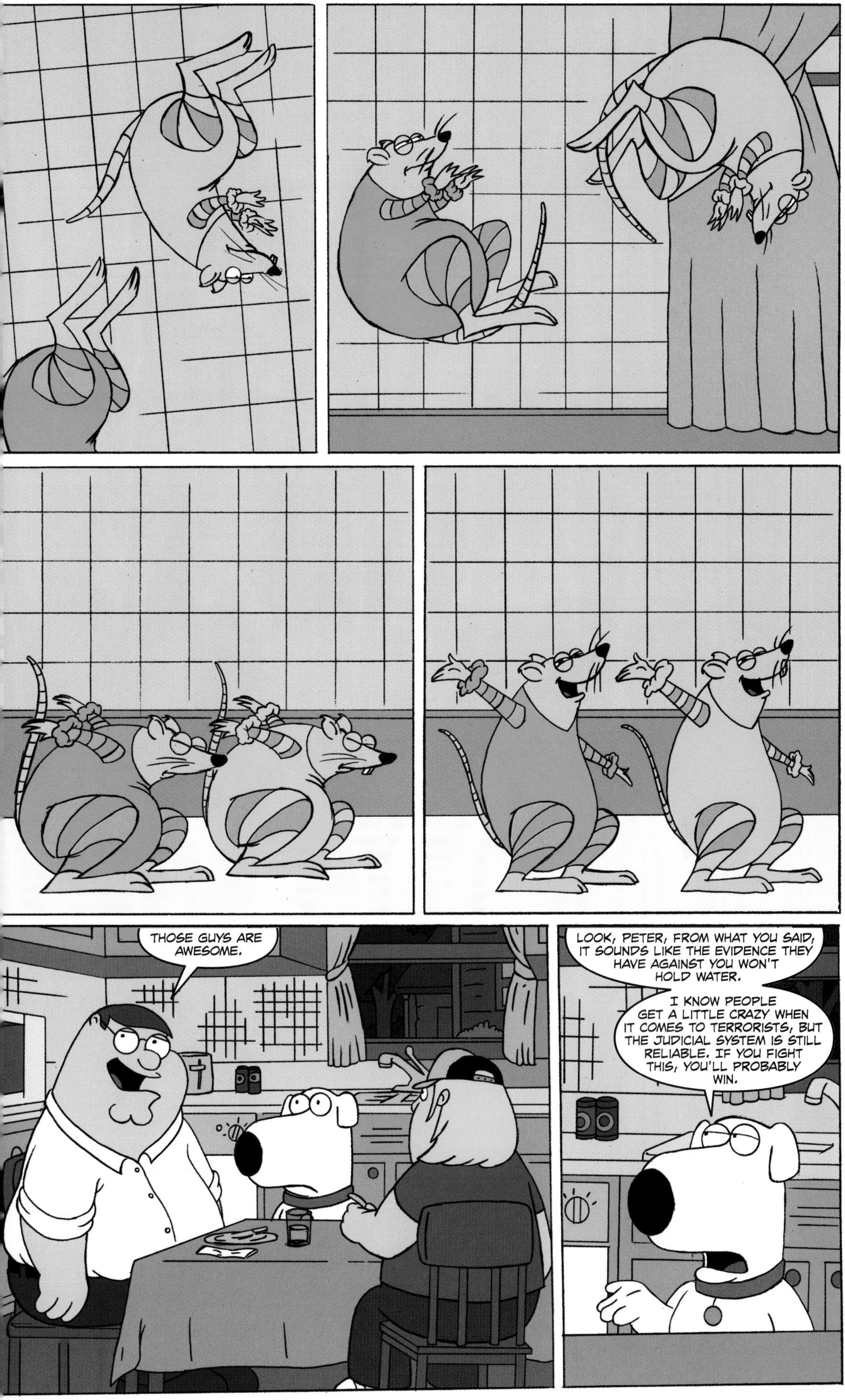
THOSE GUYS ARE AWESOME.
LOOK, PETER, FROM WHAT YOU SAID, IT SOUNDS LIKE THE EVIDENCE THEY HAVE AGAINST YOU WON'T HOLD WATER.
I KNOW PEOPLE GET A LITTLE CRAZY WHEN IT COMES TO TERRORISTS, BUT THE JUDICIAL SYSTEM IS STILL RELIABLE. IF YOU FIGHT THIS, YOU'LL PROBABLY WIN.

HE'S RIGHT, DAD. WE STUDIED SIMILAR CASES IN SCHOOL.

AT MY SCHOOL, THE GYM TEACHER MAKES US STUDY HOW HE MAKES LOVE TO HIS GIRLFRIEND IN THE BACK OF HIS SKYLARK.

THE IMPORTANT THING IS, PETER, YOU HAVE TO ABLE TO LIVE WITH THE DECISION YOU MAKE.

YOU HAVE TO LOOK INTO YOUR SOUL AND FIGURE OUT WHAT YOU NEED TO DO.

YOU'RE RIGHT, LOIS. I CAN'T LET MYSELF BE INTIMIDATED BY MEN MORE POWERFUL THAN ME. I CAN'T LET THEM TAKE AWAY MY RIGHTS AS AN AMERICAN. I HAVE TO DO WHAT'S RIGHT.

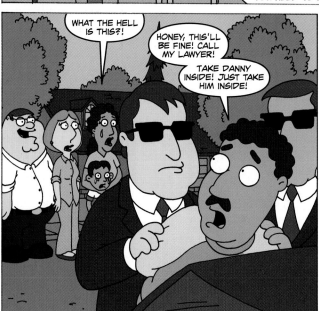

WHAT THE HELL IS THIS?!

HONEY, THIS'LL BE FINE! CALL MY LAWYER!

TAKE DANNY INSIDE! JUST TAKE HIM INSIDE!

THANK YOU FOR YOUR HELP, MR. GRIFFIN. YOU'VE DONE A REAL SERVICE FOR YOUR COUNTRY.

JUST GLAD TO HELP, SIR.

WOW, THAT IS REALLY CONVENIENT.

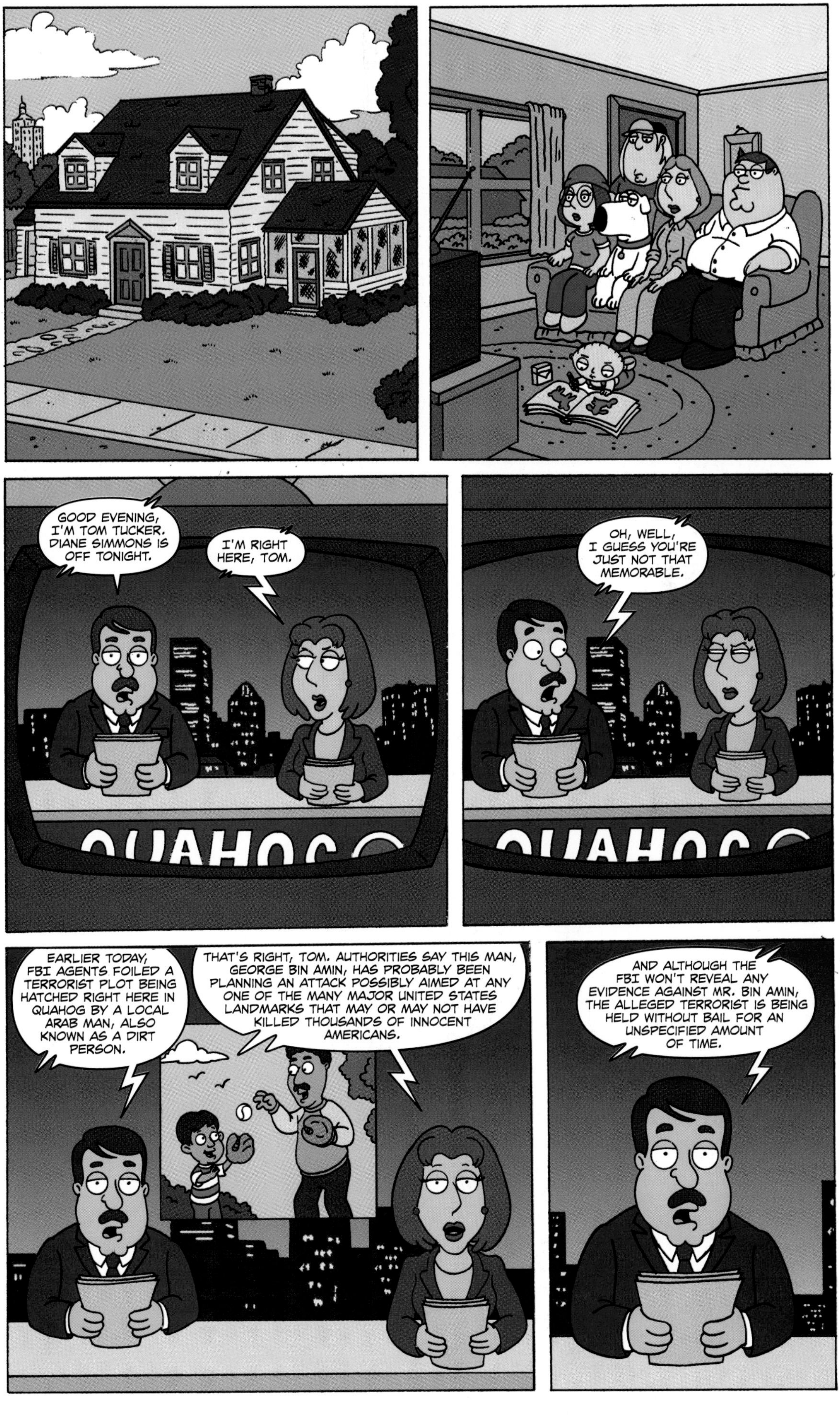
GOOD EVENING, I'M TOM TUCKER. DIANE SIMMONS IS OFF TONIGHT.
I'M RIGHT HERE, TOM.
OH, WELL, I GUESS YOU'RE JUST NOT THAT MEMORABLE.
EARLIER TODAY, FBI AGENTS FOILED A TERRORIST PLOT BEING HATCHED RIGHT HERE IN QUAHOG BY A LOCAL ARAB MAN, ALSO KNOWN AS A DIRT PERSON.
THAT'S RIGHT, TOM. AUTHORITIES SAY THIS MAN, GEORGE BIN AMIN, HAS PROBABLY BEEN PLANNING AN ATTACK POSSIBLY AIMED AT ANY ONE OF THE MANY MAJOR UNITED STATES LANDMARKS THAT MAY OR MAY NOT HAVE KILLED THOUSANDS OF INNOCENT AMERICANS.
AND ALTHOUGH THE FBI WON'T REVEAL ANY EVIDENCE AGAINST MR. BIN AMIN, THE ALLEGED TERRORIST IS BEING HELD WITHOUT BAIL FOR AN UNSPECIFIED AMOUNT OF TIME.

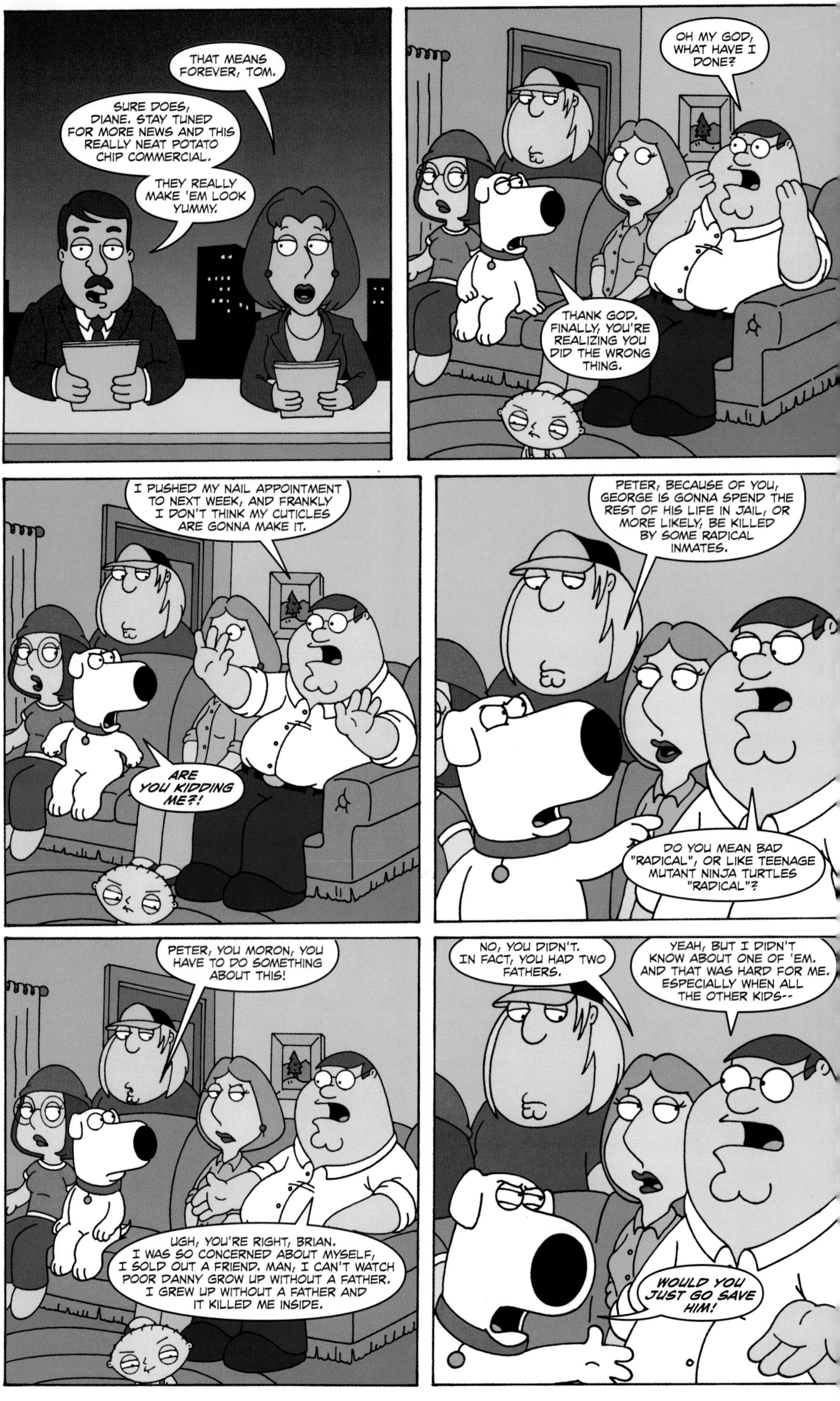
THAT MEANS FOREVER, TOM.
SURE DOES, DIANE. STAY TUNED FOR MORE NEWS AND THIS REALLY NEAT POTATO CHIP COMMERCIAL.
THEY REALLY MAKE 'EM LOOK YUMMY.
OH MY GOD, WHAT HAVE I DONE?
THANK GOD. FINALLY, YOU'RE REALIZING YOU DID THE WRONG THING.
I PUSHED MY NAIL APPOINTMENT TO NEXT WEEK, AND FRANKLY I DON'T THINK MY CUTICLES ARE GONNA MAKE IT.
ARE YOU KIDDING ME?!
PETER, BECAUSE OF YOU, GEORGE IS GONNA SPEND THE REST OF HIS LIFE IN JAIL, OR MORE LIKELY, BE KILLED BY SOME RADICAL INMATES.
DO YOU MEAN BAD "RADICAL", OR LIKE TEENAGE MUTANT NINJA TURTLES "RADICAL"?
PETER, YOU MORON, YOU HAVE TO DO SOMETHING ABOUT THIS!
UGH, YOU'RE RIGHT, BRIAN. I WAS SO CONCERNED ABOUT MYSELF, I SOLD OUT A FRIEND. MAN, I CAN'T WATCH POOR DANNY GROW UP WITHOUT A FATHER. I GREW UP WITHOUT A FATHER AND IT KILLED ME INSIDE.
NO, YOU DIDN'T. IN FACT, YOU HAD TWO FATHERS.
YEAH, BUT I DIDN'T KNOW ABOUT ONE OF 'EM. AND THAT WAS HARD FOR ME. ESPECIALLY WHEN ALL THE OTHER KIDS--
WOULD YOU JUST GO SAVE HIM!

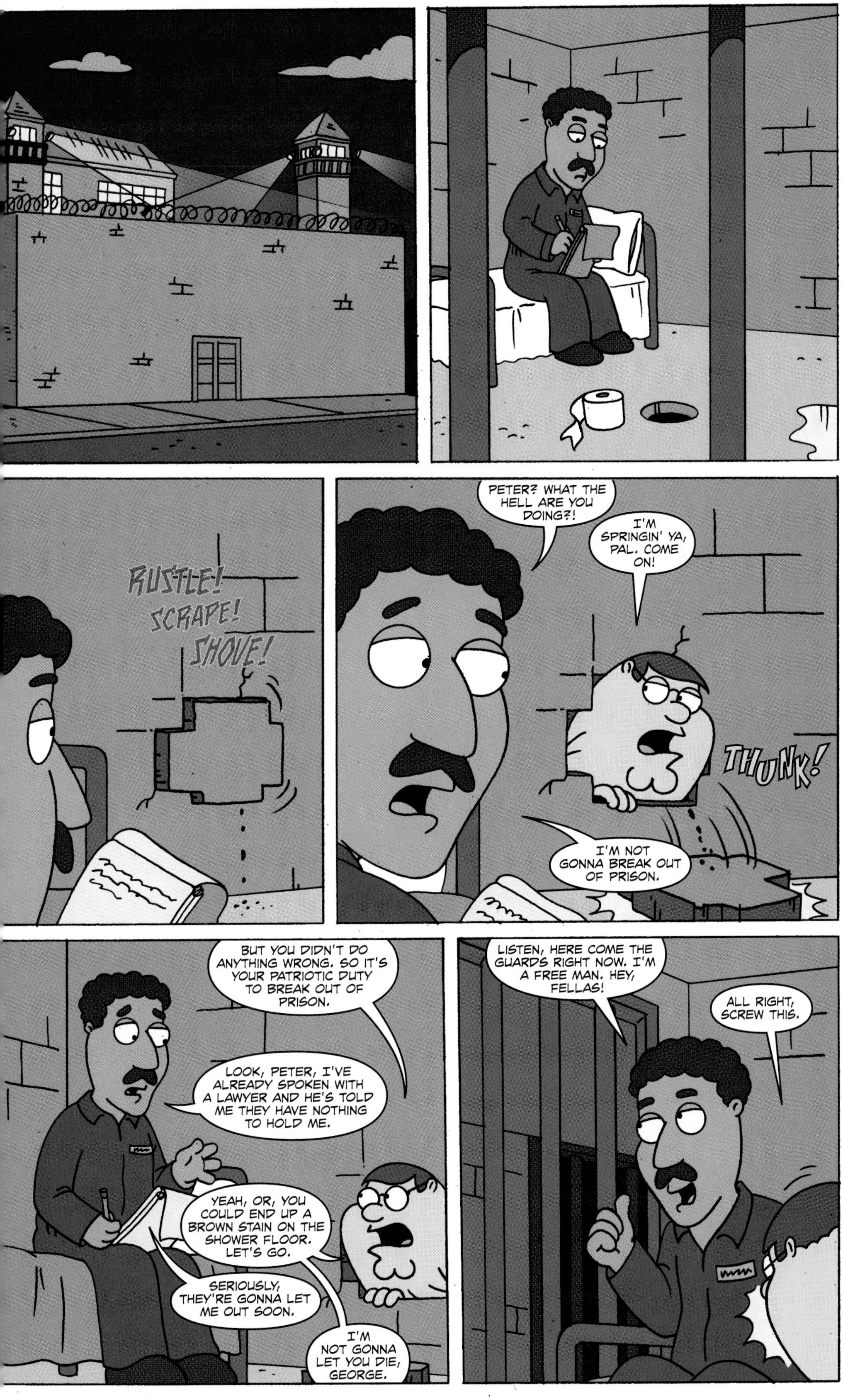
RUSTLE!
SCRAPE!
SHOVE!
PETER? WHAT THE HELL ARE YOU DOING?!
I'M SPRINGIN' YA, PAL. COME ON!
THUNK!
I'M NOT GONNA BREAK OUT OF PRISON.
BUT YOU DIDN'T DO ANYTHING WRONG. SO IT'S YOUR PATRIOTIC DUTY TO BREAK OUT OF PRISON.
LOOK, PETER, I'VE ALREADY SPOKEN WITH A LAWYER AND HE'S TOLD ME THEY HAVE NOTHING TO HOLD ME.
YEAH, OR, YOU COULD END UP A BROWN STAIN ON THE SHOWER FLOOR. LET'S GO.
SERIOUSLY, THEY'RE GONNA LET ME OUT SOON.
I'M NOT GONNA LET YOU DIE, GEORGE.
LISTEN, HERE COME THE GUARDS RIGHT NOW. I'M A FREE MAN. HEY, FELLAS!
ALL RIGHT, SCREW THIS.

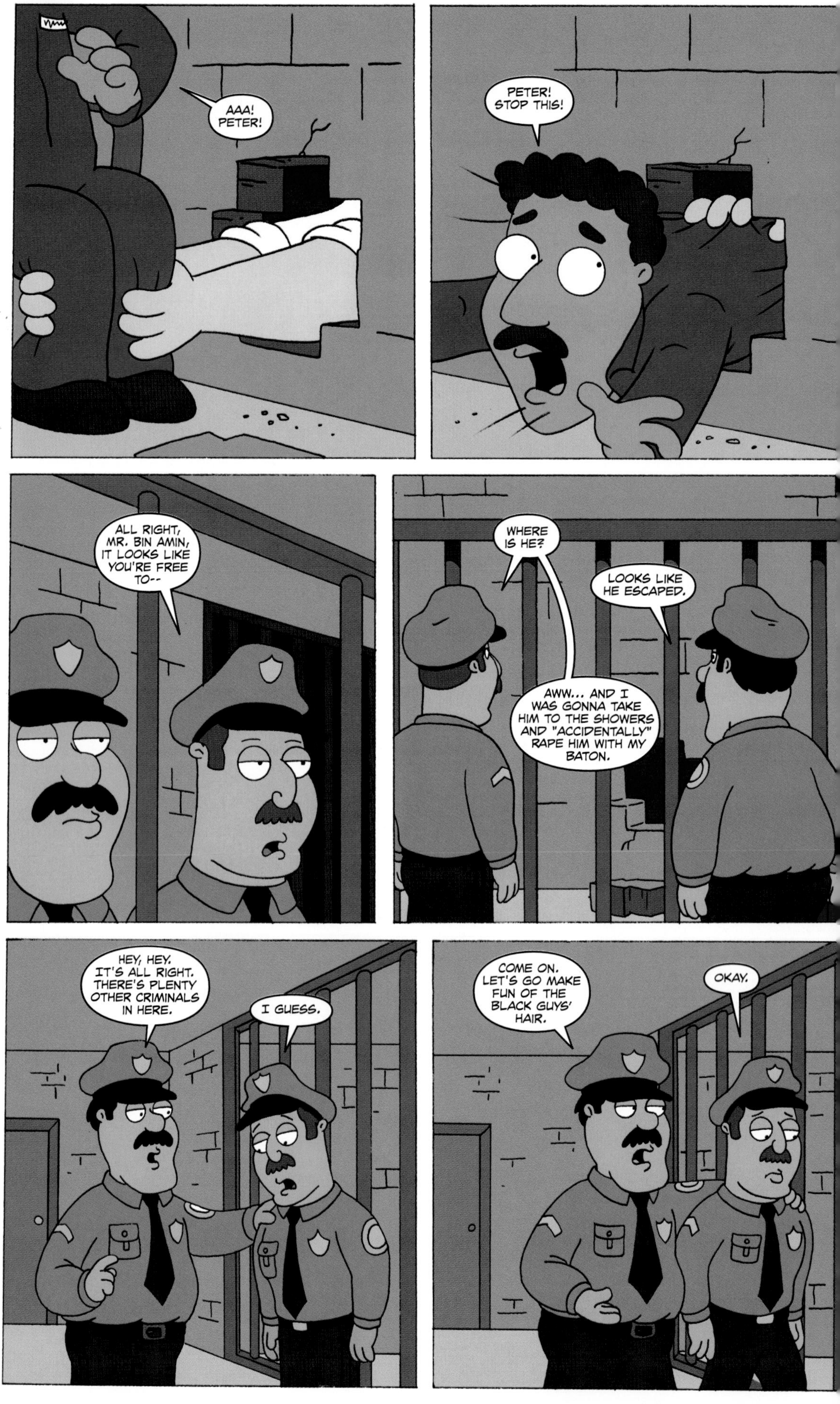
AAA! PETER!
PETER! STOP THIS!
ALL RIGHT, MR. BIN AMIN, IT LOOKS LIKE YOU'RE FREE TO--
WHERE IS HE?
LOOKS LIKE HE ESCAPED.
AWW... AND I WAS GONNA TAKE HIM TO THE SHOWERS AND "ACCIDENTALLY" RAPE HIM WITH MY BATON.
HEY, HEY. IT'S ALL RIGHT. THERE'S PLENTY OTHER CRIMINALS IN HERE.
I GUESS.
COME ON. LET'S GO MAKE FUN OF THE BLACK GUYS' HAIR.
OKAY.

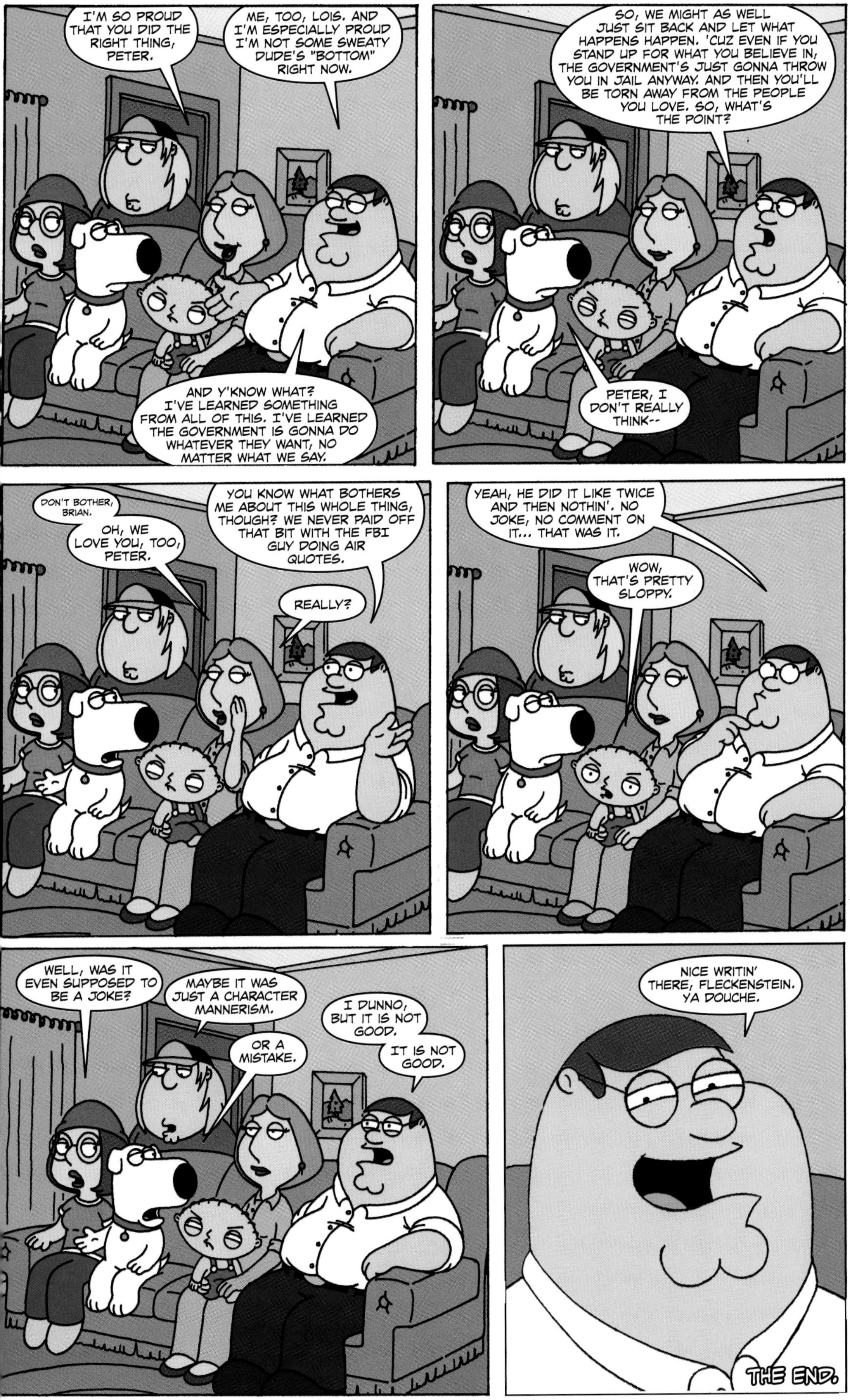

I'M SO PROUD THAT YOU DID THE RIGHT THING, PETER.
ME, TOO, LOIS. AND I'M ESPECIALLY PROUD I'M NOT SOME SWEATY DUDE'S "BOTTOM" RIGHT NOW.
AND Y'KNOW WHAT? I'VE LEARNED SOMETHING FROM ALL OF THIS. I'VE LEARNED THE GOVERNMENT IS GONNA DO WHATEVER THEY WANT, NO MATTER WHAT WE SAY.
SO, WE MIGHT AS WELL JUST SIT BACK AND LET WHAT HAPPENS HAPPEN. 'CUZ EVEN IF YOU STAND UP FOR WHAT YOU BELIEVE IN, THE GOVERNMENT'S JUST GONNA THROW YOU IN JAIL ANYWAY. AND THEN YOU'LL BE TORN AWAY FROM THE PEOPLE YOU LOVE. SO, WHAT'S THE POINT?
PETER, I DON'T REALLY THINK--
DON'T BOTHER, BRIAN.
OH, WE LOVE YOU, TOO, PETER.
YOU KNOW WHAT BOTHERS ME ABOUT THIS WHOLE THING, THOUGH? WE NEVER PAID OFF THAT BIT WITH THE FBI GUY DOING AIR QUOTES.
REALLY?
YEAH, HE DID IT LIKE TWICE AND THEN NOTHIN'. NO JOKE, NO COMMENT ON IT... THAT WAS IT.
WOW, THAT'S PRETTY SLOPPY.
WELL, WAS IT EVEN SUPPOSED TO BE A JOKE?
MAYBE IT WAS JUST A CHARACTER MANNERISM.
OR A MISTAKE.
I DUNNO, BUT IT IS NOT GOOD.
IT IS NOT GOOD.
NICE WRITIN' THERE, FLECKENSTEIN. YA DOUCHE.
THE END.

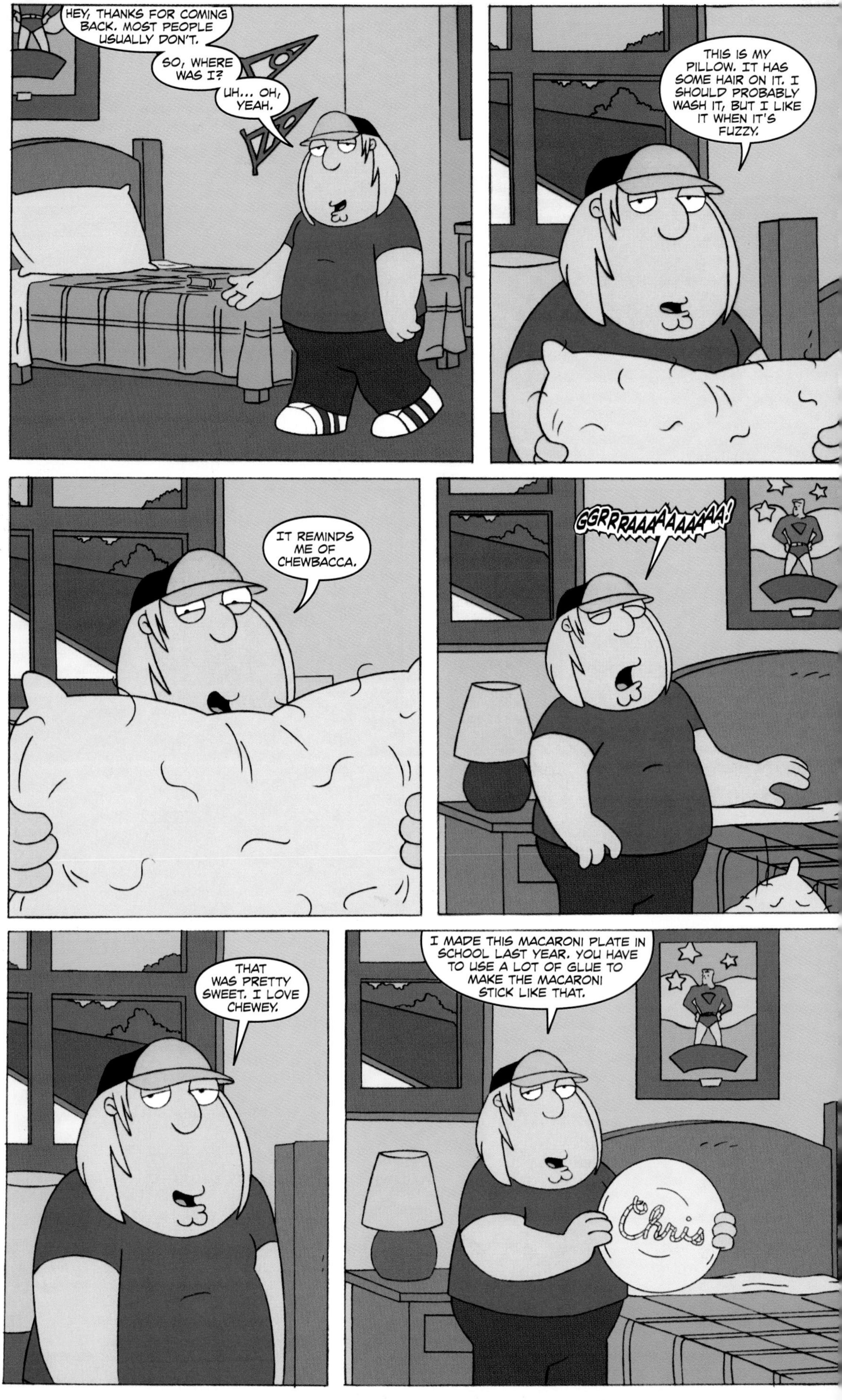
HEY, THANKS FOR COMING BACK. MOST PEOPLE USUALLY DON'T.
SO, WHERE WAS I?
UH... OH, YEAH.
THIS IS MY PILLOW. IT HAS SOME HAIR ON IT. I SHOULD PROBABLY WASH IT, BUT I LIKE IT WHEN IT'S FUZZY.
IT REMINDS ME OF CHEWBACCA.
GGRRRAAAAAAAAA!
THAT WAS PRETTY SWEET. I LOVE CHEWEY.
I MADE THIS MACARONI PLATE IN SCHOOL LAST YEAR. YOU HAVE TO USE A LOT OF GLUE TO MAKE THE MACARONI STICK LIKE THAT.
Chris

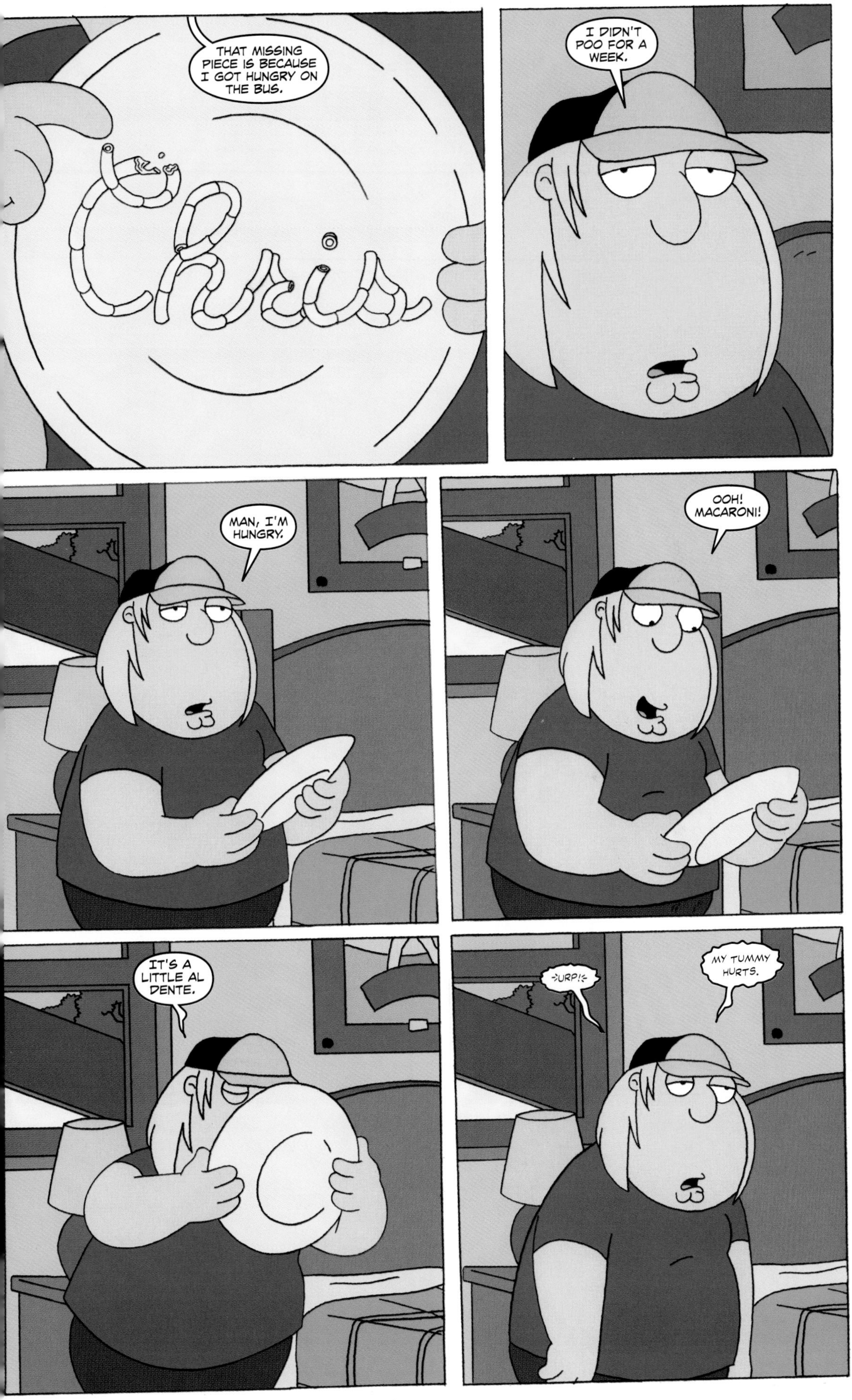
THAT MISSING PIECE IS BECAUSE I GOT HUNGRY ON THE BUS.
Chris
I DIDN'T POO FOR A WEEK.
MAN, I'M HUNGRY.
OOH! MACARONI!
IT'S A LITTLE AL DENTE.
URP!
MY TUMMY HURTS.

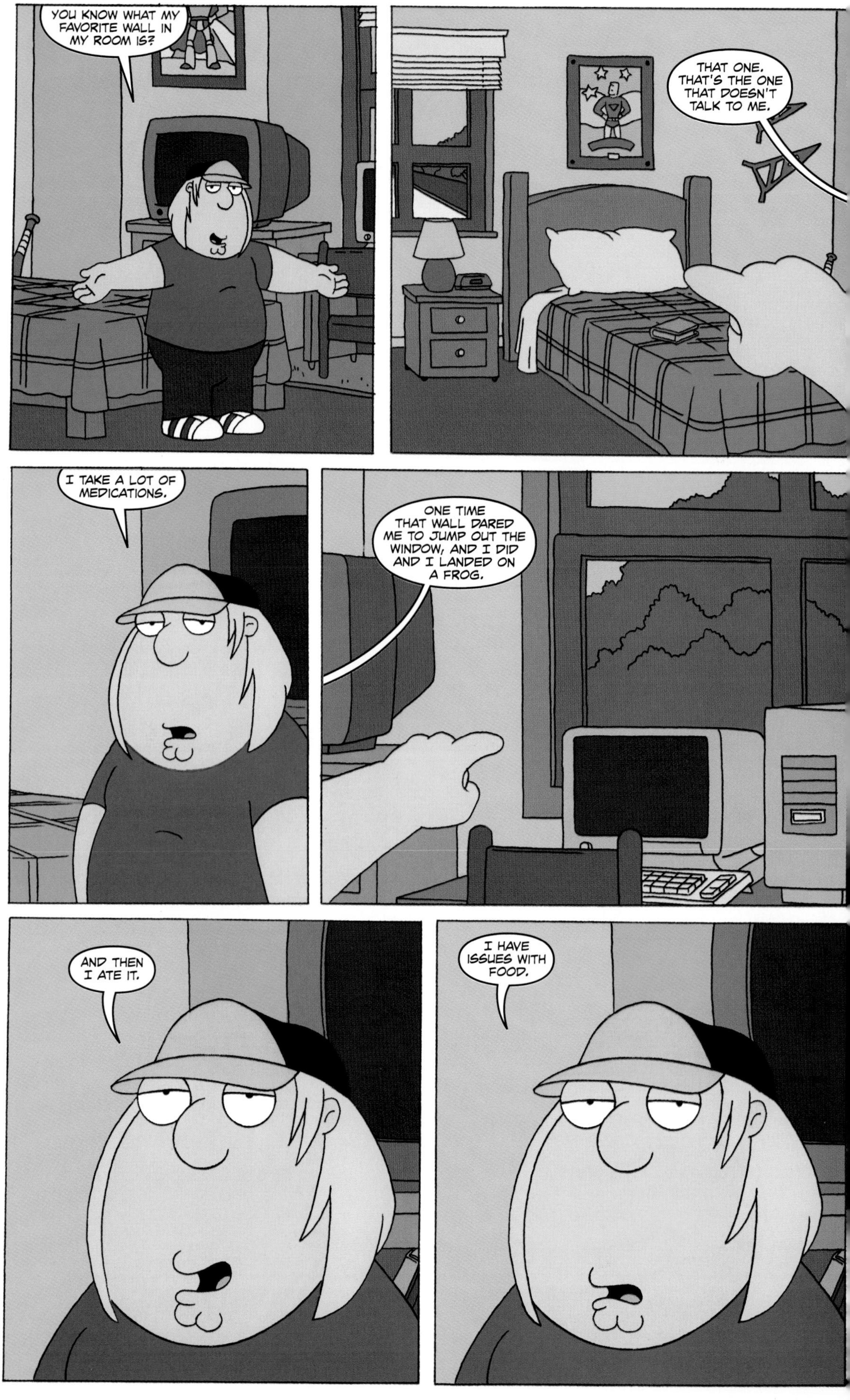
YOU KNOW WHAT MY FAVORITE WALL IN MY ROOM IS?
THAT ONE. THAT'S THE ONE THAT DOESN'T TALK TO ME.
I TAKE A LOT OF MEDICATIONS.
ONE TIME THAT WALL DARED ME TO JUMP OUT THE WINDOW, AND I DID AND I LANDED ON A FROG.
AND THEN I ATE IT.
I HAVE ISSUES WITH FOOD.

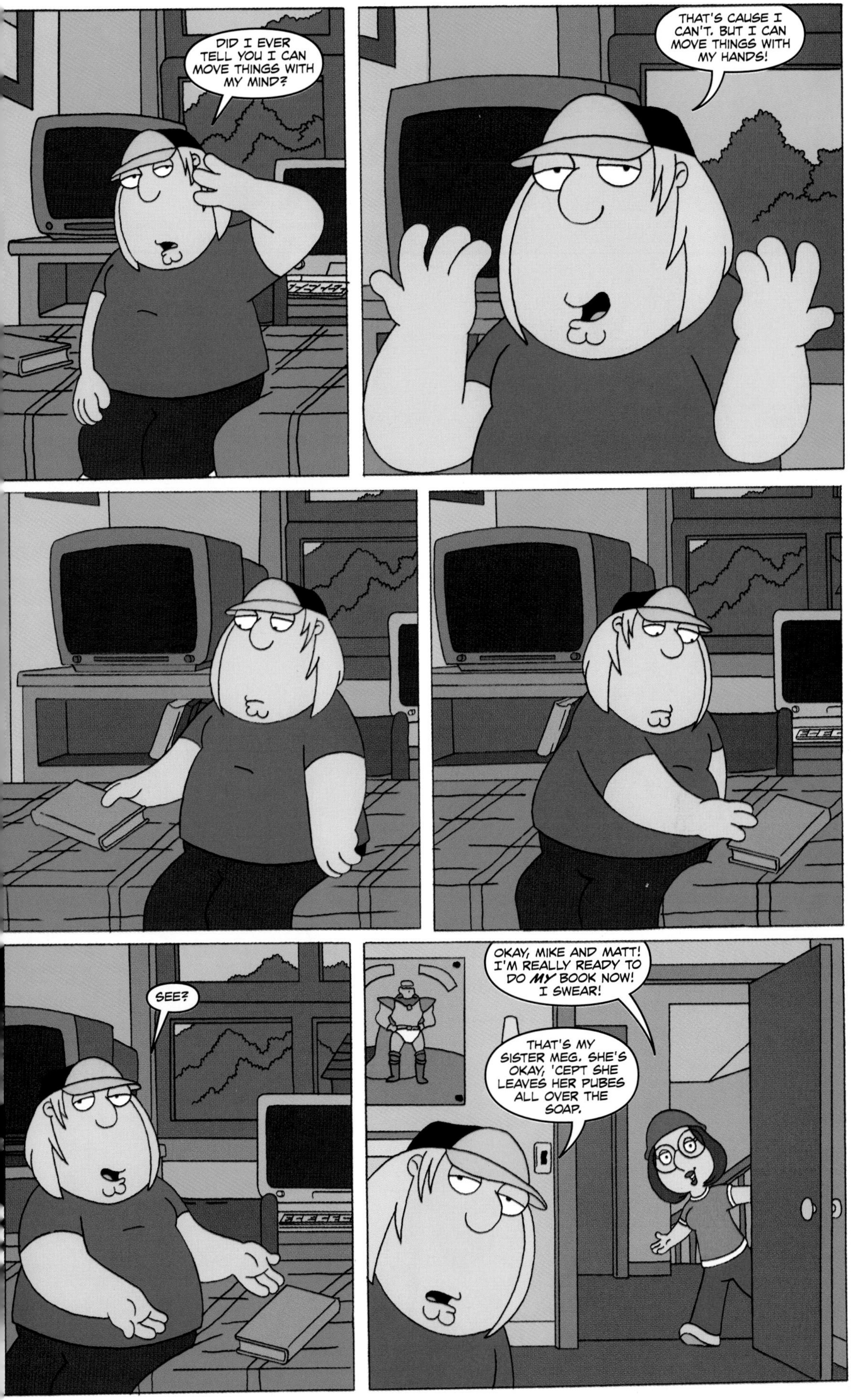
DID I EVER TELL YOU I CAN MOVE THINGS WITH MY MIND?
THAT'S CAUSE I CAN'T. BUT I CAN MOVE THINGS WITH MY HANDS!
SEE?
OKAY, MIKE AND MATT! I'M REALLY READY TO DO *MY* BOOK NOW! I SWEAR!
THAT'S MY SISTER MEG. SHE'S OKAY, 'CEPT SHE LEAVES HER PUBES ALL OVER THE SOAP.

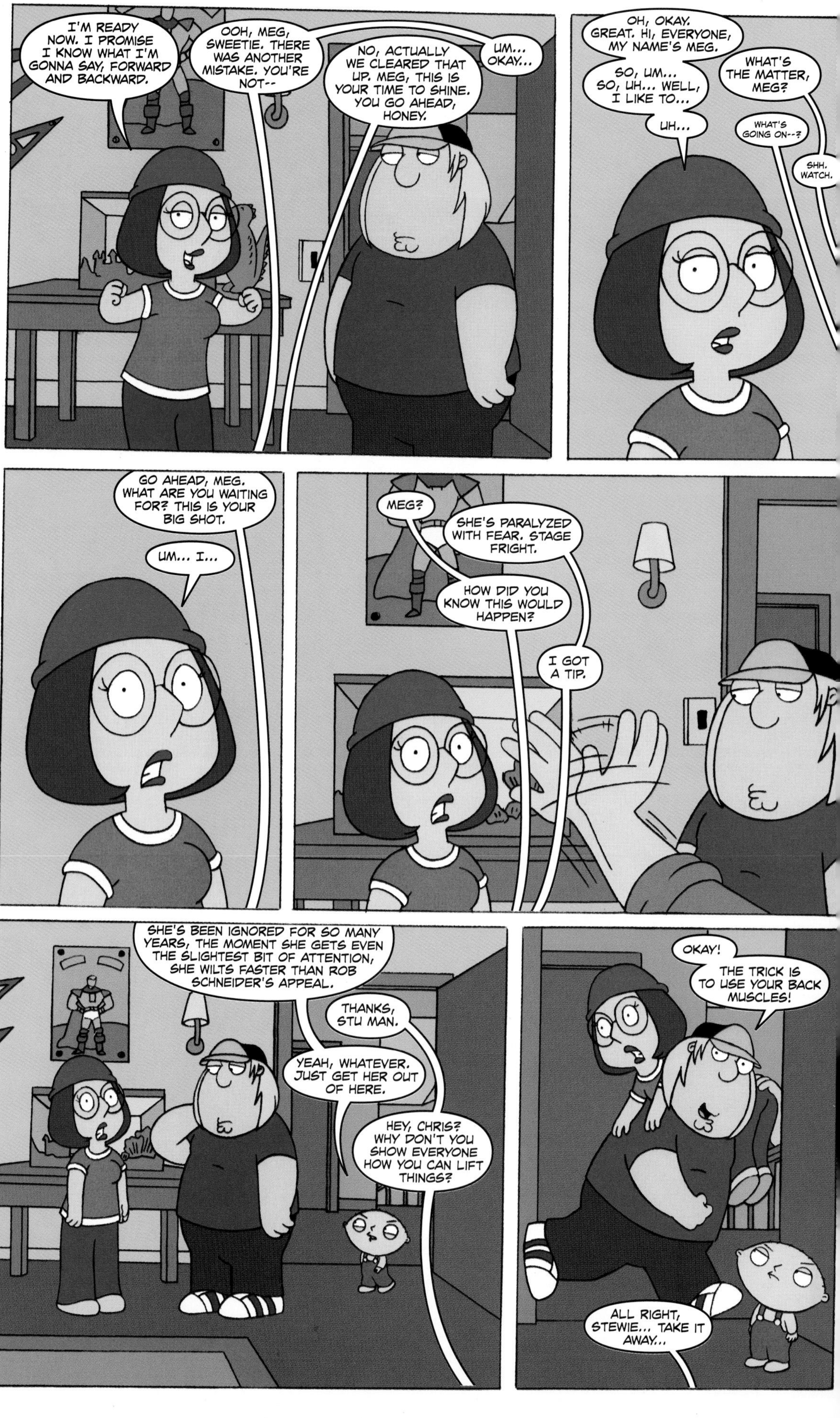
I'M READY NOW. I PROMISE I KNOW WHAT I'M GONNA SAY, FORWARD AND BACKWARD.
OOH, MEG, SWEETIE. THERE WAS ANOTHER MISTAKE. YOU'RE NOT--
NO, ACTUALLY WE CLEARED THAT UP. MEG, THIS IS YOUR TIME TO SHINE. YOU GO AHEAD, HONEY.
UM... OKAY...
OH, OKAY. GREAT. HI, EVERYONE, MY NAME'S MEG.
SO, UM... SO, UH... WELL, I LIKE TO...
UH...
WHAT'S THE MATTER, MEG?
WHAT'S GOING ON--?
SHH. WATCH.
GO AHEAD, MEG. WHAT ARE YOU WAITING FOR? THIS IS YOUR BIG SHOT.
UM... I...
MEG?
SHE'S PARALYZED WITH FEAR. STAGE FRIGHT.
HOW DID YOU KNOW THIS WOULD HAPPEN?
I GOT A TIP.
SHE'S BEEN IGNORED FOR SO MANY YEARS, THE MOMENT SHE GETS EVEN THE SLIGHTEST BIT OF ATTENTION, SHE WILTS FASTER THAN ROB SCHNEIDER'S APPEAL.
THANKS, STU MAN.
YEAH, WHATEVER. JUST GET HER OUT OF HERE.
HEY, CHRIS? WHY DON'T YOU SHOW EVERYONE HOW YOU CAN LIFT THINGS?
OKAY!
THE TRICK IS TO USE YOUR BACK MUSCLES!
ALL RIGHT, STEWIE... TAKE IT AWAY...

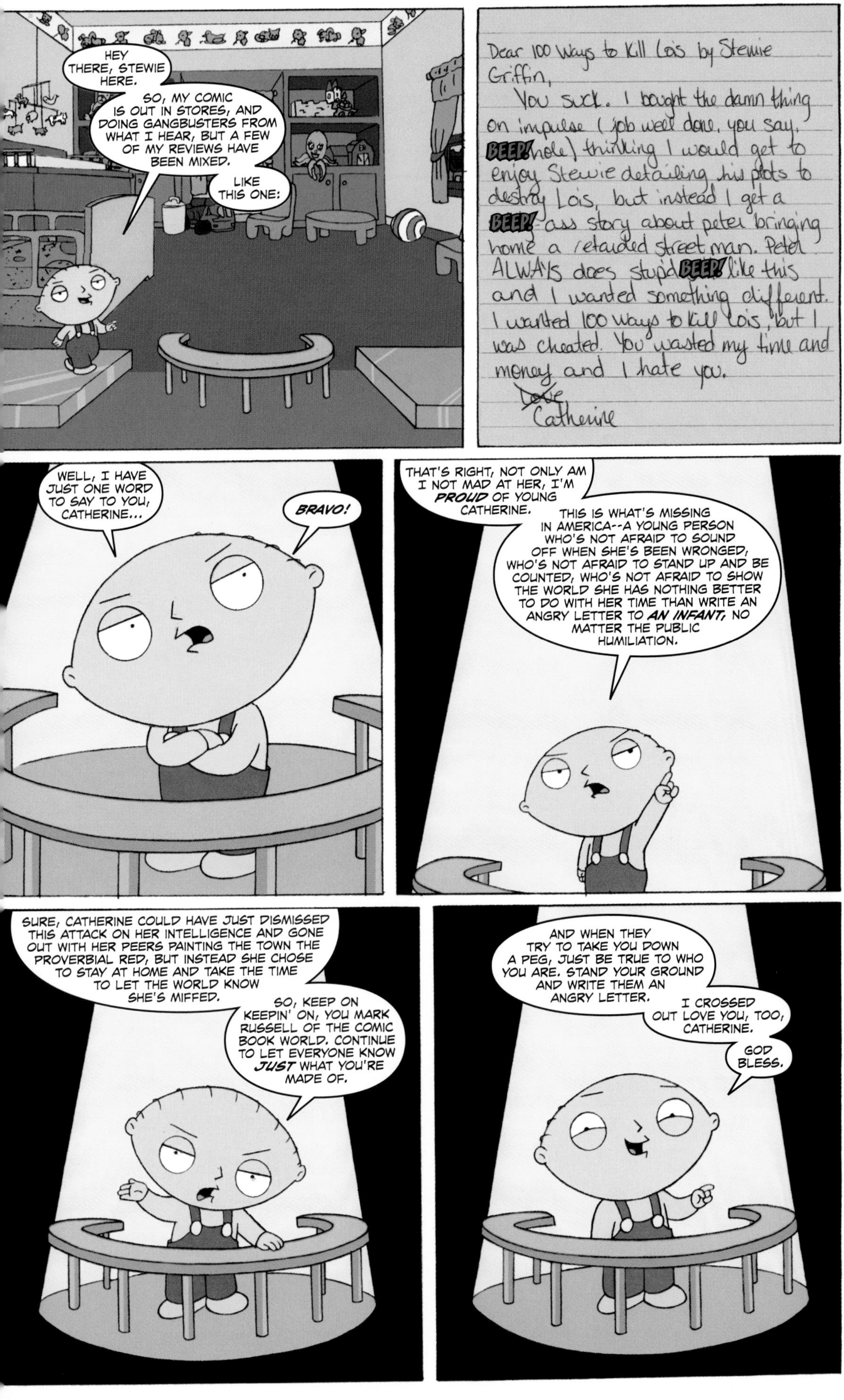
HEY THERE, STEWIE HERE.
SO, MY COMIC IS OUT IN STORES, AND DOING GANGBUSTERS FROM WHAT I HEAR, BUT A FEW OF MY REVIEWS HAVE BEEN MIXED.
LIKE THIS ONE:
Dear 100 Ways to Kill Lois by Stewie Griffin,
You suck. I bought the damn thing on impulse (job well done, you say, BEEP!hole) thinking I would get to enjoy Stewie detailing his plots to destroy Lois, but instead I get a BEEP! ass story about peter bringing home a retarded street man. Peter ALWAYS does stupid BEEP! like this and I wanted something different. I wanted 100 Ways to Kill Lois, but I was cheated. You wasted my time and money and I hate you.
~~Love~~,
Catherine
WELL, I HAVE JUST ONE WORD TO SAY TO YOU, CATHERINE...
BRAVO!
THAT'S RIGHT, NOT ONLY AM I NOT MAD AT HER, I'M PROUD OF YOUNG CATHERINE.
THIS IS WHAT'S MISSING IN AMERICA--A YOUNG PERSON WHO'S NOT AFRAID TO SOUND OFF WHEN SHE'S BEEN WRONGED, WHO'S NOT AFRAID TO STAND UP AND BE COUNTED, WHO'S NOT AFRAID TO SHOW THE WORLD SHE HAS NOTHING BETTER TO DO WITH HER TIME THAN WRITE AN ANGRY LETTER TO AN INFANT, NO MATTER THE PUBLIC HUMILIATION.
SURE, CATHERINE COULD HAVE JUST DISMISSED THIS ATTACK ON HER INTELLIGENCE AND GONE OUT WITH HER PEERS PAINTING THE TOWN THE PROVERBIAL RED, BUT INSTEAD SHE CHOSE TO STAY AT HOME AND TAKE THE TIME TO LET THE WORLD KNOW SHE'S MIFFED.
SO, KEEP ON KEEPIN' ON, YOU MARK RUSSELL OF THE COMIC BOOK WORLD. CONTINUE TO LET EVERYONE KNOW JUST WHAT YOU'RE MADE OF.
AND WHEN THEY TRY TO TAKE YOU DOWN A PEG, JUST BE TRUE TO WHO YOU ARE. STAND YOUR GROUND AND WRITE THEM AN ANGRY LETTER.
I CROSSED OUT LOVE YOU, TOO, CATHERINE.
GOD BLESS.

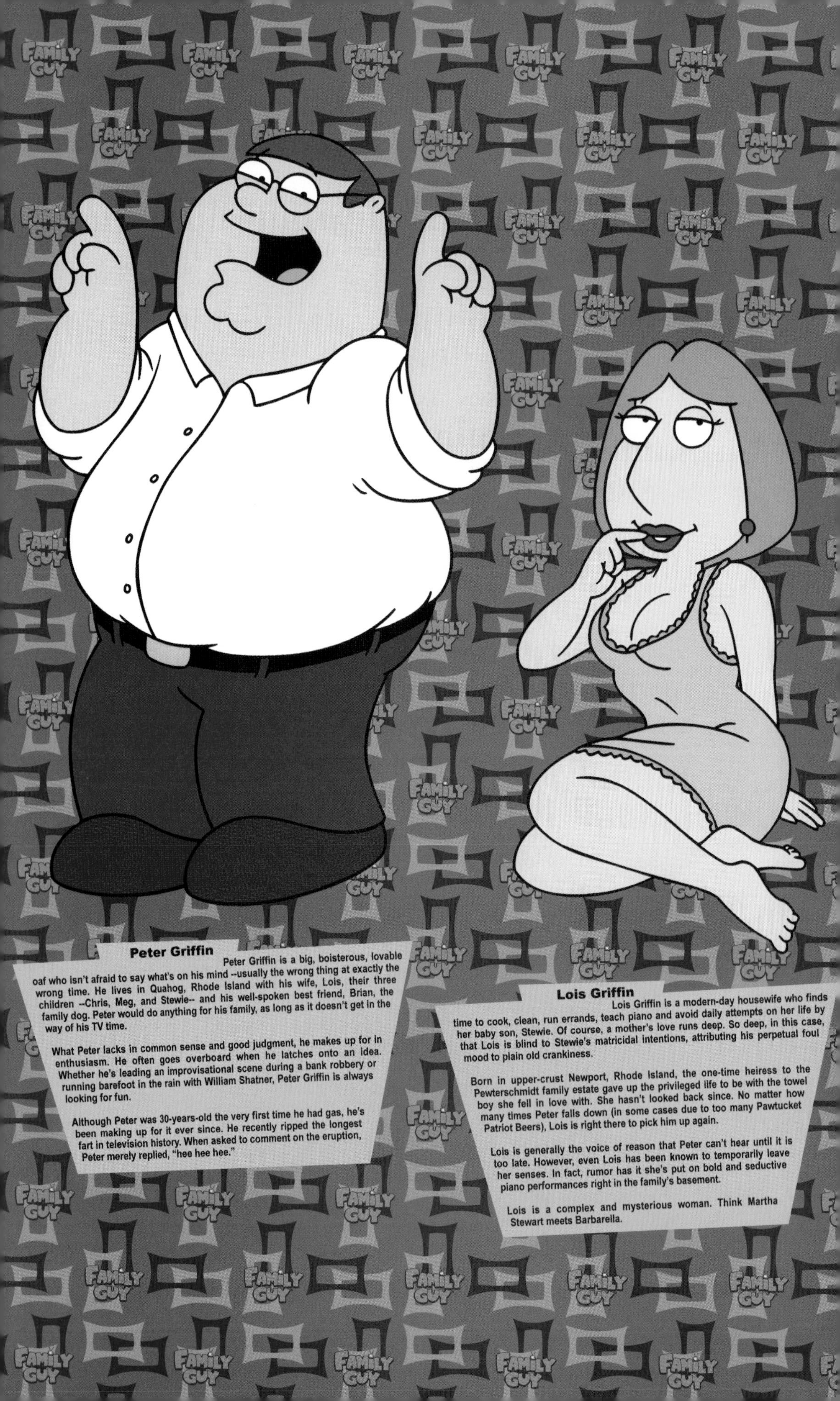

Peter Griffin

Peter Griffin is a big, boisterous, lovable oaf who isn't afraid to say what's on his mind --usually the wrong thing at exactly the wrong time. He lives in Quahog, Rhode Island with his wife, Lois, their three children --Chris, Meg, and Stewie-- and his well-spoken best friend, Brian, the family dog. Peter would do anything for his family, as long as it doesn't get in the way of his TV time.

What Peter lacks in common sense and good judgment, he makes up for in enthusiasm. He often goes overboard when he latches onto an idea. Whether he's leading an improvisational scene during a bank robbery or running barefoot in the rain with William Shatner, Peter Griffin is always looking for fun.

Although Peter was 30-years-old the very first time he had gas, he's been making up for it ever since. He recently ripped the longest fart in television history. When asked to comment on the eruption, Peter merely replied, "hee hee hee."

Lois Griffin

Lois Griffin is a modern-day housewife who finds time to cook, clean, run errands, teach piano and avoid daily attempts on her life by her baby son, Stewie. Of course, a mother's love runs deep. So deep, in this case, that Lois is blind to Stewie's matricidal intentions, attributing his perpetual foul mood to plain old crankiness.

Born in upper-crust Newport, Rhode Island, the one-time heiress to the Pewterschmidt family estate gave up the privileged life to be with the towel boy she fell in love with. She hasn't looked back since. No matter how many times Peter falls down (in some cases due to too many Pawtucket Patriot Beers), Lois is right there to pick him up again.

Lois is generally the voice of reason that Peter can't hear until it is too late. However, even Lois has been known to temporarily leave her senses. In fact, rumor has it she's put on bold and seductive piano performances right in the family's basement.

Lois is a complex and mysterious woman. Think Martha Stewart meets Barbarella.

Meg Griffin

16-year-old Meg Griffin lives a difficult life. She is a total outsider at school as well as at home. The constant butt of the joke, Meg is forever reminded what a loser she really is. She is constantly struggling to gain acceptance from the "in" crowd, or any crowd for that matter.

A bit of a drama queen, Meg pines for her hunky new neighbor, Kyle. Unfortunately, not even a clingy new dress or an eleven-hundred-dollar Prada bag seem to get her any closer to first base.

Like most girls her age, Meg is often embarrassed by her family. However, most girls don't have Peter Griffin as their father, who has turned embarrassment into an art. He once interrupted Meg's class to chide her about shaving her legs in the shower, complaining that "it's like a carpet in there!"

But Meg will survive. And one day she'll get the popularity she so richly deserves. Yeah, right.

Chris Griffin

Chris Griffin is an overgrown, sweet-hearted 13-year-old who wouldn't hurt a fly... unless it landed on his hotdog (Chris' favorite food). In that case, Chris would probably treat the fly as a condiment.

Chris doesn't have many friends. He often stays to himself, sometimes spending time alone in his bedroom. Or that is what you may think. He is, in fact, tormented by an evil monkey residing in his closet. Though Chris shares his tales of the pointing and sneering primate with his parents, they are forever indifferent to his cries of catarrhine abuse.

Chris idolizes Peter and works hard not to disappoint him. It's a good thing for Chris that his father's expectations are so low. Still, Chris does have some hidden talents, especially his ability to draw. He should probably spend more time cultivating his skill and less time with Peter in front of the boob tube, looking for boobs.

A true individual, Chris lumbers to the beat of his own drum. Although physically he's matured early, he still has a way to go intellectually. But just because he's still not clear on where babies come from doesn't mean he's not eager to learn.

Brian Griffin

Brian Griffin is more than just the family dog. He is a gentleman and a scholar, and undeniably the most eloquent member of the Griffin household. Brian is the first person Peter will turn to in times of crisis. But the sarcastic barbs that Brian doles out can be as dry as his martinis.

Yes, Brian has been known to toss back a few. Some say it's to kill the pain that comes with the social stigma of being a dog. Others say it's to help him forget the time before he met Peter, when he was a homeless stray who cleaned windshields for handouts. But Brian will tell you it's just good for his coat.

Drinking and throwing out witty bon mots aren't the only things Brian is good at. If you ask him to speak, don't be surprised if he responds in flawless French. He's also got an amazing voice --he can sing all four parts of a barbershop quartet simultaneously. In short, Brian might be the family dog, but don't tell him that. Did we mention that Brian also holds a third degree belt in taekwondo? And in seven more years he'll be a black belt. That's one more year to you and me.

Glenn Quagmire

Glenn Quagmire is the Griffins' next door neighbor and Quahog's resident sex addict. He works as a pilot, but spends most of his free time seducing women at his bachelor pad. A confirmed foot fetishist, Quagmire's trademark "Giggety Giggety Goo" is known to simultaneously arouse and repulse women all across New England.

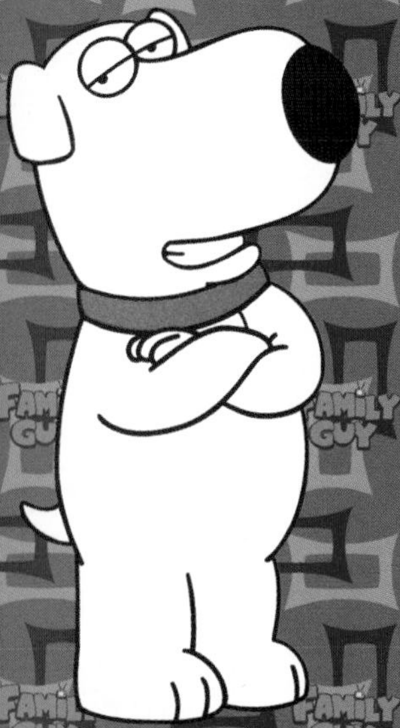

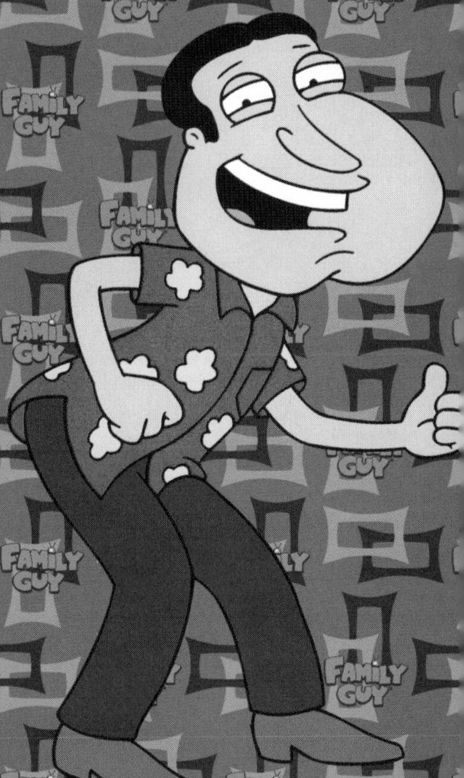

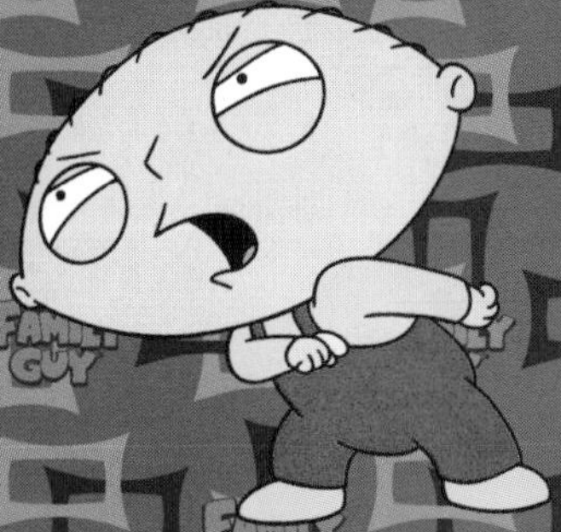

Stewie Griffin

Stewie Griffin is a 1-year-old baby with a single goal: total world domination. He has the voice and manner of an evil Rex Harrison, but he's only recently celebrated the one year anniversary of his escape from his mother's "cursed ovarian Bastille," in which he was incarcerated for nine grueling months. Stewie has vowed to defeat his mother's matriarchal tyranny and topple the "gynocracy" she rules.

Just because Lois has narrowly escaped several attempts on her life thus far (from a box of chocolates filled with active grenades to a barrage of arrows shot straight for her head) doesn't mean she's in the clear yet. Stewie might begrudge Lois a modicum of respect for being the worthy adversary she is, but don't be fooled. One day her uppance shall come!

In fact, Stewie's only friend is his gay teddy bear, Rupert. Stewie himself has shown... tendencies. If it were not for his lack of muscle tone, toilet training and his need for parentally provided sustenance, Stewie would have already gained control over most of the third world, including Canada. Until his domination over all mankind comes to fruition, anyone or anything that interferes with his grand plan shall be destroyed. And if he can create a machine that controls the weather, what makes you think he won't be able to control you, hmmm?

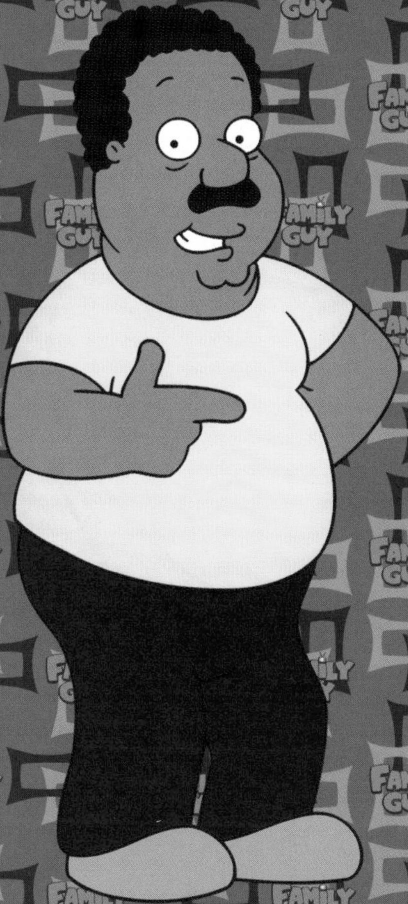

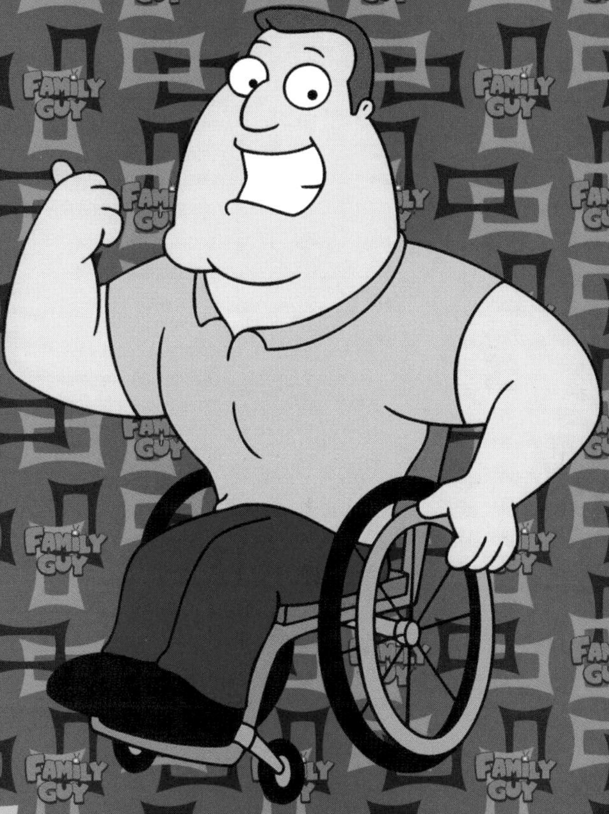

Cleveland Brown

Cleveland Brown is another resident of Spooner Street, where he lives with his sassy wife, Loretta, and his hyperactive son, Cleveland, Jr. The proprietor of Cleveland's Deli, Cleveland is another of Peter's drinking Buddies. Polite and sensitive, Cleveland wouldn't hurt a fly. He has the finest mustache in Quahog.

Joe

Joe Swanson is Peter's handicapped neighbor and drinking pal. With his wife Bonnie and son Kevin in tow, Joe came to Quahog as a cop, searching for a quieter life, following a transfer from Providence. It was during a Christmas-time orphanage robbery that Joe became a paraplegic; first shot, then falling from a snowy rooftop due to a misplaced roller-skate. He enjoys baseball games and sex. He also choreographs dance numbers for local musicals. One important thing about Joe: he always obeys the law. Always.

GRAB YOUR JOYSTICK AND GET READY TO...

UNLEASH YOUR INNER PETER!

It's too hot for TV!

AVAILABLE NOW!

FAMILY GUY VIDEO GAME!

WWW.2KGAMES.COM/FAMILYGUY

VOICED AND SCRIPTED BY MEMBERS OF THE REAL FAMILY GUY TV SHOW CREATIVE TEAM!

DISTINCTIVE FAMILY GUY HUMOR—RAUCOUS AND RACY, JUST HOW YOU LIKE IT!

HILARIOUS AND ENTERTAINING NON SEQUITUR MINI-GAMES KEEP THE LAUGHS COMING.